Voices of Difference: Studies in Critical Philosophy and Mass Communication

THE HAMPTON PRESS COMMUNICATION SERIES

Critical Studies in Communication
Leslie T. Good, supervisory editor

Voices of Difference: Studies in Critical Philosophy and Mass Communication

Thomas S. McCoy
California State University, Hayward

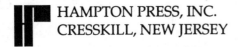 HAMPTON PRESS, INC.
CRESSKILL, NEW JERSEY

Material appearing on pages xi, 4, 9, 11, 12, 28, 30, 31, 40, 50, 58, 61, 64, 77, 78, 80, 81, 139, 140, 141, 142, 225, 275, 280 reprinted from Chris Argyris: *Behind the Front Page: Organizational Self-Renewal in a Metropolitan Newspaper*, © 1974 by Jossey-Bass, Inc., Publishers. Permission granted by the publisher.

Material appearing on pages 10, 74, 92, 93, 102 reprinted from Michel Foucault: *Power/Knowledge*, © 1972, 1975, 1976, 1977 by Michel Foucault. Permission granted by Pantheon Books, a division of Random House, Inc.

Material appearing on pages 37, 166, 178 reprinted from J. Derrida: *Writing and Difference*, © 1978 by The University of Chicago Press. Permission granted by the publisher.

Material appearing on pages 21, 209, 238 reprinted from Michel Foucault: *Beyond Structuralism and Hermeneutics*, © 1983 by The University of Chicago Press. Permission granted by the publisher.

Material appearing in Chapter 2 reprinted from Warren Hinckle: *If You Have a Lemon, Make Lemonade*, © 1974 by Warren Hinckle III. Permission granted by the Putnam Publishing Group, Inc.

Library of Congress Cataloging-in-Publication Data

McCoy, Thomas S.
    Voices of difference : studies in critical philosophy and mass
communication / Thomas S. McCoy.
        p.   cm. -- (The Hampton Press communication series)
    Includes bibliographical references and indexes.
    ISBN 1-881303-55-1 (cloth). -- ISBN 1-881303-56-X (paper)
    1. Mass media. 2. Philosophy, Modern--20th century. I. Title.
II. Series.
    P91.M373   1993
    302.23--dc20   93-357
                                                                           CIP

Hampton Press, Inc.
23 Broadway
Cresskill, NJ 07626

To Margaret and Brennan

Contents

Preface

Voices of Difference attempts to connect the phenomenological tradition to communication studies literature through the application of what I call critical phenomenology to mass communication. This approach involves an integration of phenomenology with French critical theory. Phenomenology, in its traditional form, lacks the critical edge necessary to explore meaning structures generated by media practices, which also remain largely unaddressed by positivist approaches to the study of mass communication. Critical theory, in its determination to renounce foundational, subjectivist theory, unfortunately (in my opinion) discarded ethical and aesthetic phenomenological contributions to communication theory. In an effort to remedy what I perceive as limitations of each approach, the book fleshes out some of the implications of a critical phenomenology for those interested in examining mass communication as a field of experience, as a social system, and as a matrix of power relations institutionally organized.

One can attach functions to three approaches toward the study of mass communication: A positivist, administrative approach analysis of "what is." Using the *New York Times'* coverage of El Salvador from Chapter 7 as an example, a positivist approach might focus on the number, affiliation, and relative status of news sources within a series of media stories. A phenomenological attitude attempts to describe the "experience of" what is. Journalistic depictions of Salvadoran experiences of the ravages of civil war would be phenomenologically relevant. Critical phenomenology questions "what is not." Incorporating phenomenological and positivist concerns, critical phenomenology could probe journalistic alternatives to "what is" that might alter the "experience of" the journalist, the reader, and even eventually the subject. One would question whether there are structural reasons why the *Times'* coverage of El Salvador entails a particular perspective.

Critical phenomenology, then, applies the rigor of phenomenological description as it emphasizes unconscious elements of power and
knowledge, difference and deferral, to describe and explain mass communication and society. The book examines our understanding of news
practices and addresses what I consider a moral deficit in communication studies. These studies in critical phenomenology are motivated by
an ethics based on voices of difference. The voices presented are offered
as alternatives to the natural attitude, an attitude which accepts a given
state of affairs as a natural, and therefore unquestioned, continuation of
that which came before.

So, critical phenomenology examines meaning as experienced, not
solely as an analytical problem, but as a perceived configuration. The
phenomenological approach is distinct from quantitative methods insofar as it emphasizes the art of asking questions over a results-oriented
science. The idea is to present a narrative rather than to build from a
firm foundation because phenomenology questions the very ways we
exist. Critical theory explores why we live and behave as we do. Critical
phenomenology questions subjective, intersubjective, and mass-mediated spheres of life. History and intersubjectivity intertwine in a dialectical
process susceptible to cultural critique.

Dialectic is an ambiguous term, and I employ its various facets.
Dialectic refers to a process of question and response, to thesis-antithe-
sis-synthesis development, and to the formulation of first principles not
in need of substantiation. For instance, I assert that communication is
fundamentally an ethical relation. While I don't expect a reader to merely accept such a proposition, I do hope he or she will suspend judgment
until I finish the story. I also think that the right to freedom of speech
requires no justification. Freedom of expression is an essential characteristic of being human, in other words, those who are denied their right to
express themselves are being denied an aspect of their humanity.
Dialectics rely on the interrogative primacy of process over substance.
The remedy for "bad" speech is more speech.

Critical phenomenology forms an attempt to join aspects of appreci-
ation-ethics inherent in communication with moments of critique-decon-
struction. Central to the arguments presented in this book are the ethical
phenomenology of Emmanuel Levinas and the phenomenological aesthetics of Maurice Merleau-Ponty. These theorists are supplemented by
the critical theory of Jacques Derrida and Michel Foucault. Also, I have
drawn on many others as I feel their voices contribute to the quality of
the discussion. The dialectical movement that results from this effort is
not without problems. I do not argue that the phenomenology of
Merleau-Ponty and Levinas is one with the critical theory of Foucault
and Derrida, nor do I propose that in all respects Levinas agrees with

Merleau-Ponty, or that Foucault is not wounded by Derrida's critique of his method. These differences have been noticed often by others, but no one has commented on what critical theory and phenomenology share. Communication theorists ought to move among poles of power-knowledge, freedom-discipline, gravity-humor, sublime-mundane.

With regard to both the form and substance of communication, reason is a problem. Rationality is problematic. From a phenomenological point of view, rationality is that process by which we make sense of the world. The way we educate our young and continue our culture through the transmission of norms and the development of sense is rationality itself. But from a critical point of view, rationality is the banner under which certain groups and their interests are advanced and given primacy over the interests of others who do not, for example, have access to the media. Reason is the name we give to a practice which configures certain cultural norms and practices that devalue other traditions and their cherished ideals. Critical phenomenology is an approach that urges the pluralization of reason and which recognizes various aspects of rationality—to understand is to understand within a cultural context. Reason is not univocal. So, the normative basis of critical phenomenology lies in an openness toward what is different, what is other.

For idiosyncratic reasons, sections invoking *Ramparts*, Bill Moyers, the *New York Times*, *60 Minutes*, and the Federal Communication Commission may appear not to parallel one another. They differ to the extent in which they promote or disserve notions presented in this book. I know that some readers expect a road map detailing what terrain lies ahead, and I am aware that tradition dictates the research unfold homogeneously. I acknowledge the unorthodox organization of this book, but I have chosen to oscillate between sections dedicated to theoretical development and those sections intended to apply and embody those developments. Chapter 2, for example, relies implicitly on the values and principles advanced in Chapter 1. To interpose the theoretical language within the narrative of "A Height of Audacity" would stifle the story of a magazine that projected voices of difference. It certainly is not my intention to jar the reader, but to bridge the developing theory with what I hope are worthwhile interludes that serve to elucidate the conceptual concerns that follow.

Versions of several of the studies presented here have appeared elsewhere. Chapter 6 appeared under the titles "Hegemony, Power, Media: Foucault and Cultural Studies" and "Surveillance, Privacy and Power: Information Trumps Knowledge" in *Communications: The European Journal of Communication*; an edited portion of Chapter 7 appeared in the *Newspaper Research Journal* as "The *New York Times'* Coverage of El Salvador" and part of Chapter 8 was published in *Communications and the Law* as "Revoking the Fairness Doctrine: The Year of the Contra."

The Phenomenological Method

This book on phenomenologically oriented communication theory focuses on the ways in which different, yet compatible, qualitatively oriented theorists treat human interaction. The goal of *Voices of Difference* is to introduce qualitative schools of thought, methods, and conceptions into more traditional function and effects-oriented American communication theory. The conceptions we employ shift and vary, but the theme remains constant. That theme is to bring into focus interpretive considerations affecting mass communication, its participants, values, systems, and organizational structures.

Since ours is a mass-mediated culture, we experience the world at large, and ourselves in particular, through media technologies, according to experts and professionals. The mass media really do link up social, cultural, and political planes, and these media linkages call out for descriptive and critical discussion. As we will see, the more efficient a medium, the more transparent that medium seems. Put another way, technological advances bring with them transformations of experience. That is the concern of phenomenology: how we experience the world.

I attempt to flesh out some of the implications of phenomenology and critical theory for those of us studying mass communication. This chapter attempts to integrate ideas of intentionality, responsibility, intersubjectivity, and experiential structures with critical analyses of power, knowledge, reason, and authority into a critique of mass communication theory and practice. So we move from considerations of method to ethical, cultural, political, and legal concerns.

1

To approach communication as primarily the transmission of a message from a source to an audience, through a medium or channel, does not enrich our understanding of the complexities, assumptions, or attitudes involved in sharing and developing meaning. Since sense is made and not pregiven, audiences should be thought of as active participants. From this point of view, the essence of communication is mediation, which forms the relations we regard as community. Mass media alternatively disseminate and constrain, inform and obscure, and legitimate and denounce contemporary culture. Journalism, specifically, can make substantial differences in cultural interpretations by the perspectives from which practitioners disseminate information and experience.

My goal is to draw attention to inherent ambiguities in communicating sense (meaning and direction). The phenomenological method attempts to question, descriptively, anything which can appear in experience. Simplicity is not, then, regarded with sanctity. Essences of appearances, invariant structures, are regarded as possible discoveries of the phenomenological method. For phenomenologists, an essence forms the conditions by which a phenomenon is what it is, or that which, if altered, would fundamentally alter our perception of communication and mass communication.

Traditional positivist theory divides the world into realms of subject and object. The subject recognizes objects "out there" as opposed to "in here," or internal to oneself. "Phenomenology is the whole truth from a certain point of view,"[1] writes Merleau-Ponty. Moreover, he is serious. But this should not be taken at face value. Phenomenology denies the subject-object dichotomy. Instead, phenomenologists emphasize intentionality, structures of meaning, which make up central modes for awareness. Intentionality comprises poles of experience. Such experience involves poles of self and that which is experienced; the difference lies in the emphasis on the polarity of one's experience, rather than totally unbridgeable modalities of existence. There is an intermundane structure to experience. The Hegelian notion of phenomenon suggests the notion of a frame comprising subject and object: the structure of appearance. There can be no empty awareness. Awareness or consciousness directs itself toward something. This process establishes the conditions for meaning. Thus, the perceived world is not an immediate, unfounded realm, but that which appears to us through our experience of it. Such experience occurs on many levels from not-yet-conscious perception to the most abstract and sublime reasoning.

This approach affects mass communication at the levels of practice and research. To deny the subject-object dichotomy flies against many commonly accepted practices in reporting and investigating events in the media. If communication is not merely, or even fundamentally, representation, then the responsibility of the writer or broadcaster is much more burdened than some think. The assumed values one conveys to an audience must be evaluated themselves. Ethics plays a seminal role in the communication process if expression is viewed as intentional and active rather than representational. We must, according to the phenomenological approach, reexamine the ethics of technologically sophisticated means of communication in light of their integration into and organizational effects on society.

Commitment to communicating meanings which inform and sometimes disturb us must be regarded as more authentic than messages passed along which serve to lull one's audience into quietude and complacency, that is, the buying mood. How committed ought a writer be? What really matters to people? How does one communicate essential aspects of experience? These considerations take on expanded relevance to efforts grounded on the phenomenological conception of intersubjectivity. Responsibility in communicating becomes an existential consideration rather than a professional afterthought.

If research efforts are reexamined phenomenologically, the process of studying mass communication appears more profound than if one views communication solely from a positivist position. The phenomenon ought not be reduced to its functions. Meaning, more than effect, forms the pregnant category for examining what happens when people express themselves to one another through mass media. Phenomenology allows for shifts in events, for example, shifts in public opinion. An interest level may remain constant, but transfer to various perceived issues or events. Conversely, interest groups may lose or gain intensity toward a given belief or strategy. If one process is mistaken for the other, then confused research findings will result.

For instance, how is one to make sense of the contention by the authors of a study of the American electorate that conventional political categories of liberal and conservative are as relevant as Whig and Federalist, or that traditional Republican and Democratic values bear little relation to the fractured nature of the electorate?[2] The poll cited nine basic values that drive and divide Americans, and it carved out 11 political coalitions where once two sufficed. Have times changed so? Or do the methods of the pollsters yield a more sophisticated rendering of the electorate? Or both? The positive research calls for description, analysis, and critique. What does it *mean* to report that the traditional view of the political parties—Republicans are free-enterprise oriented, affluent, and conservative, while Democrats are peace-oriented, social reformers, and liberals—holds for only one-third of the electorate? What does the contention that social justice, rather than economic satisfaction, is of overriding concern to Americans signify? Is this reflected by the media?

Should we take note that a television news anchor is judged by most Americans to be more trustworthy than a president?

So, critical phenomenology is an attempt to examine meanings within existence as experienced. It is a method. Phenomenology is descriptive as opposed to analytical, but critical theory provides the necessary analysis. We turn to a world which precedes our knowledge of it, to a life world wherein events mesh. We perceive events first and know them later. Thus seen, the world is first in the realm of participation and later in the realm of reflection. Reflection mediates straightforward, unreflected events. Thought and expression predicate something previously downplayed. Communication comes from perspective and perception plays on horizons, structuring fields of endeavor. Therefore, perception takes place on a different level of awareness than judgments about what one perceives. Merleau-Ponty tells us there is no inner man observing the outer world. Man is in the world and makes sense only to the degree he is committed to that world.

Perception is not truth itself, but our access to and possibility for truth. All considerations about human reality stem from this prepredicative level of awareness. The world is not fundamentally what one thinks about it, but what one lives through. We do not possess the world; we communicate with it. We base the possible on what is real and should not opt for the real limited by considerations of possibility.

Individual awareness directs itself perpetually toward a world it does not possess, but inhabits. Dimensions of the world deliver meaning to us in a reciprocal relationship with the world and others. We are constituted by being-in-the-world. Merleau-Ponty asks:

> Should we try to understand a doctrine from its overt content, or from the psychological make-up of its author? We must seek an understanding of all these angles simultaneously, everything has meaning, and we shall find this same structure of being underlying all relationships.[3]

This structure of being can be fleshed out only through pursuing relationships and not primarily by isolating events from the fabric of the situations in which they take place. Meaning must be generated; it emerges, and truth is realized through sedimentation of related meanings through situations, which lend perspective. Merleau-Ponty tells us that the value of the phenomenological method is the gain accrued from uniting the extremes of subjectivism and objectivism in phenomenological notions of rationality and world. Rationality is measured by the rational. This implies that the sense is deciphered by the experience through which it arises; the integration of perspectives confirm one another to evoke meaning. All our knowledge is sustained by communicating with the world and others. But reality calls for clarification through the questioning of what we perceive through communication, otherwise known as rationality. "Something of the nature of the question passes into the answer,"[4] says Merleau-Ponty.

But when isolation of views allows for the presentation of one overbearing stance, irrationality and cultural repression result. Obviously, this ought to concern those in the media. To a large extent, the media determine not only what people think about, but how people perceive the world. Do the media inform and entertain, or do they manipulate and indoctrinate? Do the media energize their audience, or do they anesthetize readers and viewers? If the media, even partially, work to manipulate, indoctrinate, and anesthetize audiences, who is to blame? Can we find fault, or are we to shrug our shoulders at the inescapable polluting "side effects" of media technology and world complexity?

Certainly, the argument against publishers controlling media content needs to be made. Everyone is aware that much of advertising is less than enlightening and emancipatory in its effects on an audience. But what about writers, broadcasters, and editors in the trenches? Are they guilt-free pawns of the powers-that-be? In the effort to capture the excitement of a story, journalists sometimes cover superficial, surface aspects of that story, pouring a real-life event into a two-dimensional mold of the inverted pyramid. In the competitive rush, factors get trampled underfoot of facts; reasons lose to events; and understanding falls prey to impact.

The media are not neutral. Even the guise of impartiality masks a perspective, usually conservative in nature. Impartiality often conceals a message: "That's the way it is." Nothing simply is the way it is. For example, when CBS covers the Middle East, a position, whether stated or assumed, is taken up. If Israel drives over the national borders of another country, such as Lebanon, the way it is described, and put into perspective *essentially* confirms a choice of message. If a reporter tells us Israel is attempting to maintain peace by invading Beirut, is he not enforcing a biased position? Or, if CNN reports that Moslems are outraged by the Israeli invasion of a nationally sovereign nation, is not a position implicitly advanced? Factors, interpretations, situations, and perspectives call for admittance. Reporters and commentators ought to admit to partiality and interpretation.

Merleau-Ponty hinges meaning and history on contingency, which is the condition of sense. Events take place in history and, consequently, fit into patterns. These patterns, at any given moment, can be only partially recognized. The texture of events within this historical fabric are multifaceted, and the patterns presented form structures only approximately recognizable when viewed too closely. The media ought to admit to such considerations. The phenomenological approach attempts a motivated, intentional description of the appearance of events. Events viewed in a context give rise to some sort of sedimentation over time, but they can be construed variously, depending on the position from which one lives events.

Often, actual, life-world events are confused by audience members with the media presentation of those events. The word or image is taken for the real world. Words become objective and are taken for objects, when they are really indicators, that is, indicating other words, or images. Does freedom of speech have any relation to freedom of thought or freedom of choice? If one man or woman is free to deny freedom to another, and the media are free to report it to insure the freedom of the person whose freedom was originally infringed and the freedom of the public to know, is everyone then equally free?

From our point of view, communication is primarily an ethical relation, not sometimes or to a certain degree, but fundamentally and essentially. Communication is essentially ethical in the phenomenological sense, that which makes something appear as it is. If ethics are choked, suffocating mediation and interpretation for special effect and immediacy, then communication has been smothered, injured. Communication forms relations between subjects; it is *the* formative process, and mass communication denotes communication among many people belonging to different social backgrounds attempting to express something within a shared culture. Nonetheless, mass communication does elicit unique structures and fosters competing interests. So, our phenomenology must entail a critical sense because we take seriously the theory that freedom of speech and press are the prerequisites, not only of other freedoms, but of the democratic form of government itself. Consequently, one of the chief obstacles to freedom is the lack of access to media in our society. For if an opinion or an idea does not eventually find its way into the media, it does not gain currency.

Even so, one assumes that mass communication functions within some sort of orderly system within the culture. Culture and such a communication system, while not synonymous, would involve some sort of semiotics (study of signs) coincidental with each other. This discourse calls for recognition that no system stands alone in a vacuum and that the term "system" must be brought into question. A system is an abstraction; it is mutable and, since it is temporal, in flux. A system is, perhaps, a perspective on a series of events or conditions constituted in a rigorous way so that internal unity may be detected. It is not necessarily an illumination in a visual sense, such as a model, but a structural discourse on the phenomena which present themselves. This, in turn, brings about shifts in value. As Merleau-Ponty notes, man, when he withdraws from things in order to reconstitute them, does not find a universe of ready-made meanings; he must construct those meanings through an intentional arc, a genesis of meaning or birth of sense.[5] However, one cannot abstract oneself out of the temporal flow, or therefore, from a constant metamorphosis with one's environment, which produces knowledge and upholds reason. Knowing, a process of mediation, a dialectical process within the flow of events, involves going beyond what preceded; yet the knower assimilates his/her past at the same time, generating patterns (knowledge) and recognizing their essential coherence (reason).

We experience a reaction between the poles of knowing and known. Merleau-Ponty thinks something new is formed, "The reaction of 'knowledge' on the object and of the object on 'knowledge' is the metamorphosis of one into the other."[6] Such a dialectic subtends the undertaking, is "preobjective," and, phenomenologically speaking, constitutes a stratum of prepredicative experience. Trying to go beyond subject/object dualism, we see that the mediation invoked here is the dialectic as experience, but it must also be an ambiguous dialectic. That is, are we discussing actual experience or the concept "experience"? Is the phenomenon in our experience, understanding, and history, or does the concept constitute a category of knowing that allows us to even articulate the question? Merleau-Ponty responds that experience is both concept and life. One experiences the concept, while recognizing that mental activity itself forges a part of experience. Ambiguity is part of the makeup of the incarnate subject, the flesh of events. "In truth, we have experience of knowledge and knowledge of experience."[7] However, culture is maintained and ordained by interested forces; genealogies of ways of knowing structure this process in ways that situate us in particular contexts, horizons of living that benefit or continue the status quo. The genealogy of power and knowledge and the authority of reason make up the critical aspects of our study, aspects which I maintain are derivative, conceptually if not purposefully, of the phenomenology of Merleau-Ponty.

For our understanding, it is necessary to realize that the primary constant involved in thought and expression, ipso facto, is language. In fact, language is the pristine structure inherent in the study of mass communication. It has been noted that any system of signs contains some admixture of language. Language presents consciousness in general. Signs form a complex of associations, which present forms of convention and ritual. Semiology, the structural study of sign systems, may thus take in any of the forms of mass communication as they function through image, interview, or conversation. The basis of such a study is one of dynamic differentiation and meaning relations. Thus, we hope to glean from experience the spirit in which this essay ushers forth; "'conception' cannot precede 'execution' . . . only the work itself, completed and understood, is proof that there was something rather than nothing to be said,"[8] according to Merleau-Ponty.

The basis for the phenomenological-structural study of language was pioneered by a Swiss linguist, Ferdinand de Saussure. Saussure points out that language is a purely social object, not by option but by definition. It is the systematized set of conventions necessary for communication. This is true regardless and independent of any content. Language becomes the set of conditions structurally necessary for consciousness to arise at all. Language is the cradle of consciousness. Speech (expression) is the singular aspect of language usage. (The term in French is *parole*, and it is more general than the English term, *speech*.) Discourse also may be used; thus *parole* is not necessarily limited to verbal expression. Discourse is an act of selection from among alternatives and thus of specific expression within language. Expression, while a function of language, evolves through speech. Hence speech, discourse, must be studied prior to language as a whole, at least from a phenomenological point of view. This constitutes an inversion of traditional linguistics. The inversion invokes a dialectical method and logic which is couched in *praxis*; it is *from* the concrete situation and returns *to* the concrete discourse. Discourse is situational, involving oppositional tendencies which produce meaning in the relational world. Speech and communication are projects. Perception, communication, and mass communication, then, involve choices, choices which are embedded in a process that results in a determinate way of arranging and engaging the world; the trajectory further opens the way for understandings compatible with prior choices and seals off alternatives incompatible with established patterns of interest.

Obviously, these sorts of choices are made through the use of language. Language is made up of signs. Discourse employs signs. In expression, signification is a process which binds the signified (vehicle, phoneme, or means) to the signified (content, concept, or end). This product, for it is *produced*, is the sign in the act of signification. The sign derives its values from its surroundings. It exists nowhere without relation or reference. The value of the sign is different from its signification. It is more important. I contend that communication is political; it has to do with community. The value of the sign comes from the dialectical relationship or opposition of sign to sign. Thus, by definition, value is dynamic, derivative, and political. Meaning, therefore, can arise only through discourse; it develops from less articulated to more articulated. It is a common intention. One distills meaning from events, not by definition of terms but through creative expression and experimental discourse.

We can locate two planes involved in this conception of language. The syntagm is the irreversible linear progression of signs in discourse. Each term derives its value from its opposition to what comes before it and what follows it. This seemingly paradoxical situation arises through the second plane which forms the paradigm, the vertical axis of understanding. The terms are associated in memory and intention; they form groups and relations. The two planes are linked such that the syntagm can progress only by incessantly intertwining with units from the paradigm, and the paradigm reforms and shifts according to syntagmatic progression. This forms a linguistic dialectic through which expression *becomes* possible.

Emmanuel Levinas argues that the syntagmatic, diachronic nature of discourse is accomplished in the incarnate subject, that signs signify from somewhere and for someone. Signs are not simply distributed among a system of equivalences, gathering their meaning from a system of differences. Communication arises from solicitation, searching out and sharing with another whom, Levinas is convinced, provides the foundation for responsibility and the possibility for ethical behavior, from which various values may flow. With this in mind, we see that, most probably, the emphasis for the study of communication itself inheres in the functioning of *parole*, speech, and discourse in society. In particular, we shall stress the role of discourse in mass communication. In the following chapter, we will look at the life of *Ramparts* magazine.

While the study of language as an entity is enlightening and necessary, it falls, by and large, outside the scope or direction of these studies. Discourse forms the syntagmatic function within a paradigmatic language system. So, while some mention of language as system is necessary, we shall discuss the dialectic of individual communicators and media in community as primary, in the sense that communication originates from a unique, if historically vested, situation. This is necessarily an ethical as well as a political concern. Accordingly, one recognizes that such considerations give rise to the notion that the process of communication, especially mass communication, evidences a crisis in societal values. The media's choices in communicating with others delivers, to a large extent, society's answers. It is largely a matter of conception and attitude, as well as organization and agenda.

CLARIFYING QUESTIONS

As phenomenology is a philosophy of experience, we question human "openness on the world" from basic prepredicative experience. We do not originally look at the experience of experience, as though one passes through homogeneous levels, but neither do we absolutely divide or compartmentalize experience. The problems of "other," "self," "world" are interrelated, commingled, communal. The world is pregiven to conscious life; it is prepredicative. The world is given for our perception in an opening toward that world. The world exists for us on a level more *basic* than any logical, epistemological or thetic judgments we may exercise concerning it. These are derived modes of thought; they are not, strictly speaking, original. Our experience of self is as an "I am able to;" this gestalt joins behavior and consciousness. A human being is open to the world through his/her body. Consciousness, for Merleau-Ponty, is ec-centric, decentered; it is virtually nowhere. Who can locate "Mind?" From where does it originate and from where does it come? Man is an ec-centric unity. One's body creates expressive space (field of expressivity); this commits perception to a scene, a body in the world. The human world is constituted from a prehuman (brute) world from which we live and constitute logical and rhetorical relations. One's perspective through his/her habitual body constitutes, very basically, sense—an intentional arc, motility. One's relation to self is a global relationship; it is not localized.

A central tenet of the phenomenological method is the *"epochē,"* the transcendental reduction, bracketing assumptions to better describe them. In order to better question experience, one must step back from the all-absorbing grip of perceptual faith, to reduce facticity to phenomenon. Ideally, the manifest perspectives are unlimited; therefore, any authentic philosophic method must approach an object of possible knowledge interrogatively. Perception may be misled through the assumption of its irrevocable validity. But, paradoxically, on a more basic level, it must be viewed essentially as one's access to truth. Perception adheres to a situation; hence it cannot be a pure impression. It is in time; it is not isolable. Our world is not a metaphysical term. Our experience of it is comprised of layers beginning or originating with perception through a habitual body, a context, and up through thematic expression and intersubjectivity. Perception displays an open, unique, and preobjective field. Perception unfolds a field of original interest. It is active and affective. Because perception involves deciphering gestures, one anticipates the world in a creative fashion. We are imbued with sense. Perception hovers; it is contingent, but it maintains a basic doxic faith. Perceptual faith is original and constitutive, intertwined in awareness. Gregory writes:

> Perception is not determined simply by the stimulus patterns; rather it is a dynamic searching for the best interpretation of the available data . . . But the senses do not give us a picture of the world directly; rather they provide evidence for checking hypotheses about what lies before us.[9]

A second major tenet of the phenomenological method lies in the conception of the world as a community with fellow human beings. While the Cartesian *cogito* (I think, therefore I am) is truly indubitable, it is traditionally misconstrued. If one examines the primordial and necessary correlate of the *cogito*, one recognizes that "I am here." One is situated. This is the true and "unsophisticated" *sense* of the *cogito*, which from Descartes on has been abstracted into logical knots and metaphysical quagmires that have little to do with the human situation. Merleau-Ponty describes the "life world" in an attempt to rid thought of presuppositions in questioning, the dialectical method. According to Plato, the origin of philosophy is simple wonder at things being the way they are. As Merleau-Ponty says:

> [O]ur sensibility to the world, our synchronized relations to it—that is, our body—the thesis underlying all our experiences removes from our existence the density of an absolute and unique act, making a transferable signification of our "corporeality," creating a "common situation," and finally yielding the perception of another like ourselves, if not in the absolute of his effective existence then at least in its general outline accessible to us.[10]

Truly, the *cogito* is not a moment of essence preceding existence. We behold active consciousness and our active acquisition of it through self-consciousness, not by watching it, but as a mode, a return to ourselves within a community. This community is interrelated yet separate, surrounded by cofunctioning validity, the life world which opens onto a vital horizon in which questioning can yield rationality. We are never completely detached from our perceptive world; the reduction is itself a process somewhat dependent on sense perception, a means to an end to a means. But mass media do affect the ways we perceive and experience the world.

We measure rationality through a coherence of perspectives in perception and communication; meaning emerges through blending and sedimentation. If belief and meaning are partially fortuitous, it is because sense is contingent upon prior conditions. Thoughts are true according to existing conditions. Truth is historical. Meaning is contingent. Merleau-Ponty's phenomenology has as its heritage a tracing of Edmund Husserl's phenomenological attitude conceived in the "life world" and recognized through "transcendental subjectivity as an intersubjectivity." Being in the life world involves a mingling of consciousness in the world; this at times results in confusion. Consciousness, inseparable involvement with body (there can be no mind-body split), lends the constitutive perspective. Nevertheless, experience of the other person, intersubjectivity, cannot be deduced from subjectivity. It is an original event. Our involvement with others constitutes communication. This is not a logical progression. It is a simultaneous and multidimensional dialectical interaction. Man is and yet is not what he is; he is a temporally transcendental being. He refuses to be limited to any one or another of his determinations. Levinas refers to this refusal as anarchic. One transcends, goes beyond one's situation to return to it, to grasp it more firmly in reflection. "Groups rather than juxtaposed elements are principal and primary,"[11] Merleau-Ponty says. While each person is unique, culture, family, social position, and, especially, language—intersubjectivity—sustain that individuality; power relations, disciplinary strategies, authority, and, especially, language—constraint—organize that subjectivity. What Merleau-Ponty calls perceptual faith involves a historical process, a fundamental historicity, involving the whole of the person as a decentralized unity, unique yet interdependent. Merleau-Ponty writes:

> [D]ialectical thought is always in the process of extracting from each phenomenon a truth which goes beyond it, waking at each moment our astonishment at the world and at history. This "philosophy of history" does not so much give us the keys of history as it restores history to us as a permanent interrogation. It is not so much a certain truth hidden behind empirical history that it gives us; rather it presents empirical history as the genealogy of truth.[12]

Phenomenology embraces not only the history of a culture—sociology and the history of the individual—psychology—as a basis of understanding humanity, it also attempts to comprehend and account for various levels of human experience—archaeology. Philosophy is not the reflection of a preexisting truth, but, like art, the act of bringing truth into being. This can only be done through expression, a constitutive category for Merleau-Ponty and phenomenology in general. Interestingly, the critical theory of Michel Foucault employs genealogy and archaeology as methodological tools in an attempt to move beyond the phenomenology of his teacher, Merleau-Ponty, whom he neglects to credit but not to criticize. Be that as it may, Foucault's analytical refinements, applied to mass communication theory and electronic dissemination of database information, provide this study with conceptual tools with which to refine the critical phenomenology I hope to advance.

Critical phenomenology attempts to situate problems in experience, not as logical problems but as "real" configurations. That relations between perceiver and perceived in fact occur is obvious. But how they occur involve considerable complexities. To recognize our "openness on the world," we take a phenomenological approach. We "reduce" conscious activity. Reason's presumption, that is, that reason in and by itself is adequation with the world, is reexamined and found to be naive. Reason is based upon perception as well as prereflective, prejudgmental life. Herein lies the origin of much philosophic confusion, and, Jacques Derrida contends, oppression: Reason is not monolithic or even coextensive with the world. Furthermore, this reflective reduction is not an end in itself; indeed, it is a means of questioning to better examine reality. We reduce the natural attitude of simple, straightforward, ongoing existence. The fact becomes phenomenon, appearance. One suspends events not because one denies perceptual faith, but in an attempt to clarify various levels of experience within the field of mass communication.

Critical phenomenology is not scientific as science already presumes the relations of being, ontology,[13] and modes of knowing and knower. For science the correlation is established and complete, while philosophy must ask the questions which involve the ways of existence of the questioner. As we noted, the *epochē* and its questioning, while ongoing and continual, are to be taken as part of a dialectic. One questions *to* clarify as one clarifies the questions. The process is indeterminate to the extent that it is not goal oriented, but it remains teleological insofar as it is directional and committed. A disturbing dimension of what I call critical theory (also referred to as deconstruction, poststructuralism, and postmodernism) focuses on discrediting the understanding that man is going somewhere, that there is any progress. The phenomenology of Levinas attempts to situate the notion of direction in life and culture through an evocation of the ethical relation. Offering no guarantees against the irrationality of history, Merleau-Ponty points to the problem of dirty hands. We all have them. By the necessity to make decisions, in order to regulate conflict and responsibility, some facts and ideas must be taken as more important than others. We undertake an ordering of life with a view to a more humane society. This movement unites our cultural present with our past. In a world which is constituted by shadow as much as material, we do not arrive at final or full answers. The *epochē* is necessary as philosophy is a translation of a text. The text is our engaged life; philosophy attempts to "get at" the text by translating it. But one must be exacting and assiduous. The trick is not to fall into the immediacy of the text nor abstract oneself too far from it. In attempting to account for the obstruction of sense, while remaining open to the faith which unites us, phenomenology has moved beyond description. The translation is useless without the text, and the text is deceptively apparent without translation.

> Our only recourse is a reading of the present which is as full and as faithful as possible, which does not prejudice its meaning, which even recognizes chaos and non-sense where they exist, but which does not refuse to discern a direction and an idea in events where they appear.[14]

But at the same time, reason is not simply thought translated into language; this is another of reason's presumptions. This presumption makes the attempt to relegate communication to a mere tool, a clumsy tool. If one considers perception as the seat of reason, instead of claiming the self-sufficiency of reason, this illusion collapses. From Merleau-Ponty's point of view, one speaks in a community; language regains its unity. Language as a system is an equilibrium, constant at any moment, yet changing through time. If language is a unity, the elements of the system signify their differences with respect to all other elements. Any sign considered by itself is in abeyance. Expression is referential by its nature to our mental equipment and culture at any place or period within history. Man and communication are historical. One learns what one thinks through expression. I surprise myself when I speak to others, read a newspaper, or watch television.

> There is no event which does not bring further precision to the permanent problem of knowing what man and his society are, which does not make this problem a present concern, which does not bring back the problem of a paradox of a society of exploitation that is nonetheless based on the recognition of man by man.[15]

Expression teaches us to think. Meaning does not arise from "I think" but rather from the awareness "I am able to." The fundamental fact of expression is temporality, and the signified does surpass the signified—in speech and writing. At the same time, however, the reason that the signified does not precede speech is that is the result of speech; it is constituted by speech in language. This is Levinas' ethical relation, being-for-the-other, which is paradoxically prior to expression. Merleau-Ponty points out that for the expressive subject, to communicate means to become aware of. Thus, expression is not only to communicate with others; it also serves to illustrate intentions to the speaker. The consequences of such a *praxis* always go beyond the premises.

Merleau-Ponty contends that the phenomenology of language contains and envelops all other considerations. We bring truth through our expressions. We cannot know things in any other way. Since language is the cradle of consciousness, ethics is realized through speech. In communication it becomes possible to understand another person as a subject and not merely as another object: He/she expresses him/herself to me and what is impossible to know through logic becomes apparent through rhetoric. Merleau-Ponty agrees with Husserl: Transcendental subjectivity is intersubjectivity.

MEANING AS MEDIATION

Mediation forms an essential moment of the communicative process, and mass communication can be approached as the mediation of that mediation. The mass media regularly simplify and flatten out events, reducing communication to formula. The antithesis is annihilated from the dialectic. There remains only the thesis—passive acceptance. The audience submits to the stories related to it, accepts those values insinuated by the order of things, and becomes implicated in the continuation of policies and events that intercede on its behalf and furthers the implementation of that which is carried out in its name. The media position their audiences within the circuit of policy advanced by the state and corporations of which most media are now a part. Perceptions and ideas are presented to us within acceptable bounds of thought. The active role of reason is constricted by an emphasis on passivity, the positive moment, derailing dialectical process. Meaning and value are effectively marginalized by the truncation of communication within much print and broadcast reporting. For instance, we have all but succeeded in not only consuming nature but ourselves as well. Now, because this "appears" as logical or expedient, on the whole it is nonetheless reprehensible. This situation is not acceptable. Do the media report the deforestation of the rain forests as the outcome of value based decisions? Is the plight of migrant farm workers simply an unfortunate byproduct of the most productive agricultural system in history? Would it be "reasonable" to suggest that the systematic mistreatment of nature and people has something to do with the ways in which we value certain categories of resources and labor, harvests and hired hands. Do mass media uphold these situations by presenting events as isolated outcomes independent of cultural process, political strategy or instrumental rationality?

Meaning is mediate. Today's post-industrial society portrays meaning as immediate. Reason and fact are taken as tautological. We see an instance of this in pyramid-style journalism. A report appearing in a newspaper leads one to believe that it is objective; to the degree that it convinces, it is unquestionable. It is fact. Fact is reality. Our recognition of reality is implicitly upheld by reason in the correspondence of factual event and by objective reporting of the event and passive acceptance of the truth of the reporting, or the structure of presentation, of the event. Interpretation, instead of being recognized as pervasive, is hidden under this structure of "objective truth." The syntax employed in such societal communication is so closed as to leave no space for understanding as seen from a reflective standpoint. There are no gaps, no room for meaning to arise: there is only formula. Where there is no space in the syntax, semantics suffocate, communication is reduced to convention, habit, acceptable acceptance. Can anyone really tell if the real (conscious) functions of the mass media are to inform and entertain or to indoctrinate and entertain? A critical phenomenology suggests an alternative to one-dimensional existence that would entail a subversion of existing media practices. That is, since it is obvious we cannot create a new language, we must undermine old habits, images, and practices to accommodate reflective thought and interpretation.

Critical approaches must be distinguished from administrative positions. National and international affairs are too often framed by sources rather than journalists. As speech molds language, it is experimental. Pyramid-style journalism is not. This is the thesis: to interpret and interpret again human experience and not be content to accept that that's the way it is or nod our head at all the news that is fit to print. Because there can be no truth when there is a refusal to recognize the situation or maintain successive points of view, truth cannot be abstracted from reality. It is a sedimentation. This is a dynamic process; our world is always in a state of becoming what it is not. It is only sensible that we speak of this dynamic in terms which interpret concepts that cannot be quantified or always broken down into simpler parts. Phenomenology teaches us that it is our mediation with the world which shows that truth does not have the substance of an object; it may be an objective, but certainly truth is not objective. It is a relation. It lies in the opposition of what is and what is not yet. It is our concern that journalism (such as the sort embodied by *Ramparts*) be philosophy realized. Our truth can lie only in the relationships of men and women, institutions, and culture. "In the crucible of events we become aware of what is not acceptable to us, and it is this experience as interpreted which becomes both thesis and philosophy,"[16] says Merleau-Ponty.

Conceived phenomenologically, truth is structured, but within a field that configures various branches of knowledge. Phenomenology describes living and real relations which have consequences among forces, people, objects, and institutions. In this sense, it attempts to present Heidegger's being-in-the world, while affirming Husserl's intentional structure. Furthermore, I think phenomenology—a critical phenomenology—capable of encompassing Foucault's genealogy of power/knowledge and the deconstruction of Derrida. For, if Merleau-Ponty and Levinas teach us how to live, Foucault reminds us how to be wary, and Derrida urges us to play with our traditions. These tools are helpful for our study of mass communication, the air which we breathe. As Merleau-Ponty notes about awareness itself (and mass communication is awareness of, a medium of knowing), it does not lend meaning, but to be aware is to give shape and distance within a field which preexists one's awareness of it, a field all around one, where mediation takes place only through actions that, in turn, transform awareness as well as its field.[17] Merleau-Ponty refined Husserl's approach, a phenomenology of pure consciousness, by placing intentionality within an embodied subject among others and introducing intentionality to dialectical process—history and intersubjectivity—providing the genesis of a critical phenomenology; critical phenomenology no longer limted to the description of individual, autonomous consciousness, but a phenomenology able to carry out a radical cultural critique without lapsing into the dense solidity of pure materialism or rocketing to an airy idealism. Merleau-Ponty points to the double nature of man as the being who is seeing/seen, feeling/felt, and thinking/thought, which explains how truth enfolds us. Kindred to Merleau-Ponty, Levinas locates in the saying/said aspect of man's polar character the fundamental condition for ethical behavior. Not only is the saying/said essential for ethics, but their correlation outlines the derivative subject-object structure that Western thought mistakenly assumes to be primary.[18] The polarity of the being who embodies the saying/said embodies the mediation interconnecting these modes and forms the normative ground from which this critique develops. Truth is thereby not an object held by the mind; it takes place in that field with others, so truth and intersubjectivity, rationality and freedom, or authority and domination are traced out together within an intersubjective field of experience. The doubling, or the fold of man, relies on perception (one's point of view) and expression (differentiation). Knowledge and communication are mediated by perceptual and cultural life, while continually transforming that life insofar as the incarnate subject inserts him/herself into it and symbolizes what he/she experiences.[19] We inhabit one world within various experiential levels. Phenomenology emphasizes the lived and reflective orders of experience, while critical theory articulates the organizing and over-organizing institutions and strategies of control through which the lived and reflective dimensions are positioned and pronounced. Mass communication participates in this dialogue and this manipulation; the media protect and victimize, blame and praise, uplift and debase, and safeguard democracy and prevent it from ever being totally realized. Correspondingly, technology is inseparably intertwined in the mass communication process—it is in this context that Marshall McLuhan's proclamation, the medium is the message, makes sense.

Traditionally, the study of mass communication has been concerned with effects and functions; in fact, this overemphasis was what drove McLuhan's aphoristic approach. Little to no attention was paid to form. Further, the debate over whether to emphasize form or substance goes beyond mass communication to embody one of the great debates of the 20th century. We see in it not only critical versus administrative approaches to media and cultural studies, but existential phenomenology suffering historical setbacks at the hands of structuralists and post-structuralists. What is at stake is how we categorize "man". If existentialism is a humanism, postmodernism disavows its emphasis on an individualism that cannot account for disciplinary societies, the marginalization of the Third World, or the engineering of consent within Western democracies.

Ought we concern ourselves with the proper methodical order capable of creating particular situations, the technical mode: form? Or is it adventitious to question the quiddity at the heart of the situation, the essential mode: substance? The phenomenology of technology allows for a description amalgamating these two modes. We recognize that our approach determines what is going to matter and what will be recognized as important. How we will connect these importances or distinguish facts from one another is mediated by our theory for connection and demarcation. If existentialism overemphasized the conscious control that individuals exercise over social situations, structuralism underesteemed the recognition that people, after all, create cultures. We approach society obliquely. Ours is a social fabric woven by the hands of men and women working with legal, political, philosophical, and economic threads to make patterns which, while participants may be too near-sighted to recognize or preoccupied to premeditate, nonetheless form historically recognizable designs.

In his phenomenological study of technology and man, Ihde argues what he calls his strong thesis: "Human-machine relations are existential relations in which our fate and destiny are implicated, but which are subject to the very ambiguity found in all existential relations."[20] Ambiguity arises from the life world and can be recognized in the difference between experience and our reflections on that experience; this critical distinction is what Ihde contends will prevent our total submersion in technocracy. However, we are linked to this technology, we form a moment of an intentional arc which is experienced as being-in-the-world and reflected by consciousness of a phenomenon. We are then involved with the world through mass-mediated technology, but we are simultaneously involved with the technology. We see that television as a window on the world is taken literally by many people, yet is a mediation of a mediation, a creation, an experience itself, but one quite distinct in kind from the experience it professes to portray. As the technology of television is refined, and the more sophisticated the medium becomes, the more "natural" or transparent becomes one's perception of and through that medium. The human-technology relation seems so simple. But does television news bring the world to us, does television technology create a world for us, or does technology create us within its technosophere? Ihde employs the phenomenological notion of embodied subject to offer a description of embodied relations with technology, in this example, television. Here, too, we delineate levels of experience. The machine displays oscillating degrees of transparency, that is, when one turns it on or changes channels or a commercial deflects awareness, the viewer becomes aware of the medium, the technological object becomes thematic. During the course of a program, this objectification of the TV flutters in and out. When watching life and death situations on national news, I forget I am not watching through a window on the scene, I suspend reflection and assume I'm watching events unfold in the world. But the news director knows better.

The medium, at the level of viewing, has removed incarnation from the subject of my perception, reduced the opulence of life to a screen, removed the flesh from the scene. Yet while restricting these dimensions of perception of other people, the medium extends perception and access to other times and places. Accordingly, embodiment relations provide for the withdrawal of the medium as awareness extends through the focus of the camera, while interpretive relations allow for a reading of the scene. Through the television, one is "informed". The constituted nature of mediated presentations are produced by experts, and this editorial, synthetic nature of the medium carries with it political and cultural interpretations, providing an instance of the exercise of power through knowledge, patterns of information presented as credible. Technological advances result in a phenomenological transformation of the perceived object and the subject's modes of knowing. The scale is expanded while context is reduced. Additional aspects of experience are revealed within the horizon of perception, but the field is homogenized. Ihde describes the tension as not so much a relationship between the viewer and the viewed, but between the truth and reliability of the content, "the representations produced by the instrument which is always presumably *of* the world."[21]

Not only does the information relayed over the airwaves impart editorial content, it gives form to experience. It in-forms. The classic example of the presidential Nixon-Kennedy debate comes to mind. Those who heard the debate over the radio reported that, so far as they were concerned, Nixon won. Those who watched the debate on television perceived Kennedy's winning style and were sure Kennedy had vanquished his dark, sweating adversary. It was form over content. Here we see rationality influenced by technology. Neurophysiological research suggests that television provides its own dimension of social reality, one based on the values of entertainment, disseminating knowledge and value systems as persuasive and pervasive as the world views inculcated by everyday experience and science.[22] Moreover, given that electronic media control major cognitive processes in viewers, television constitutes a reality system in which the viewer is passively connected to the programming stimulation. Chesebro suggests that this reality system is quite distinct from other realities, and, in fact, may be in competition with them over cultural dominance. He reports that television does not actively involve the viewer; it is an experience of *passive* reception of massive amounts of information—generating, in turn, few thoughts—which allow for minimal links to the viewer's life—producing amorphous responses to whatever is seen. Television serves as a metaphor of reality, invoking identifiable mental patterns that may become habitual and which finally achieve a cerebral dominance, so to speak. A heavy television viewer begins to perceive not that television is like the world, but that the world is like television.

> [F]or the electronic format isolates an emotional state, concentrates solely upon that emotional state to exclusion of other emotions, and then orchestrates or coordinates the situation, dialogue, actors, and actions to evoke and to reinforce the emotion desired.[23]

That the print and electronic press orchestrate the news is hardly news. But what emotional states do the press strive to reinforce? Are strategies put in place by which the press communicates some points of view to the exclusion of other considerations? Of course. One can discern an intentionality within the field of mass communication discourse. Mass media do their work within a field, displaying intentional structures, but this intentionality must be described as intersubjective. By this I mean that the methods deployed, the tactics advanced, and the news disseminated are not produced by any identifiable author. Rather, the process is part of the role of an institutionalized press with a historical development and focused on certain essential and interrelated goals, that is, maximizing profits and expanding or at least maintaining circulation or ratings; this is in part achieved by not offending either sources of information or advertisers.

The method of objectively reporting the news can be seen as a historical development of these two interests. As is well known, European journalism is much more partisan along the political spectrum than is ours, and up until the early part of the 20th century, American journalism displayed similar loyalties. Partisan journalism came to be perceived as counterproductive and unprofessional in the United States. A committed press was also a press that aggravated and further polarized the community, which displeases advertisers and official sources. So information was made more impartial, unbiased, objective. Objective reporting can also be seen as a contagion. As occurs on a regular basis, concepts and ideas spread across the boundaries of the natural sciences to the social sciences, and wanting to appear in control, even if to a lesser degree than in a laboratory, the press cultivated this scientific attitude of neutral observation. To be objective is by definition to be responsible, professional, detached, and, above all, credible. It mollifies those in power while domesticating the audience. Events set down as objective fact are perceived more passively than occurrences described as contingencies, developments flowing from specific attitudes and policies. As Bagdikian puts it, objectivity has "widened the chasm that is a constant threat to democracy—the difference between the realities of private power and the illusions of public imagery."[24]

If we step back and perform the phenomenological reduction, from the ongoing practices of the press in culture, we can trace out within the intentional structures of the press active and passive moments. Intertwined with the phenomenon of objectivity within American journalism (I expect to see the notion exported as the number of corporate voices in the worldwide media decreases) is the growing articulation of passive modes of relaying news and information. Essential to the objective method is the reliance on expert and official sources. This is problematic insofar as these sources are often the very parties interested in affecting the "spin" placed on a news story by structuring the information imparted to the journalist who, in turn, passes it on or writes it up. A sort of circuit of passivity is formed by this pervasive "source" journalism. Experts, those adept in articulating the views of power, to paraphrase Henry Kissenger, conceive of a policy, pass it along, let us say to the New York Times reporter who is on a first-name basis with his source, and this "news" is dutifully picked up by the networks and passed along to the viewing public, who is, according to research findings, already in the passive mode, ready to be informed about the events of the day, which he or she assumes truly to have occurred in the world on that day.[25]

Embodying an active moment in what I refer to as the intentional structure of the press practicing passive, source-oriented reporting, Karp recounts an ironic instance in the tradition of admiring servility in the guise of objective reporting.[26] Time ran a story in December 1982 critical of the level of preparation and quality of Ronald Reagan's decision-making process concerning matters of extreme gravity. The sources of the story were Reagan's aides, "who thought it would help them club him awake." Months later, Reagan aid Michael Deaver lunched with a New York Times reporter at the White House to impress upon him Reagan's hands on approach. The Times ran a front-page story emphasizing the president's grip on the issues concerning an upcoming economic summit conference. The image of Reagan's competence was dutifully relayed by the national networks in their covering of the summit. It is not that television reflects the world, but the world becomes like television. The viewer's awareness is expanded to take in events of the world, but alternatively, the viewer's understanding of the event is reduced by the coverage and manipulation inherent in media reporting methods.

PHENOMENOLOGICAL POSSIBILITIES FOR MEDIA RESEARCH

We have seen that the two essential concepts for any phenomenologically based investigation are reduction and intentionality. Now, these instruments of qualitative analysis may be applied at diverse levels of experience to describe consciousness, perception, dialogue, and relations between individual and group or among groups of people. The potential formulations are limitless. Lemert, while not purposefully employing the phenomenological method, employs similar notions of reduction and intentionality in his research on the effects of mass communication and public opinion. Using the method he refers to as "effects analysis," Lemert criticizes latent assumptions—insupportable reductions—made by researchers in mass media, political science, and sociology. These reductions came about when social scientists employed methods of the natural and biological models of science. Traditional media research tends to quantify and homogenize attitudes and phenomena.

The resulting reductionism has led researchers to at least questionable operational assumptions. Lemert defines reductionist as the attempt to explain social-level phenomena according to the structure of individual-level phenomena. Today, public opinion is viewed, generally, as the sum of everyone's attitudes about something. Lemert feels this "bad" reduction has three correlates which he calls correspondence rules:

> First, if mass communication does produce massive attitude change toward an issue, that change is *sufficient* to have produced a change in public opinion. Second . . . if mass communication has not produced attitude change among its audience, public opinion change cannot have occurred. . . .Third, the attitude of all members of media audiences count as same. . . .[27]

According to these correspondence rules, individual behaviors are correlated to mass behavior.

Lemert argues that the correspondence rules and the original reduction (public opinion equals the sum of everyone's attitudes) are inaccurate. Like Husserl, Lemert asks, Upon what do these reductive assumptions stand? They stand upon a method borrowed from a science of quantities, applied to phenomena marked by differences and qualities (people). Some people are more susceptible to attitude change than others; certain individuals' motives for using the media differ in degree and number from the motives of others; the jump from individual to group is not necessarily an arithmetic or even geometric progression. Lemert concludes we need a new reduction which will, in turn, generate new correspondence rules. One method Lemert views sympathetically is coorientation: the attempt to analyze linkage between one person or group and another with regard to respective perceptions of what the other thinks about some intentional attitude object. Effects analysis points to the need for a new reduction; one that specifies a "greater number of interrelationships among more variables . . ."[28] For example, he cites the interrelationships of participation, power, and influence frameworks.

This leads to intentionality, which Lemert calls "attitude." "An attitude is a state of affect felt by the individual toward what is, for that individual, a psychological object," says Lemert.[29] Any intentional attitude has two components: affect (intention) and attitude object (anything perceived). This process exhibits dimensions of direction, intensity, and salience. Direction and intensity determine salience, that is, how positively, negatively, or neutrally something is perceived determines how clearly it stands out from the background. Traditional theory considers two broad categories of intentionality with regard to the audience and the media. They are attitude change and attitude reinforcement. Lemert's attitude change refers to "the movement of affect toward a new sign."[30] He defines reinforcement "as an increase in the intensity of affect felt toward an object without a change in sign."[31] Besides the permutations of attitude recognized within traditional research, Lemert posits "attitude formation" and "attitude object change." These two descriptive categories exhibit a marked similarity to the phenomenological reduction to better describe previously unrecognized intentional structures. Lemert's conception of attitude formation "involves recognition of object and the learning of an effective response to it."[32] Attitude object change substitutes one attitude object for another, leaving the attitude untouched. "The importance of attitude object change is that it might lead to changes in the way we react and behave *without any change in the affect felt toward either the old or the new object.*"[33]. He cites as example Nixon's "protective reaction strikes" in Vietnam, and Kennedy's "quarantine" of Soviet ships during the Cuban missile crisis. Generally, euphemisms work as changes in attitude object. Advertising supplies many: "Remember Lanolin (sheep grease)?"[34] Lemert asks. Additionally, one remembers Reagan's comparison of the American founding fathers to the Nicaraguan contras, whom Reagan called "freedom fighters," although many recognized, nonetheless, as terrorists.

Traditional mass communication research, Lemert says, measures only affects and not attitude objects. To help define or identify a situation, any attitude object change must be recognized (if such change occurs, of course). This means placing an event or attitude object in a social context, from a situation viewed from a grounded perspective as lingual and differential; difference implies social and political consequences. Lemert writes:

> At the moment, object change seems the best available concept for explaining how certain changes in public opinion processes are produced. The reason for its importance is that most members of the population do not seem spontaneously to have worked out very many relationships among their political attitude objects.[35]

Lemert locates three components of his conception of public opinion: efficacy—one's feeling that through participation something can be accomplished; participation—expressing issue-related attitudes; and power—the relative quality of the participation. Here is another parallel to Merleau-Ponty's phenomenology: transcendental subjectivity and intersubjectivity. Lemert emphasizes, "Power is not the possession of political actors, but instead will be used as a convenient label to describe one or more of a number of *relationships* among actors, and . . . these relationships are not fixed; power can change."[36] This prefigures our later discussion of Foucault's theory of power as relational, not substantial, and to that extent power is nominal. Power produces knowledge. The arrangement of patterns of information embodies power. Mass communication, Lemert argues, can change the amount and intensity of participation, attitude change and formation, object change and relative power of participants. By mobilizing information, the media influence public opinion, contrary to current beliefs among mass media researchers. Nondecision as well as conscious decision influence participation within the media whose efforts, Lemert proclaims, are to persuade and mobilize public opinion.

In the process of mobilization and persuasion the media rely on statistics because numbers seem objective and unbiased. "It is a safe kind of journalism. You can't generally be accused of ideological or political bias," quips a consultant to the Gallup-Times Mirror survey organization. The statistics survey industry is expanding at about 15% per year from earnings of over $2 billion a year. While a great deal can be learned from analyzing statistics and polls, they, of course, are not unbiased or objective, either. Someone decides parameters, questions, ordering of those questions, terminology of those questions, the inflection of the terminology, and the order of those questions put to people who most certainly are not unbiased. The point of polling is, in part, to map out and tally biases. Take the abortion issue. If a question in a survey is framed in terms concerning the right of privacy or of the right of individual choice by a woman in consultation with her physician, then most Americans appear to be pro-choice. But if the issue is presented from another perspective, for example, should abortion be made illegal or be permitted only if the woman's health is in jeopardy, then people's responses appear more anti-abortion.

When the GOP polled Americans in 1984, 2% of the voters listed crime and drugs as uppermost on their minds. By October 1988, 20% listed crime and drugs.[37] In the spring of 1989, from a list of 11 issues that had been *in the news recently*, Gallup reported 74% of its respondents paid a great deal of attention to the problem of crime and 73% to the drug problem. The U.S. trade deficit captured the same level of interest in only 36% of the respondents.[38] The operative terms, I would suggest, are "in the news recently." The 1988 presidential campaign was noteworthy for the attention paid by the Bush campaign to "red meat" attacks on Michael Dukakis' positions on what were substantially peripheral issues, such as a prisoner furlough program and the Pledge of Allegiance in classrooms. Very little attention consequently was paid to the trade deficit. An agenda was put into place. The agenda was transmitted by the media, but the strategy was designed according to a particular tactic, authored by Bush campaign aides including his campaign manager, his pollster, and his media consultant. In May 1988, a Gallup poll placed Bush well behind Dukakis. That poll also claimed that five voters were favorably disposed toward Dukakis for every one who did not care for him; Bush supporters and detractors were evenly distributed.

The alarmed Bush strategists traveled to New Jersey where they had assembled two groups of 15 Democrats each who had supported Reagan in 1984. Behind two-way mirrors the managers of the presidential campaign observed their subjects reactions to issues like the prisoner furlough plan, the Pledge of Allegiance, and other matters that these media experts had been amassing for months and which became the sensational 30-second commercials the rest of the public viewed for the duration of the presidential campaign of 1988. Assuming that one of the groups was a control group, the result was that by the end of the "market test" on the "focus groups," 15 of the 30 experimental subjects had abandoned Dukakis. "'I realized right there that we had the wherewithal to win . . . and that the sky was the limit on Dukakis' negatives,' Atwater, Bush's campaign manager, said."[39]

A PROBLEMATIC

Mass communication research and practice largely have ignored philo-sophical and ethical concerns and have focused more on empirical and individual issues. I hope to illustrate that the very structure of communi-cation as mediation forms a breathing system for a larger order. Information as value focuses on the kinds of positions posed by Merleau-Ponty and Levinas, and mass communication as value system provides a matrix for the problems articulated by Foucault and Derrida.

Great attention has been paid to the notion of media as tech-nique. Media are technique. They mediate and convey. Clearly, com-plexity calls for ethical considerations for values do come into conflict. Ethics and technique ought to be scrutinized before our situation is unrecognizable (from our current vantage point). Technique and ethics are as means and ends; so goes the archaic dichotomy. The world *has* changed. Technology is not simply acquired, leaving values unaffected. Most would agree that value structures have shifted during the last, say, 50 years. Certainly, values have altered. We must seek out new ethical constructs that might deal with current contradictions and totalizing fac-tors better than Kant's categorical imperative or pragmatism. If values and society are ethically unquestioned, then uncriticized ethics will arise. Intentionality must be brought into play at an empirical as well as phenomenological level.

Jacques Ellul reports that such an uncritical ethics has taken hold of society; he straightforwardly calls it technological morality. This ethics supplies two tenets: "1) it is behavioral (in other words, only correct practice, not intentions or motivations, counts), 2) it rules out the prob-lematics of traditional morality (the morality of ambiguity is unaccept-able in the technological world)."[40] This system recognizes success, power, certainty, and earnestness (opposed to play) as functional con-cepts, concepts of authority—concepts traditionally associated with ends rather than means. Means engulf ends, perverting the process and dis-torting their objects—us. Thus, conceptual and practical ethics must be sought out to challenge the positivistic state of affairs. Ellul asserts the need for a new ethics with the power to preserve the role of traditional ethics, preserving the control of man (as individual) over life, and including the qualitative development of society and personal relation-ships. The categories Ellul suggests are "non-power, freedom, conflict, and transgression."[41] The functional touchstone, considering the calami-ties possible today, would be choosing *not* to do that which one has the power to do. For example, the refusal to continue to compete destruc-tively, or the refusal to overemploy simplicity merely to sell more issues of a publication. For, our problem, as Ellul posits the issue, is one of meaning—fear of meaninglessness. "Uncertainty as to whether life means anything is the sickness of modern man, and the rediscovery of meaning is conditional upon the choice of nonpower."[42]

Another voice calling for difference is that of John Merrill. Although limited in depth and scope, the tenor is sincere and vital. Merrill has come up with his unique brand of commitment following existential thought. It is to be opposed to quietude and blind acceptance. "Rather, existential journalism is that aspect of journalism mainly manifested in an attitude of freedom, commitment, rebellion, and responsibility. It makes no a priori assumptions as to the direction journalism should take."[43] Merrill's thought is really classical liberalism in contemporary clothing, but it is sincere. He falls, however, into traditional concepts instead of searching for new perspectives. For him, the subject vs. object, mind vs. body, us vs. them splits reflect the structure of the social world. Merrill divides writers into mainly scientific-objective or mainly subjective-artistic types. The existentialist, unmistakably, is of the latter group. He admits that this is not an either-or dichotomy but more a predominant disposition. Merrill asks, "How involved and committed should journalists be? What is reality and how should journalists best get at it? And, finally, how should they pass on such 'reality-information?'"[44]

He divides those who work in mass communication into two camps: Existential or Rational. Does this imply existentialists are not rational and rationalists not existential? He continues to call existentialists romantic and rationalists Platonic. He has set up—once again—realism vs. idealism or even more fruitless, emotion against intellect. It ought to be clear upon inspection that emotion is not pitted against intellect. They are different levels of experience, separate yet intertwined. The life world grounds both. Logic, as well as intuition, is founded on perception, Husserl points out. Perhaps if Merrill had looked at the tradition he borrows from a bit more widely, he could have avoided this rather obvious error. Merleau-Ponty goes to great pains to illustrate the murkiness of objectivity and the many levels of knowing. Existentialism sprang from phenomenology, ran its course, and remerged with the phenomenological tradition or split off into Neo-Marxism.

"The only valid ethics is that which is within each person,"[45] Merrill says. If each person is a self-enclosed entity, responsible to himself, from where does validity come? Apart from the solipsism implied by the statement, phenomenology and gestalt psychology have shown conclusively that human reality is intersubjectively constituted, and along with the social environment, the values arising within the life world are anchored concurrently in the other. Merrill enthrones the person, not the group. In his reaction against the theory of social responsibility, he omits half the discourse. One sees that behind the cry for existential authenticity lies classical 19th-century liberalism with all its beliefs and doctrines.

The individual desires recognition, communication from within an asymmetrical relationship. Communication constitutes a dialogue. It makes no sense as a monologue. His faulty punctuation distorts his message. Sharing information requires at least two persons discoursing about something (the third term). Merrill's conception of individualism, while incomplete, is valuable. Individualism, he points out, "means that how he looks on the world as a reporter is the world; and as a reporter he transmits at least a portion of his total perceptions to his reader as his world."[46] This, he continues, articulates an ethical situation. The life world is quite complex and heterogeneous. To venture to communicate is risky. One can err. Responsibility in part means accepting that risk to communicate. Merrill finds too many in the media accept subservience, timidity, and conformity. The emphasis on function and technique fosters such indoctrination. Merrill pleads with us to listen to the voice of conscience—to be ethical.

Another intentional arc is instituted by the other. The other, "mass" man, presents a profound challenge to a writer and the media, as well. Jean Baudrillard relays the common assumption that more information ought to accelerate circulation of meaning, creating increased value through its exchange. Baudrillard displays information as waste, serving to maintain injustices in society. This is not only information overload, but also what he calls the creation of circular hyperreality. The representation of an event becomes, through the media, more real that the event itself. Pollution occurs. Hyperreality and information-overload have all commonly acknowledged effect-difference. "All the media and all information cut both ways: while appearing to augment the social, in reality they neutralize social relations and the social itself, at a profound level."[47] A destructuring of the social life world takes place. People become impervious to information on the one hand, and grow excited by the trivial on the other. Look, for example, at soap operas and prime-time "dramas." A "universalization" of difference takes place. Interchangeability shows itself to be more devastating than Derrida thinks. Confusion of signifier with signified is a malfunction, a disturbance of psyche. Thus, media overtake the life world of interaction for consumption of indifference. The media fuzz the distinction between form and content. Meaning unmediated loses value, sincerity, sense. Baudrillard writes:

> That, strictly speaking is what implosion means: the defusing of polarities, the short circuiting of the poles of every differential system of meaning, the obliteration of distinctions and oppositions

between terms, including the distinction between the medium and the real.[48]

Circularity destroys dialectics. Triviality becomes dramatic. Stereotypes replace archetypes. Indifference to what is essential in life—value, interaction, desire, difference, death—spreads through the media, causing not overt resentment but insincerity. Baudrillard does not claim to romanticize the mass man, to offer the title of "alienated" or "manipulated." The power of the mass man is his silence. This, Baudrillard seems to say, is a protective reaction, a strategic resistance which takes on the style of the system itself. If the news shows, newspapers, and magazines look alike, so do their audiences. This amounts, according to Baudrillard, to holding up a mirror to the mirror of society, fighting sameness with the same, signifier with signified. This, then, is anything *but* passive, although it may not be fully conscious. This phenomenon must be investigated in all its positivistic blatancy. "Is it the media which dissolve meaning and produce the formless or 'informed' masses, or is it the masses which defeat the media by perverting or silently absorbing all the messages which they produce?"[49]

Evidently, there are those who see technology as neutral. Maybe. But to agree with Ellul and Levinas (technique as totalizing), our identity is an ethical struggle for freedom-in-depth. This depth must come through maturation in dealing with technique. Ellul writes:

[E]thics is a useful instrument [as value system, symbolic order] for achieving liberation . . . *we must decide (and the decision carries with it grave consequences) that is it not technique which frees us but rather it is from technique that we must free ourselves.*[50]

Thus conflict becomes, in Ellul's view, an ethical principle, along with play. Through play one can make the necessary holes in the social fabric. Writing involves a playful dimension. However, since the values of freedom and nonpower create conflict and tension, Ellul elevates or focuses them on an ethical plane. People, he says, exist in conflict.

Ramparts magazine embodies an example of a publication that attempted to persuade and influence its readers as well as to criticize American social and political policy. *Ramparts* presented stylized, nonobjective, committed writing and a no-holds-barred brand of dedicated, perspectival journalism. In short, *Ramparts* approached journalism from an ethical standpoint; the magazine emphasized context and exuded a sense of engagement with its fellow man.

NOTES TO CHAPTER 1

1. M. Merleau-Ponty, "Philosophy and Non-philosophy since Hegel," trans. H. Silverman, *Telos*, 29 (Fall 1976), pp. 39-105.

2. "The People, the Press & Politics," Times Mirror Study, conducted by the Gallup Organization, September 1987.

3. M. Merleau-Ponty, *Phenomenology of Perception*, trans. C. Smith (New York: Humanities Press, 1962), p. xix.

4. M. Merleau-Ponty, *In Praise of Philosophy and Other Essays*, trans. J. Wild and J.M. Edie (Evanston, IL: Northwestern University Press, 1988), p. 14.

5. M. Merleau-Ponty, *Sense and Non-Sense*, trans. with preface by H. and P. Dreyfus (Evanston, IL: Northwestern University Press, 1964), p. 19.

6. Merleau-Ponty, "Philosophy and Non-philosophy since Hegel," p. 69.

7. Ibid., p. 81.

8. M. Merleau-Ponty, *Adventures of the Dialectic*, trans. J. Bien (Evanston, IL: Northwestern University Press, 1973), p. 138.

9. R.L. Gregory, *Eye and Brain, The Psychology of Seeing* (New York: World University Library; McGraw-Hill Book Company, 1966), p. 11.

10. M. Merleau-Ponty, *The Prose of the World*, ed. C. Lefort, trans. J. O'Neill (Evanston, IL: Northwestern University Press, 1973), p. 139.

11. Merleau-Ponty, *Sense and Non-Sense*, p. 48.

12. Merleau-Ponty, *Adventures of the Dialectic*, p. 56.

13. Being as Being, becoming.

14. Merleau-Ponty, *Sense and Non-Sense*, p. 169.

15. Merleau-Ponty, *Adventures of the Dialectic*, p. 38.

16. Ibid., p. 3.

17. M. Merleau-Ponty, "Themes from the Lectures at the Collège de France, 1952-1960," trans. J.O'Neill, in *In Praise of Philosophy*, p. 115.

18. See E. Levinas, *Collected Philosophical Papers*, trans. A. Lingis (The Hague: Martinus Nijhoff, 1987), pp. 79-83, and Levinas, *Otherwise than Being*, trans. A. Lingis (The Hague: Martinus Nijhoff, 1981), pp. 45-48.

19. M. Merleau-Ponty, "An Unpublished Text by Merleau Ponty: A Prospectus of His Work," in *The Primacy of Perception*, ed. with an intro. by J.M. Edie (Evanston, IL: Northwestern University Press, 1964), p. 7.

20. D. Ihde, *Technics and Praxis* (Dordrecht: Reidel, 1979), p. 4.

21. Ibid., p. 33.

22. J.W. Chesebro, "The Media Reality: Epistemological Functions of Media in Cultural Systems," in *Critical Studies in Mass Communication* (June 1984), p. 126.

23. Ibid., p. 122.

24. B.H. Bagdikian, *The Media Monoply*, 2nd ed. (Boston: Beacon Press, 1987), p. 180.

25. See W. Karp, All the Congressmen's Men: How Capitol Hill Controls the Press," in *Harper's* July 1989, pp. 55-63.

26. Ibid., p. 57.

27. J.B. Lemert, *Does Mass Communication Change Public Opinion After All? A New Aproach to Effects Analysis* (Chicago: Nelson-Hall, 1981), p. 2.

28. Ibid., p. 213.

29. Ibid., p. 20.

30. Ibid., P. 22.

31. Ibid., p. 22.

32. Ibid., p. 22.

33. Ibid., p. 25.

34. Ibid., p. 25

35. Ibid., p. 28.

36. Ibid., p. 36.

37. L. Cannon, "President Defends Bush Tactics, *The Washington Post*, October 28, 1988, p. All.

38. "The People, the Press & Economics," Times Mirror Study, conducted by the Gallup Organization, May 1989, p. 24.

39. P. Taylor, D.S. Broder, "Evolution of the TV Era's Nastiest Presidential Race," *The Washington Post*, October 28, 1988, pp. A1, A10.

40. J. Ellul, "The Power of Technique and the Ethics of Non-Power," trans. M. Lydon. *The Myths of Information: Technology and Postindustrial Culture*, ed. K. Woodward (Madison, WI: Coda Press, 1980), p. 244.

41. Ibid., p. 245.

42. Ibid., p. 246.

43. J.C. Merrill, *Existential Journalism* (New York: Hastings House, 1977), p. 50.

44. Ibid., p. 41.

45. Ibid., p. 132.

46. Ibid., p. 54.

47. J. Baudrillard, "The Implosion of Meaning in the Media and the Implosion of the Social in the Masses," trans. M. Lydon. *The Myths of Information*, p. 139.

48. Ibid., p. 141.

49. Ibid., p. 141.

50. Ellul, "The Power of Technique," *The Myth of Power*, p. 246.

A Height of Audacity, Ramparts

To recognize a standard, it will help to describe the efforts of a publication that attempted and often succeeded in raising the banner that articulates the values heralded in critical phenomenology. One need not peer too far into the past to locate voices of difference that evoked values consistent with critical phenomenology, a magazine written for citizens (as opposed to demographic parameters) criticizing power relations, offering a dimension of ethical responsibility within a sphere of playfulness, approaching journalism in an effort to map out critical terrains while promoting issues from a definite perspective, and fusing theory to practice, reporting to thinking, and facts to values. This magazine attempted to communicate to all members of our society the recognition that events were neither the way they had been announced to us by both the media and policymakers, nor, for example, that academic institutions were independent from military and surveillance interests, as so many had assumed. Since communication is intentional and proceeds along lines of perspective, intentional structures could be reported whereby meaning could be produced that contested the objective version of the times. This amalgam of perspective, style, and dedication is apparent in, what from the point of view of this study, founds an authentic attempt at mass communication, issuing from the level of group involvement and incorporating the commitment of individuals.

While mainstream media represent the voices of conformity, *Ramparts* embodied a moral and journalistic commitment to others, while exposing the genealogy of power at work within the American tradition of relying on the beneficence of authority. Undergirding its style was a conviction that while meaning and history are contingent, they depend on something, a publication which would try to get at a truth more truthful than the offical version. *Ramparts'* crusades attempted to reconsider social issues from the perspective of those who suffered the brunt of decisions made by those in control. The Vietnam war and racism were the two issues claiming much of *Ramparts'* dedication. *Ramparts* attempted to give a voice to those of draft age and victims of racism.

Ramparts furnishes numerous instances of the style and commitment Merleau-Ponty urged writers to evolve when communicating about human affairs. In May 1962, *Ramparts* began with the general idea of defending the Catholic Church, in an articulate and compassionate fashion, against secularism. The idea was to strike forth from the ramparts. The magazine presented highbrow, classical, and what it recalcitrantly came to recognize as totally unrealistic, misguided beliefs and ideals. One of the more serious and consequential chimeras in which *Ramparts* put faith was that the Catholic Church desired a broadened debate with laymen, enlightened or otherwise. The people at *Ramparts* grew in their dismay at the chicanery and devious methods asserted by the church. *Ramparts'* trepidation shifted to skepticism which eventually fostered hostility. By 1964, this Catholic layman's magazine began to dissociate itself from the church.

The civil rights movement and the war in Vietnam served as the focal pivots around which *Ramparts* rallied. These issues spawned the progressive alienation of the magazine from the church and, later, from the very fabric of established American domestic and foreign policies. The cloth ripped. Walter Hinckle, prime mover of the magazine, writes of the period:

> Almost everyone started off believing in something—moral persuasion, civil disobedience, education, gradual progress, voting rights, effective new laws, good will among men—but those beliefs all ended as rumpled illusions.[1]

Ramparts evolved almost by accident, certainly without plan. Its development was contingent on the exterior events of those turbulent times from the early '60s through the early '70s. The magazine's metamorphosis spanned four years, while those who worked for *Ramparts* awakened to a situation that grew progressively worse than what they imagined at the outset. The church was indeed involved in Vietnam; the United States did play a part in the death of Che Guevara; the CIA and the FBI illegally manipulated persons and events here and abroad; and much of the civil rights conflict was orchestrated by those in positions of political power and social respect. *Ramparts* unearthed a path from the Catholic particular to the political universal. Those at *Ramparts* certainly exercised commitment, at first to the church, later to the New Left. They were committed, sincere people. These were hysterical times and if Ramparts at times erred, it erred in judgment, not motive.

We approach *Ramparts* from three perspectives: editorial issues and development, financial-managerial problems, and critical appraisals of *Ramparts'* effort by other publications. The significance of *Ramparts'* editorial positions is obvious. The financial convolutions and marketing innovations flesh out the magazine and aid in illuminating the development and eventual demise of the publication. Critical views afford a sense of perspective to the efforts of *Ramparts* during its short life.

EDITORIAL ISSUES

It is not true that the world is divided into two empires of good and evil. It is not true that we cannot think without weakening nor be strong without talking nonsense. It is not true that good intentions justify everything, nor that we have the right to the opposite of what we want. The comedy of history, the switching of roles and the frivolity of the actors do not prevent us from discerning a clear enough course of action, provided only that we take pains to know what is going on rather than nourishing phantasms, and provided that we distinguish anguish from anxiety and commitment from fanaticism.[2]

This manifesto, written by Merleau-Ponty, appeared on the back cover of the first edition of *Les Temps Modernes* in 1946; it expresses the essence of *Ramparts'* undertaking. While it had a definite point of view, *Ramparts* embraced no ideology. Its effort was critical. The magazine took up traditional threads of the muckraking tradition, largely abandoned since *McClure's* suspended publication. *Ramparts* increasingly served to expose the government, to reveal the truth—a task which it felt to be humanistic and ethical, not primarily logical or ideological—to interpret events according to their human impact. In it the New Journalism emerged full-blown and unafraid, stylish, even trendy, yet men of such stature as Bertrand Russell and Jean-Paul Sartre contributed to *Ramparts*. Editor Hinckle never ignored the facts, even if others after him at times did. "There is nothing ideological about the facts."[3] Hinckle advised younger writers hoping to influence events by dramatizing a story. He claimed to edit out self-aggrandizing.

As Hinckle fused the energies and organized the considerable talents that formed *Ramparts*, Edward Keating provided the funds and actually founded the magazine. Two men more different in style and temperament would be difficult to bring together. Hinckle—bold, young, outrageous, incredibly innovative, radical—played havoc with the finances while Keating, a convert to Catholicism, staid, a middle-aged nonpracticing lawyer, a millionaire, came across like an alert banker, a stabilizing force in the careening lurches of *Ramparts'* forays. After all, it was Keating's money. Keating considered *Catcher in the Rye* a dirty book. Keating hired Hinckle in the autumn of 1961, fired him in January, and rehired him in November. Hinckle never asked why he was fired nor the reason he was rehired. It wasn't his style. He simply forged ahead. However, he did form impressions.

> He [Keating] didn't look like a millionaire to me, but then I had never met one before. His shoes were black FBI issue, his socks had clocks in them. His pants bagged at the bottom as if there were several marbles in the cuffs.[4]

The storm caused by their collision abated only when Keating left the magazine, a beaten and weathered man some years later.

Keating courted the Jesuits; he felt they would provide the other side of *Ramparts'* dialogue. When Hinckle wrote an article critical of the Jesuits, calling them narcissistic and worse, Keating responded in what became an archetypical fashion. "You're too rough on them," he said. "We've got to be reasonable in our criticism. You can't describe the Jesuits as Rome's caterpillars! I'm seeking a dialogue."[5] But the dialogue was not forthcoming. A knife in the back was. Hinckle interested *Time* magazine in doing a story on *Ramparts'* layman efforts to originate a discourse with the Jesuits. Inexplicably, *Time* killed the story. *Time* had "discovered" that *Ramparts* was a right-wing fanatical magazine, manned by cranks. Hinckle reported that he responded to this with a laugh, adding jocularly that he bet the reporter got that from the Jesuits. "Yeah,—how'd you know?"[6] The Jesuits did not want any criticism, no matter how well intentioned. They refused to answer Keating's phone calls or send any promised manuscripts. This situation was pivotal in the turning-to-the-left of *Ramparts.* The ramparts were to be used in the future for attacking the church, not defending it. This occurred in 1964. *Ramparts'* personality had begun to take shape.

"I Quit. The Whole Thing Was a Lie! by a Special Forces Hero."[7] So ran the cut line under the photo of Special Forces Master Sergeant Donald W. Duncan that appeared on the February cover of *Ramparts* in 1966. Sgt. Duncan was dressed in his uniform, resplendent, arms folded, wearing his Bronze Star, South Vietnamese Silver Star, Combat Infantry Badge, and United States Air Medal, his breast covered with ribbons and, on his head, the green beret. Of course, Duncan was referring to the Vietnamese war.

Upon his return from Vietnam, Duncan repeatedly was asked whether he resented young people, who had never seen Vietnam, protesting the war. Duncan replied:

> On the contrary, I am relieved. I think they should be commended. I had to wait until I was thirty-five years old, after spending ten years in the Army and 18 months personally witnessing the stupidity of the war, before I could figure it out. That these young people were able to figure it out so quickly and so accurately is not only a credit to their intelligence but a great personal triumph over a lifetime of conditioning and indoctrination.[8]

Duncan attempted to tell his story to the establishment press time after time; they would not listen. As was to happen again and again, *Ramparts* scooped the establishment press through that press' inabilities and poor gatekeeping. Duncan's conclusion—the message he had for the American people—was, simply, that the world is not full of good guys and bad guys, and anticommunism is a poor substitute for democracy.

An amusingly ironic, yet fortuitous, incident flowed from the February 1966 issue of *Ramparts*. Hinckle recalled that the newsstand business was "about the biggest closed club this side of Sicily."[9] *Ramparts* prior to February 1966 had failed miserably in obtaining *any* newsstand distribution. No one would handle the magazine until luck and a liquid lunch intervened. The general manager of a newsstand distribution concern had just refused *Ramparts* as usual. Before the executive removed *Ramparts* from his desk:

> [I]n lurched the chairman of his board of directors, weaving like a sloop in a hurricane from the effects of what appeared to be a ten-martini lunch. . . .The chairman grabbed the copy of *Ramparts* with Duncan on the cover that was lying on the manager's desk. "'Now this is wonderful!'" he exclaimed. "It's a pleasure to see a magazine that has the guts to put one of our fighting men on the cover at a time when all those punky kids and peaceniks are criticizing our boys in Vietnam." The chairman banged out the door leaving the irrevocable orders to distribute the patriotic paper called *Ramparts*.[10]

Although they did not use that particular distributor, the magazine used that offer to negotiate a deal with one of the other distributors.

Also during this watershed year, *Ramparts* published a review of a sociological study that, while hardly illuminating the enterprise of responsible journalism, not only affords a unique perspective on the character of *Ramparts*, but says something less than laudable about journalistic professionalism. *Ramparts* ran a review of *Time of Assassins* by Ulov G. K. Lebouef, a Franco-Russian sociologist. The 4-volume set narrated the sequence of events of the Kennedy assassination. The two reviewers[11] favorably reported Lebeouf's findings. Had it not been for this book, the contents of the pick-pocketing of an FBI agent at a New Year's eve party might never have been brought to light. Among the papers, "were a compromising photograph of Robert Kennedy and Marilyn Monroe, a sizable I.O.U. from Ronald Reagan, a United Airlines credit card in the name of Senator Ralph Yarborough."[12] The contents of this wallet were linked to the death of President Kennedy. Lebeouf claimed, further, that there was not only a second Oswald, but also a third, fourth, and fifth, all 5'9", weighing 165 pounds.

The Boston Globe ran a front-page feature story heralding this study. The feature story, while highly critical of *Ramparts* (irresponsible and unbelievable), called for reopening the investigation of the assassination, partially because of the new findings of Ulov G. K. Lebeouf. It became apparent *The Globe's* investigative reporters had not read *Time of Assassins*, not even one volume. They could not; *Time of Assassins* did not exist, nor did Ulov G. K. Lebeouf! The book was the invention of the two reviewers.

More serious and essential was *Ramparts'* 1967 exposé of the National Student Association's co-option by the CIA. For this it won the George Polk Memorial Award for Excellence in Journalism. "The award cited *Ramparts'* explosive revival of the great muckraking tradition,"[13] writes Hinckle.

In 1967, more than 400 colleges and universities belonged to the National Student Association (NSA). During the 1960s, NSA supported the student movement against the war in Vietnam and the draft; NSA championed the civil rights movement. Only a very few of the organization's top leaders understood the CIA connection. The relationship lasted for 15 years and greatly benefited those involved. They were paid very well; they traveled, did important government work, and, according to the *Ramparts'* authors, felt loyal to their stated cause, the NSA. They also were assured student draft deferments. "The agency looks after its own,"[14] writes Sol Stern.

The NSA prided itself on its "independence" from government alliances or controls. It was this, NSA boasted, that made it different from similar organizations in communist nations. After the disclosure of CIA ties and funding, NSA leaders argued it should be kept secret to not embarrass or weaken the "enlightened" wing of the CIA. In an epilogue to this story, Marcus Raskin writes, "We are left with the fact that one generation attempted to corrupt the young by paying them off, buying and renting them on the installment plan."[15]

In glaring distinction to the NSA leadership, the editors of *Ramparts* ran a photo on the cover of the December 1967 issue depicting four arms raised, a burning draft card clenched in each hand. The caption read, "Hell No We Won't Go!"[16] One could clearly read the names of Walter Hinckle, Robert Scheer, Dugald Stermer, and Sol Stern on the ignited cards. For this the editors were made to face a grand jury. Hinckle denounced the proceedings, claiming, "An indictment of the *Ramparts* editors . . . must be interpreted as a direct and unmistakable attempt to close down the leading organ of dissent in the American press."[17]

These examples are not intended to form a definitive portrayal of *Ramparts*; rather, they are offered as differing and various illustrations of the magazine in the hope of illuminating angles on the multifaceted physiognomy of the complex existence that was *Ramparts* magazine and to exemplify values inherent in critical phenomenology.

FINANCE AND MARKETING PRACTICES

Ramparts' editorial success was contingent on its availability to people who had not been previously exposed to the ideas of the New Left. During the '60s, *Ramparts* was *the* publication representing those who otherwise agreed on very little. Hinckle referred to the New Left as "a concept about as cohesive as marbles boiled in butter."[18] The plan was to climb down from the soapbox and onto the newsstand. It was very well for magazines like the *New Republic* and *The Nation* to carry the banner of thoughtful, traditional liberalism. But how many minds changed because of what they printed? Hinckle did not believe very many. His idea was to make *Ramparts* as slick as *Vogue* and as highly visible as *Time*. This, he felt, was necessary if *Ramparts* was to affect American policy.

The magazine achieved this goal through financially uncertain practices of nerve and credit. The editors bluffed their creditors. This practice ultimately caved in, but the success lasted a good while due to the guile, affrontery, and measured charm of its editors. *Ramparts* grew to a quarter-million circulation, a staff of 50, and an income of about $2 million a year from sales, subscriptions, and book publishing. Hinckle reported this income was "almost sufficient to meet operating expenses but insufficient to cope with its debt, a snake pit of turned-off investors and curdled creditors who early began to whipsaw *Ramparts* in the manner of the tail wagging the dog."[19]

During 1964, the newly created monthly's circulation hovered around 4,000, up from 2,000 circulation as a quarterly. While the view from this perspective appeared encouraging, the staff had to print 50,000 to sell 4,000. Publisher Keating informed Hinckle that he was broke and could no longer foot the bill. Hinckle, dazed and in disbelief, pushed the issue. At this, Keating mentioned that, yes, he did have one shopping center left.

This conversation took place within the murky confines of a bar in New York. When Hinckle picked up the bar tab, Keating thanked Hinckle, who thought Keating displayed admirable sarcasm—the money he paid with was Keating's. When Hinckle pointed this out, Keating replied that he knew, but he liked the way Hinckle took charge of the situation. This incident reveals aspects of the publisher's relationship with his executive editor. The shopping center was sold, and *Ramparts* was back in business.

Nonetheless, Keating's money would not last forever; clearly, other funding had to be solicited. *Ramparts'* employees began by attending fund raisers for other causes, observing the amount of checks, hoping to procure funding by poaching.

After honing their fund-raising techniques, they succeeded in obtaining several financial backers. The first was Irving Lauks, an effervescent, vital 81-year-old liberal with a son aged 9. Lauks, a somewhat eccentric man held to causes dear: peace and women. His logic grounding this polarity sprang from *Lysistrata*. Lauks invented plywood. He invested $75,000 in *Ramparts* in 1965. Next came Bill Honig, part owner of the largest advertising firm in California; he became head of *Ramparts'* finance committee. His contribution came to $100,000. Fredrick Mitchell, a 31-year-old graduate student in Aztec civilizations at the University of California, Berkeley, asked Hinckle if it would be all right if he invested $100,000. It was.

Keating owned all the stock in *Ramparts*. The stock had to be diluted to make room for the new investors. Howard Gossage, an avant-guard advertising executive, who hated the advertising industry, came up with the solution. Keating, while remaining the publisher, was to offer some of his stock to the staff to vote. Then, the investors would buy in, thus forming three spheres of influence with no one in absolute control. Keating, while willing, was not altogether pleased with this development. He was subsequently convinced by staffers to run for Congress against Shirley Temple Black, while the reorganization took place. Keating lost the election as well as control over *Ramparts*.

Howard Gossage signed onto *Ramparts'* ship as a consultant of Generalists, Inc. Gossage's reason for despising his own business was that he felt the advertising industry had disenfranchised the American people. Once, thought Gossage, the press had been responsible to the people and aimed its communication efforts toward them. But, as the advertising industry expanded and emphasis shifted from direct sales to advertising sales, the target of the press became, more and more, the advertisers. Gossage felt this interfered with the right of the freedom of the press. So, *Ramparts* attempted to emphasize reader financing of the magazine.

Gossage hired Dugald Stermer as art director. Stermer completely redesigned the magazine into the trendy, slick format that *Evergreen Review, Harper's, Atlantic, New York* magazine, and *Esquire* were quick to adopt.

Hinckle recalls this period of innovation:

> I ran the paper with a sort of Israeli toughness about what had to be done, driving our wayward bus at comet speed, getting across the necessary hurdles at any cost, while the passengers were bounced around in the rear and occasionally thrown out a window.[20]

The editors did not hesitate to completely rip the magazine apart at the last minute to alter layouts, articles, or covers. This practice, of course, induced printer's fits and compelled the "wayward bus" to operate from crisis to emergency. While hysteria often reigned within the editorial and production staffs, *Ramparts'* survival depended on not paying the printing bill during 1966. Hinckle spent a 5-hour, 15-martini lunch with his printer, who had not been paid in seven months. *Ramparts* owed him $270,000. Hinckle not only convinced the printer to lend Ramparts the $270,000 with which to pay the printing bill; he convinced the man to advance another $100,000 credit. By way of gratitude, Hinckle hired the printer's daughter.

A year later, in 1967, arose what was to be known as "High Noon." Ed Keating and the 3-man business department concluded that *Ramparts* had run amok. The business department saw that new management practices were necessary. This translated into a showdown between Keating and Hinckle. Following a very bloody battle, events came down to who held the most stock and proxy votes. It was not close. Keating lost the vote 13 to 1. He told the press, "They threw me out like an old shoe."[21] According to Hinckle, the rift was caused by the different outlooks of the two camps; sides were divided according to age. In the business department, the average age was 40; they paid the bills—or tried to. Within the editorial department, the average age was about 23. They did not even see the bills.

Not only did *Ramparts* lose its business department, but it ran into financial trouble from its backers as well. Some of the wealthy investors remained willing to fund *Ramparts* as long as their political views were favorably reflected in the magazine. But when divergencies in editorial views arose, funding slowed to a trickle. Concerning the Six Day War, *Ramparts* took a pro-Israeli stance, though not adequately doctrinaire for two of *Ramparts'* liberal Jewish investors, Marty Peretz and Dick Russell. As a result of *Ramparts'* investigative work on the CIA, these men invested heavily in the magazine. Taking issue with Hinckle and Scheer's editorial posture on the Six Day War, they withdrew $1 million from *Ramparts'* coffers. Peretz later bought the *New Republic.* Hinckle writes:

> Thus sank the Good Ship Lollipop. *Ramparts* for five years had been a remarkable robust terminal case, but to lose a million under those circumstances was a blow even its moonshine-based financial nervous system could not survive; at least it was an honest way to go.[22]

Clearly, Hinckle felt this was the beginning of the demise of the magazine. With a loss of this magnitude, massive monetary transfusions were called for to sustain life. The transfusions supplied proved inadequate. *Ramparts* managed remissions, but the illness became terminal. In the mad scramble for new life-blood, Hinckle, Scheer, and Stermer unearthed a professed donor who plunked down $50,000 with a pledge to later infuse another $500,000. The donor, Stanley Weiss, made his fortune from precious metals and importing Russian vodka. The story of *Ramparts'* attempt to lay hands on the $500,000 informs and reveals the dire conditions into which it had lapsed.

Hinckle believed Weiss' motivation lay in an attempt to buy some meaning in his life. The millionaire, who lived in Cuernavaca, Mexico, fell into the editors' lives direct from central casting. As the talks went on and the deal almost closed, Weiss invited the editors to Mexico for a few days rest and a chance to meet Erich Fromm—the trip to be paid for by Weiss. Of course, the invitation was extended without the host's slightest consideration of refusal. So, the *Ramparts* entourage flew to Cuernavaca.

The group, invited to Dr. Fromm's for a seminar, sat around a table where "the psychoanalyst sized us up as if one of our number were singlehandedly guilty of the primal crime,"[23] says Hinckle. The upshot of the "seminar" hit the editors squarely on the chin: They were being tested in a debate with none other than Erich Fromm, while the potential investor sat back, pared his fingernails, and enjoyed the contest between Old World Liberal and New Left. As the debate between gradual progress and cultural revolution waxed, mutual respect waned. A circus atmosphere replaced the austerity of the editors' entrance. Tongues were bitten, smiles forced, teeth clenched until Fromm observed that Hinckle was obviously politically unsophisticated. Insult lapsed into comic incredulity. Fromm told Weiss, in no uncertain terms, of his distaste for the *Ramparts* people.

> The seminar ended as a shoe-banging summit meeting. Fromm was standing, shaking a gold pen at Scheer. Mrs. Fromm, a pleasant lady with yellow teeth who was a foot taller than her husband, was at his side, trying to give him a glass of water and a tiny white pill. The art director, a former lifeguard at Southern California beaches, was on his feet, saying that for two cents he'd bust this psychiatrist right in the mouth.[24]

One-half million American dollars went directly down a Mexican drain in the home of a German psychiatrist.

The circulation department had problems of its own. The February 1967 issue of *Ramparts* took five weeks to reach subscribers through the mail. The cover of this issue featured Robert Kennedy; inside ran an article critical of Kennedy. This occurred during the Johnson administration. While this incident may have been a mere malfunction, it has been since documented that early in 1967, the CIA's Directorate of Plans assigned counter-intelligence agent Richard Ober the job of "putting together information on *Ramparts*, including any evidence of subversion (and) devising proposals for counteraction,"[25] says Angus McKenzie. The CIA met with Thomas Terry, assistant to the commissioner of the Internal Revenue Service, to request information about *Ramparts'* backers through *Ramparts'* corporate tax returns. This information was delivered to Ober and the CIA and then the IRS was asked to investigate certain individuals for tax violations.

Different forces worked at bringing about *Ramparts'* insolvency. They all hung, however, on one peg—*Ramparts'* unfalteringly aggressive investigative reporting practices. Those at *Ramparts* made errors in judgment, but those errors, by themselves, may not have caused *Ramparts'* financial downfall. *Ramparts'* enemies were none other than the U.S. government, its agencies and departments. *Ramparts* did not think the CIA had any business co-opting Americans. For this, attempts were made to co-opt *Ramparts*. On the other side, *Ramparts* never claimed neutrality; it never assumed innocence until guilt was proven. *Ramparts* ushered forth to attack the government for what it considered the government's culpability.

The following is a list of news departments in the proposed publishing plan for a biweekly *Ramparts* in June 1968: The Secret Government; The American Empire; The Blacks; The Movement; The Church; Lies and Mistakes; The Other America; People Not in the News;

The American War Machine.

Ramparts was first in nationally exposing America's involvement in Vietnam, unmasking lies that most of the American press at that time accepted. The magazine pointed out before the Kerner report that white racism was the basis for racial tensions. Further, *Ramparts* attacked Cold War policies as counterproductive. Hinckle writes:

> *Ramparts'* purpose as a magazine is to shatter that predisposition to treat the secret covenants of government and power as sacrosanct, and it has had continual financial problems because it has been so effective in that goal. As we broke one explosive story after another and took unpopular stands on major issues, we consistently lost both advertisers and investors who either disagreed with the magazine or became afraid to associate with it.[26]

Financial trouble led *Ramparts* to what some consider, in retrospect, its fatal error. Editors decided to go from monthly to biweekly. The hope was to bring in more revenue directly from subscribers so the magazine, in turn, would be less dependent on advertisers. The editors turned the economic future of *Ramparts* over to the readers by charging them the cost of publication. So went the theory. It was disastrous. For a multitude of reasons, readers either could not, or would not, foot the bill. In June 1969, *Ramparts* reverted to monthly publication. *Ramparts* managed to publish until September 1975, when it uttered a last cry that few heard.

THE CRITICS

From the beginning, the establishment press looked at "the magazine for the rest of us" with a mix of superior amusement, begrudging admiration, rabid hostility, and sullen disdain. *Time* magazine referred to the fledgling *Ramparts* in 1966 as a contentious Roman Catholic magazine firing broadsides in a shrill campaign against U.S. Vietnam policy. In the '60s, *Time's* hostility towards *Ramparts* went undisguised, while *Newsweek* affected bemusement. However unfortunate (*Ramparts* advocated U.S. withdrawal from Vietnam), *Newsweek* admitted that in 1966, the little magazine had increased circulation from 2,500 to 50,000 in just four years. *Newsweek* predicted the American audience could expect more controversy and iconoclasm, hallmarks of *Ramparts*manship. William F. Buckley's *National Review* recognized the enemy, but gave *Ramparts* an amount of respect, admitting *Ramparts* avoided much of the scatological language and excited labeling of the '60s and '70s. *National*

Review perceived *Ramparts* fairly clearly as the muckraking periodical it was, "of the sort crammed with arcane statistics and anecdotes of allegedly typical alleged atrocities (Greece and Chile, you know)."[27] Admitting *Ramparts'* status, a certain sobriety and maturity, *National Review* applauded *Ramparts'* condemnation of the SLA (Symbionese Liberation Army) as downright immoral. The *New York Times* vacillated in its attitude from severe to benevolently paternal. The *Times* seemed to enjoy *Ramparts'* feisty attitude. James Ridgeway writes:

> Ramparts went right after the Catholics in the first issue: "You preach social justice and love for fellow men. But on racism, on poverty, on nuclear war, the Catholic Church stays comfortably silent, does little. You just don't want to rock the boat."[28]

Interestingly, when *Ramparts* broke the story of Michigan State University's involvement with the CIA in Vietnam (1966), it was not *National Review*, but *Time* which, by selecting its quotes, maligned *Ramparts'* efforts. Speaking of MSU sending a colony of Ph.D's to Vietnam, *National Review* reported, "From the beginning, this 'educational' mission was, in large part, a mask for the CIA . . ."[29] It continued that even *Ramparts*, the least aware of the monthlies, had caught on. The implication that others knew of the involvement may have been true; if so, none of the others wrote the story. If they knew, they remained silent. *National Review* concluded that next to President Hannah (MSU's president), *Ramparts* seemed almost coherent. *Time* ran quotes from political scientist Wesley Fischel calling *Ramparts'* story a scurrilous, silly hatchet job—which it was not. *Time* pointed out through Fischel that the authors of the *Ramparts'* story were advocates of the Viet Cong and hoped to see a communist victory in Vietnam. This was untrue; *Ramparts* merely advocated Vietnamese self-determination.

True to its nature, *Ramparts* did not hesitate to fight fire with scintillation. It ran on the January 1967 cover the Crucification with U.S. infantrymen as Roman guards. The editors also placed the photo in the *New York Times*. Within the same issue appeared an explicit account of U.S. actions on the native civilian population, quoting the secretary of defense as saying that we simply didn't have any idea of the number or nature of civilian casualties in Vietnam. A quote from the 1967 *Ramparts'* article is included here to emphasize the graphic portrayal of suffering at a time of public adversity to *Ramparts'* position.

> Luan, age eight, was on of the two children brought to Britain last summer. . . .He came off the plane with a muslin bag over what had been his face. His parents had been burned alive. His chin had

'melted' into his throat, so that he could not close his mouth. He had no eyelids.[30]

Time was livid over this reporting:

Ramparts magazine greeted the New Year with a straight left jab to the public jaw. A full page ad in the *New York Times* last week featured a blow up of the January cover: a nauseous photo of a crucifixion complete with a pudgy Jesus and two U.S. infantrymen standing guard with bayonets. The magazine . . . contains what it claims are pictures of some of the 'one million children killed, wounded or burned in Viet Nam.'[31]

Time did not see fit to criticize The *New York Times* for running the advertisement. *Time* continued that no other leftist magazine pursued shock more relentlessly or distorted facts to the extent of *Ramparts*. It quoted editor Hinckle as saying that *Ramparts* looked at things from a moral viewpoint. *Time* considered this reprehensible. *Time* rested its case with the warning that *Ramparts* was slick enough to lure the unwary into accepting flimflam as fact.

By 1969, the nation reeled under massive protest of the Vietnamese war. One was no longer stamped a pariah to oppose the war. The *New York Times*, by this time, opposed U.S. involvement, and *Time* began to ask questions. It even altered its attitude toward *Ramparts* from active hostility to amused observance of the "*Ramparts* gang." There was even a tinge of sympathy and guarded admiration as Time admitted that even though bankrupt, *Ramparts* continued publication, on time, with each issue less hysterical than the last:

When last we left the *Ramparts* boys they were in a pretty tight fix: the phones were out, there was no more booze in the closet and, worst of all, they owed a million and a half dollars to angry creditors—including their arch enemy, the Internal Revenue Service.[32]

At the time *Ramparts* suffered bankruptcy, the *New York Times* ran an in-depth look at the magazine, noting its unique style and committed journalism, as well as questionable business practices. James Ridgeway wrote in the *Times* that, in his opinion, *Ramparts* should not be termed a radical magazine. This opinion would raise resistance from both those to the left and right of Ridgeway. *Ramparts*, he argued, popularized for a more divergent audience what the smaller left-liberal publications had espoused for years.

At this time, jumping the burning ship, Hinckle left *Ramparts* to found *Scanlon's*, an ill-fated offspring of *Ramparts*. Consequently, Robert Scheer became editor. Scheer was a dedicated writer on the New Left; he encouraged the Black Panthers, got Sgt. Duncan to relate his thoughts on Vietnam for *Ramparts*, and almost single-handedly obtained Che Guevara's diary from Castro for exclusive publication in *Ramparts*. Always, Ridgeway writes, Scheer set the political-editorial line for the magazine, but Hinckle put the package together and promoted it. "I have no politics," Hinckle said. Then he added: "I hate magazines."[33]

According to Ridgeway, the Big Mistake was made in Spring 1968, when *Ramparts* decided to go biweekly. It always had a tough time meeting deadlines—often it did not. The biweekly schedule wreaked havoc. When it missed a publication deadline, newsstand sales dropped from 125,000 to 60,000.[34] Added to the deadline difficulties, readers then had to pay $15 a year instead of $8.50 for an annual subscription. *Ramparts'* largest asset was its subscription list, which plummeted from 120,000 to 60,000 in 1969. So, the situation festered. By March, the magazine compiled a $2 million debt. They owed writers $50,000, $40,000 to the IRS, and another $19,000 to the telephone company.[35]

Ramparts managed to avoid folding, but it was never again the vital magazine it once was. With the disappearance of the '60s, its totem, *Ramparts* lost its magic power—people no longer believed—for reasons largely unclear. In *Ramparts'* last issue appeared these telling lines:

> The magazine is as small as nine people, but it is as big as the generation of commitment that made it possible. In a way, *Ramparts* was an accidental institution, produced by a fortuitous conjunction of money and people, issues, politics, and exposes, a vital coincidence unlikely to be repeated soon.[36]

NOTES TO CHAPTER 2

1. W. Hinckle, *If You Have a Lemon, Make Lemonade* (New York: C.P. Putnam's Sons, 1973), p. ix.

2. M.A. Burnier, trans. with an additional chapter by B. Murchland, *Choice of Action* (New York: Random House, 1968), pp. 26-27.

3. Hinckle, *If You Have a Lemon, Make Lemonade*, p. 119.

4. Ibid., p. 35.

5. Ibid., p. 48.

6. Ibid., p. 50.

7. R. Duncan, "I Quit. The Whole Thing Was a Lie." *Ramparts,* Special Issue (1968), p. 41. (Article reprinted.)

8. Ibid., p. 46.

9. Hinckle, *If You Have a Lomon, Make Lemonade,* p. 159.

10. Ibid., p. 159.

11. J. Brackman and F. Levine, "Ephemera" *Ramparts,* 5:5 (November, 1966), p. 59.

12. Ibid., p. 60.

13. Hinckle, *If You Have a Lemon, Make Lemonade,* p. 179.

14. S. Stern, "NSA and the CIA." *Ramparts,* 5:9 (March, 1967), p. 36.

15. M. Raskin, Co-Director, Institute for Policy Studies, "And a Judgement." *Ramparts,* 5:9 (March 1967), p. 39.

16. "Hell No We Won't Go." *Ramparts,* 6:5 (December, 1967).

17. S. Zion, "Four Editors Facing Draft Card Prosecution" *Ramparts,* 7:3 (November 24, 1968), p. 4.

18. Hinckle, *If You Have a Lemon, Make Lemonade,* p. 180.

19. Ibid., p. 180.

20. Ibid., p. 181.

21. Ibid., p. 195.

22. Ibid., p. 337.

23. Ibid., p. 344.

24. Ibid., p. 353.

25. A. McKenzie, "Sabotaging the Dissident Press." *Columbia Journalism Review* (March/April, 1980), p. 57.

26. W. Hinckle, "Apologia." *Ramparts,* 6:10 (June 15, 1968), p. 1.

27. M.J. Sobran, Jr., "Voice of the Old New Left" *National Review,* 26 (October 13, 1974), pp. 1048-9.

28. J. Ridgeway, "The Ramparts Story:. . . Um Very Interesting" *The New York Times Magazine* (April 20, 1969), p. 34.

29. R. Kirk, "Spies Behind the Red Cedar" *National Review,* 18 (June 28, 1966), p. 630.

30. W.F. Pepper, "The Children of Vietnam." *Ramparts,* 5:7 (January, 1967), p. 53.

31. "A Bomb in Every Issue." *Time,* 89 (January 6, 1967), p. 35.

32. "The Ramparts Gang" *Time,* 93 (June 6, 1969), p. 53.

33. Ridgeway, "The Ramparts Story," p. 34.

34. Ibid., p. 43.

35. Ibid., p. 44.

36. "A Matter of Life or Death," *Ramparts,* 13:10 (August/September, 1975), p. 5.

The Problem of Language

In the spring of 1989, thousands of Chinese students led a nation-wide protest against corruption and for the right to speak their minds. The protest spread from the universities to workers, intellectuals, Party members, and journalists. Originating in Beijing's Tiananmen Square, the protest was quickly taken up in other cities; a dialogue about expression itself had flared up within the culture. The democratic appeal was brutally crushed. "We do not approve of great democracy. Great democracy is avoidable, and this requires having small democracy," writes Deng Xiaoping in the official press and broadcast on national news, the voice of power.

This "avoidability" reflects one concern for language. A phenomenology of language concerns itself with dialogue. Monologue—official pronouncements—constrict the dialogical situation, which forms the foundation for communication. Through the mass media, Deng mediates "democracy." By linking the populist uprising ("great" democracy) to the state's policy of control ("small" democracy), the semantic shift appears to be one of modulation and not the repression it in fact was. Deng employs a strategy of "small democracy." Allowing the masses a marginal influence "is better than not having supervision," he writes. Free speech in the service of cultural critique challenges the institutional structure and leads to "anarchy," a condition no "rational," responsible person would champion.

Clearly, the battle in China is being fought over what is to be considered sense and non-sense, and the matrix of the conflict is language. This struggle articulated by free speech issues takes place within differing contexts in the Western nations as well. American troops defended democracy in Grenada in the same spirit as the Chinese troops were the "defenders of the nation." From the perspective of a critical phenomenology, we do well to describe the various levels of meaning: subjective, intersubjective, and mass-mediated planes of expression that intertwine the phenomena of language and discourse. Civil liberties, implicit in the term democracy, were erased, that is to say, during the days of protest one could detect (through the mediation of the media) the tracing of freedom of spirit. This spirit, symbolized by the statue of the goddess of democracy placed in Tiananmen Square, marked a difference from what came before it. This difference was placed in abeyance as events unfolded. As time passed, a scene played itself out in which what was not came to pass. Then events were wrenched away from the protesters. Authority, in the name of reason and order, returned violently, flooding over the deference previously displayed by the government. But things have not returned to the way they were before the demands for change. Change altered the course of events in China. The discursive practices of the state have been ruptured; that rupture has torn the social fabric, afflicting individuals as it has distressed the system. Traditional conceptions of meaning lead us to view events as full, sequential, and continuous. I hope to show through a discussion of phenomenology and critical theory that events are porous, contingent, and discontinuous. The various possible interpretations derive from implicit understandings about the nature of perception, sense, expression, and rationality.

We see that expression becomes institutionalized even as language forms an original institutional system. Language and perception mark two essential modes of concern for phenomenology. I consider a description of the thought of Edmund Husserl as the starting point in any exploration of the problem because his transcendental phenomenology, and reactions to it, resonate throughout our study. From the existential phenomenology of Merleau-Ponty to Levinasian ethics of desire, and from Derrida's deconstruction of the eidetic conception of language to Foucault's genealogy of discursive strategies, Husserl is the intellectual precursor of critical phenomenology. Since phenomenology is an attempt to pick out particular facts and values from a field and to integrate them in such a way as to highlight specific patterns, in order to explore the contexts configured by the arrangement of what is perceived as figure from background, I will attempt to describe various levels of the problem of language from the acquisition of language to the relations of critical thought to traditional phenomenology. A discussion of objectivity provides a further opportunity to look at the media presentation of various modes of expression.

Even as we come to understand human events and facts through a reading of them, we interpret through signs, or even signs of signs, what we mediately know as reality. "Reality is not a crucial appearance underlying the rest, it is the framework of relations with which all appearances tally,"[1] writes Merleau-Ponty. We are able to orient ourselves to the shifting appearances of perspective precisely because events and objects are presented within a relational context, and as we shall see from the work of Noam Chomsky, the strucure of awareness is articulated to equate successive perspective presentations with one another so that an event or understanding is presented as a continuum. Phenomenology does not, indeed, attempt to prove pregiven or divine propositions, but comes to a recognition of reality through a description based on our openness in perception and expression. As our determinations are contingent and multifarious, our explanations, Merleau-Ponty writes, "must, therefore, be subjective, since there is subjectivity in the situation—but that is not to say that we must be arbitrary."[2] One must attempt to describe and explain what is observed; news reporting, for example, is an active interpretation of events. Expression and interpretation involve situations, and because the process is situational and dialectical, it is subject oriented.

An investigation into nursing homes can have an impact on public attitudes, and what is said can ring true *and* unique, that is, situational. Thus, we will consider analysis as interpretation of expression; speech and language are constitutive of the human condition. The world and communication escapes a personal solipsism in our awareness that knowledge is not fundamentally "objective," but intersubjective and communal. This is not a purely or principally technical consideration, rather, it is the traceable founding of awareness in daily life. A mass-mediated presentation of life does, however, entail a technological reduction of experience and this reduction allows us to expand our awareness of events. The printed presentation of an interview with someone who may affect one's life is an experience of a person without his "presence," but it is nonetheless gripping. One may attempt without total success to remark on phenomena to make sense of a text through its structure. It is difficult to focus, and impossible to absolutely delimit, the sign in communication, as it is never absolutely "there" as existent, it is a referent. A referent refers not to "things," for example, the word/image of a man does not refer to "a man" or "the man" or "that interviewee." Speech and symbols take on significance through man's desire to communicate, indicate, express something. These terms are not different in kind but interact in a gestalt of expression in language. How does this work? Husserl provides the classic explanation with his eidetic theory of language.

TRANSCENDENTAL PHENOMENOLOGY

Perhaps if we turn to Edmund Husserl's conception of language, expression, and meaning, we can clarify differences between remarks made in this essay and the classical position. Husserl is presented here as an example of traditional linguistic theory. He maintains that, at bottom, language is founded on logic, not rhetoric. It is the logical, grammatical configurations which lend meaning to language. Thus, there is a basic difference between signs and what they signify. There is an ontic (as opposed to ontological) bond between the sign and its referent—the sign must refer to a "thing." Also, one must distinguish between thought-pure meaning and speech-indication. Language is a founded realm. It indicates thought through expression. Indication functions to externalize thought or pure meaning to someone exterior from oneself. Therefore, indication is impure meaning. It is meaning bound in words like passengers in an automobile. We are consequently faced with distinctions among indication, language usage, speech, expression, pure meaning, and thought. Words, in essence, have timeless meaning; they go beyond any single referent into a realm of ideal meaning. For example, the word "person" would include all possible persons according to this theory. Thus, one has a purely logical determination, not dependent on the usage or on "this" person or "that" person. Meaning is possible outside of indication and apart from communication. Moreover, indication in its logically pure state would be virtually empty, an empty intention. A sound with no meaning is pure indication, and a thought with no sound is pure meaning.

Meaning exists subjectively in a pure state until it is mixed in indication—language in the sign. Meaning, for Husserl, is nonlingual. This conception makes meaning, in its logically pure relation, completely subjective as thought. It is private. It is unity in duration.

The distinction:

word:	sense:
means to inner sense,	what is actually meant,
merely expressed by the	pure expression;
word as vehicle;	
co-incidence	
signifier	signified

The sign (combination of word and sense) is the logical constitution of the signifier (word) in the signified (sense). The sign is an act of bestowing a meaning. The sign gives meaning; it makes public the intentions of the subject, the monadic independent ego, the interior mental life of the speaker. Again, the essential distinction is among indication, the empirical movement of association which has no meaning content of itself, the signifier, and the expression which conveys (or is) meaning content. Sense is the signified content, the meaning or pith. "Communication, then, would be a re-presentation of what primordially occurs in the inner sphere."[3] "If there is to be pure expression at all—and, consequently, pure meaning—it must take place wholly within the internal sphere, in the *absence* of indication; it would be a `silent' monologue,"[4] says Jacques Derrida. One sees that, logically, communication clouds meaning and impairs clear thought.

It is Husserl's contention that once we know enough about the grammatical judgment patterns involved in propositions within the individual languages, we will be able to abstract pure, universal, absolute patterns which function and determine the forms of all languages. This would result in a body of knowledge which would guide us in our understanding, similar to Kant's system of categories of thought in the *Critique of Pure Reason*. Here, the classical attitude and the scientific or quantitative attitudes are similar; both would "see" a body of pre-established language as already existing and analyze it. The predicate concept would thus be present in the form of the subject concept. The paradigmatic proposition would present itself in the form of the copulative judgment: all S is P. This is a positivistic conception of language; meaning can be understood by a set of assertions in form. This method accounts for the past by reference, cannot account for the present adequately, and can say very little about the future except that it will resemble the past in its determinations. Such is the account of logic as the primary determinator of communication, without reference to rhetoric; rhetoric must follow the forms of logic. In fact, this is a system built to preserve the status quo.

But Levinas is able to supplement this logic with ethics. While meaning is constituted intersubjectively, for the later Husserl, meaning is always a mode of validity for an individual consciousness, or elementary intentionalities, constituting further meanings through intentional syntheses.

> And meaning is never anything but meaning in modes of validity, that is, as related to intending ego-subjects which effect validity. Intentionality is the title which stands for the only actual and genuine way of explaining, making intelligible.[5]

Even if this analysis cannot account for social problems, language acquisition, unconscious processes, or media epistemology, it was groundbreaking theory at the level of describing individual consciousness. Husserl's analyses of the relation between logic and perception provided Levinas with insights into his research into questions of ethics and language. Husserl's meditations on the production of meaning, his methodological account of awareness, how one realizes an intentional structure within the world, is of inestimable import for the development of phenomenology. Husserl's phenomenological method pointed the way for Levinas. Once Husserl had shown how we discover meaning within our lives through an original contact with the world, breaking through the *cogito*, through being always more than consciousness—a consciousness of (x)—then Levinas could posit the contact from a distance of the face-to-face relation, manifesting ethics as responsibility. "The interhuman is thus an interface: a double axis where what is 'of the world' qua *phenomenological intelligibility* is juxtaposed with what is 'not of the world' qua *ethical responsibility*,"[6] From this ethical responsibility, upon which this entire study depends, comes morality, which forms the norms of social behavior and public duty. Morality, for Levinas, structures our interests with one another while ethics is the exposure of one person to another.

This conception, I believe, is lacking in the critical theory of both Derrida and Foucault. Difference is not enough: It is quite true that it is more interesting to view intersubjectivity as difference rather than as unity, as social rather than as identical being. But as Levinas warns us, if the moral and political arenas forego the ethical foundation completely, we no longer have a standard by which to evaluate better from worse; we may no longer urge pluralistic over totalitarian, democratic over fascist, forms of government. Evaluation depends on some standard, and moral distinctions finally rely on some absolute. Critical theory must take into account why freedom is better than enslavement and not simply content itself with deconstructing authority; by what measure do the exhaustive critiques of the traditions offer help? Critical theory needs phenomenology as phenomenology requires social critique.

Returning to Levinas via Husserl, intentionality evolves into desire and desire, then, has an intentional structure, poles of appreciation, and signification becomes sensibility. If the hallmark of subjectivity is sensibility, then the condition of sensibility is found in a vulnerability of the process: signification is one-for-another. This, as distinct from Foucault's constraint, is manifested as "enjoyment." One enjoys sensibility. We will take up Levinas' study of enjoyment, sensibility, the other, and desire in the following section. Suffice it to say that being one-for-another institutes an opening, an active generation of awareness of self and other, from which justice is realized. Justice is responsibility for the other through oneself, prior to its manifestation as a legal, regulatory system, or as a technique for harmonizing the competing interests among men and women. In this derivative—actually secondary, if all embracing dimension—law may be rightly regarded by critical theory historically as a means of violation of the weak against the powerful, a tool for maintaining the status quo. But the originary sense of justice occupies Levinas.

DECONSTRUCTING PRESENCE

If, for Husserl, language functions to make public the fullness of a sense that is primarily subjective, that is, private, Merleau-Ponty wishes to posit a dialectical notion of language as presented in speech mediated by the incarnate subject toward another by what he terms a "coherent deformation." Merleau-Ponty emphasizes "as a fundamental fact of expression *a surpassing of the signifying by the signified which it is the very virtue of the signifying to make possible.*[7] There must be a situation in which communication occurs, a past, and an anticipation in any dialogue that allows for sense to be made. The intention, the urge to communicate, is not a derivative of thought because signifying is its condition. This brings out the essence of Merleau-Ponty's conception of expression: Thematization of what is being expressed cannot precede its articulation because this thematization is itself made in the process of signification. There is, then, for Merleau-Ponty and, subsequently for Derrida, no pure thought. As Ferdinand de Saussure taught, there is no sense without language. Articulation, even stream of consciousness, depends on the structure of the sign. Language is a system of words, sounds, and concepts, a system of relations, a system of pure value, not substance. Saussure says, "Language can also be compared with a sheet of paper: thought is the front and the sound the back; one cannot cut the front without cutting the back at the same time."[8]

Accordingly, 20th-century thought has fixed on the paradigm of language as constitutive of consciousness in general. Only through expression, considerations of meaning and truth are advanced, accepted, or rejected. Merleau-Ponty, however, emphasizes the process of expression over the study of language as a system. He taught that this is in fact Saussure's emphasis. While this version of de Saussure is not accurate,[9] it seems typical of Merleau-Ponty's strategy of emphasizing those portions of a theory which aid him in developing his own ideas.[10] Language is an institution upholding and yet developed through culture. But, Saussure points out, it is incomparable to any other of society's institutions insofar as it is an original institution. The very structure of this institution underlies various forms of emotion, thought, and conduct. These behaviors are realized through language. Our natural and cultural worlds are linguistically structured.

Expression, as we have seen, does not substitute for or package thought: It is thought. This, I think, is Foucault's point in arguing that truth is produced through strategically motivated discursive practices.

Signs link meanings through intentional processes, and temporality works to incorporate what is said with what is understood. For example, the 17th-century decision to construe form as an aggregate of physical "simples" was first discussed, then effected. Existential phenomenology holds that the world is presented through perceptual-operational consciousness on the one hand and lingual-cultural intersubjectivity on the other. These processes are co-present and, of course, resemble the two sides of Saussure's sheet of paper.

As in politics, it seems those closest together exert more energy denying similar positions than disagreeing with obvious opponents. Derrida and Foucault were trained in phenomenology, yet both deny its influence in their work. While Derrida berates phenomenology for its reliance on the concept of presence (along with the whole of Western philosophy) and for its maintenance of logocentrism (centrality of reason in human existence), his work is dependent on phenomenology, springs from it, and forms a critical moment questioning the assumptions of intentionality and reduction. Although he most certainly would disagree, Derrida's conceptions of difference, supplementarity, play, and the trace are essentially phenomenological conceptions stemming from the very notions he denigrates: reduction, intentionality, and life world. The locus of his critique can be found in the emphasis phenomenology, particularly Husserlian, places on subjectivity and presence. Nevertheless, the similarity of not only some of his ideas but of his techniques seem akin to existential-phenomenological notions of Merleau-Ponty, especially that of figure-ground, foreground-horizon, and reality as decentered frameworks or relations. The deconstructive work of both Derrida and Foucault has been positioned as "post-Merleau-Pontyean."[11] Ihde has commented on the parallelism between Derrida's deconstructive strategy of approaching a text and marginalizing what is usually perceived as the dominant theme, while placing in the foreground what was previously unnoticed in the background,[12] and the phenomenological conception of figure-ground corresponding to perceptual patterns presented by the relation of perceiver and environment. Existential phenomenology and critical theory concur in the idea that language is differential. The conception is based on the recognition that in order for a word to maintain its currency, language must mark out a space for that term by differentiating it throughout the network of what it is not. This is an implicit critique of transcendental phenomenology insofar as one recognizes that this differential system, or any particular part of it, is not produced by consciousness. Expression is in part produced according to processes independent of subjectivity. Language is a system of pure value, not substance. Continuity is not logically prior to discontinuity. "[I]n language there are only differences. Even more important: a difference generally implies positive terms between which the difference is set up; but in language there are only differences without positive terms,"[13] says Saussure.

Opposed to the logic of identity, the critical attitude attempts to emphasize establishment of a future necessarily different from the past, resting on the attempt to grasp living language usage. Such an attitude toward language is through a dialectical mode of thought, which reshapes itself through the direct questioning of rhetoric, recognizing that statements of the form "all S is P" have, at best, secondary interest in determining meaning within a linguistic community. One cannot definitively abstract sense out of the spatial and temporal flux of events. The attempt to understand language involves living relations which are not reducible to the logical forms of identity. Meaning is not constituted in identity. On the contrary, the concept most germane for the project of acquiring some understanding of the sense within the world is difference. Difference does not even imply a hint of the possibility of the reduction of meaning to a static series of positivistic assertions, implicit in journalistic objectivity, for example. Merleau-Ponty writes, "In a language, Saussure says, all is negative; there are only differences, and no positive terms. The side of the signified amounts to conceptual differences, the side of the signifier to phonetic differences."[14] Words are references used in *praxis*, according to general rules, but these rules are generative; change and alteration can always affect our considerations on sense.

In deconstructing Husserl's conception of presence, Derrida presents the present moment as difference; the moment, "now," springs out of a nonidentity with moments passed, yet it retains an empty trace, a retention of what has been. Derrida is attempting to shatter the idea that the present is all encompassing, a series of immediate moments which somehow cohere in a fullness of sense. The identity of the subject ought to be thought through on the basis of a retentional trace. So, Derrida argues: "Sense, being temporal in nature as Husserl recognized, is never simply present, it is always already engaged in the 'movement' of the trace, that is, in the order of 'signification'."[15] A trace provides a time; it opens upon a scene. The vestige is not, however, simple residue. It is a shadow, visible and yet not candid, a fossil in the sense of what was has passed but not completely; the subject continues. The present, in its difference, molds and shifts, redirects what cannot be inscribed completely in the now. There is no static existence or *archē* (first cause) upon which or from which the shadow springs. Our opacity does not blend or form from a bed of clarity; rather, any sedimentation of sense results from our metamorphosis in difference, in movement. One makes sense in and through the temporal movement which is a "spacing," in that one uses structure to produce or align an order of some particular sort. Sense is spatial as it is positional, perspectival; it is temporal due to its incessant flowing in a swirling current.

To better designate the complementary significance and divergence, Derrida presents a term which serves to indicate an aggregate movement, an expressive stratum which also is an end or product: différance. Différance, with an "a," serves to indicate and separate inclusive functions. It makes "things" differ from themselves and others. Difference evokes mediation in the form of a detour; it suspends the desire which Levinas has shown to be constitutional. To differ is to redirect through process. Therefore, to differ is to defer, to suspend action or reduce judgment. We wait while differing or choosing. The other sense of difference is more comfortable to us as we are more used to it. This sense of the term evokes nonidentity, discernible variance, or dis-similarity. To differ is not to be same but to be other. It is an ordering, putting in position, a continuous and active re-forming of perspective. Like the constituents of a sign, differing and deferring are but aspects of the same process, that is, one cannot dissect the process and have the original remain. The analysis remains dialectical. Derrida writes:

> The verb "to differ" seems to differ from itself. On the one hand, it indicates difference as distinction, inequality, or discernibility; on the other, it expresses the interposition of delay, the interval of a *spacing* and *temporalizing* that puts off until "later" what is presently denied. . . .[16]

This movement or dialectic is complementary to the realization that, in accordance with linguistics, meaning is produced through an oppositional difference, a lateral tension between terms. A sign is not identity, not full, but differential and partial. Meaning arises through difference as historical fabric, a gauze folded upon itself, porous but structured. In a sense it is always the same, but never identical; meaning and history are relations to self, but produce difference from self. This happens in language, a referential code, and by expression, meaning's designative movement. "Différance," according to Derrida, is what makes the opposition and mediation of meaning possible. It is the middle term, the conjugation. It is the "play" in discourse; "différance" embodies the strategic note, the "functional condition." It differs and defers. To speak of "différance" is to speak about speaking, to write about writing. It is a separating and co-mingling with a text. Thus, it is no-thing in itself but energy as a structure and movement. "Différance" inscribes and yet is itself inscribed in the chain of the dialectic. Derrida refers to it as "the possibility of conceptuality"[17] itself, not merely a concept, but conceptual insofar as it is recognizable at all. Difference is ironically constitutive, a task not an alibi. It constitutes the possibility of intersubjectivity. Because, as

Merleau-Ponty notices, "It is our very difference, the uniqueness of our experience, which attests to our strange ability to enter into others and re-enact their deeds."[18] The *"différance"* of style (individual affective meaning) sustains thought much more primordially than it serves as a mere vehicle of information. Sense is intersubjective, dialectical, elliptical; meaning is not egocentric, self-contained, or circular. The tracings of difference involve Husserlian notions of retention and protention, but they are simultaneous and discordant, historical and unified. The present is not constituted on a first principle, but essentially is multifarious and dependent upon antiquarian trace. The echo of the past presents the possibility of the future: "The trace would not be the mixture or passage between form and amorphous, between presence and absence, etc., but that which, in escaping this opposition, renders it possible because of its irreducible excess,"[19] says Derrida.

The trick involved is the attempt to visualize *"différance"* as a concept or a principle. It is neither. It is an opening and closing, a mediation and direction, a movement and closure; it is difference in a dialectic, a positing in negative terms of the possible activity of meaning in transformation. The movement differs and defers, yet traces out meaning. One cannot emphasize or isolate any term in the process. Its behavior is not a quantity in itself; rather, it is the quality of expression. Thus, one grasps the intuition of the present as a scene, a temporal and spatial stage. The trace is, says Derrida, a "relation to what it is not, to what it absolutely is not; that is, not even to a past or future considered as a modified present."[20] One feels Derrida's effort to put the dialectic in radical, meaningful terms, to follow the path which he marks out:

> [T]he other as "differed" within the systematic ordering of the same (e.g., the intelligible as differing from the sensible, as sensible differed; the concept differed-differing intuition, life as differed-differing matter; mind as differed-differing life; culture as differed-differing nature; and all the terms designating what is other than *physis—technē, nomos*,[21] society, freedom, history, spirit, etc.—as *physis* differed or *physis* differing: *physis in différance*.[22]

Therefore, one eschews the oppositional nature (expression/indication) of the classical theory of meaning as exemplified in Husserl. Meaning is not pure or complete or ideal. It is combinatory in our relations with one another in time and thus incomplete, interrelatedly concrete and expressed. Meaning involves a sedimentation of sense validated in our experience. At the level of expression, formal, logical and grammatical determinations are interdependent with rhetorical, intentional, and substantial. One fundamentally is present to others through others as decentered subjects in discourse.

RECONSTRUCTING THE SUBJECT

The subject has not fared well by critical theory. Much of the reason for the subject's demotion is political. We have seen that theories that focus on individual consciousness do not seem to be able to take into account political, cultural, economic, and ecological crises. From the critical perspective, the emphasis on the individual's "awareness" seems misplaced, luxurious, and indulgent. Approaching social relations as systems of constraint has led critical theory to emphasize the negative moments of the dialectic; control of individuals and collectives by impersonal forces does not lend itself to ready interpretation by describing subjective processes. The subject does not appear to be in control. Individual awareness seems too puny to explain social conflict. The idea that we actually know what we do does not seem to hold up upon examining consequences of actions undertaken for stated reasons that time and again produce untoward results, which in turn reaffirm and expand uncertainty. Foucault's warning that while everything is not bad but dangerous proves apt.

Let's return to Merleau-Ponty's statement about the surpassing of the signifying by the signified, which the signifying in fact actualizes. How does one account for this movement in expression, this desire to communicate what can only be said through an expression constituted by expressing? Does this explain communication? No. This is a description of the process of signification, of making sense. What sets the boundaries which allow for the possibility of mutual recognition? It has been pointed out that Merleau-Ponty's emphasis on expression over the study of syntax, and his refusal of linguistic universals leads to a truncation.[23] Critical theory has noted the preoccupation with consciousness is inadequate to explain cultural phenomena or unconscious drives.

Taking a look at the process by which we acquire language may prove beneficial in placing the problem of the subject into context. Examining how we acquire the language we use is an important aspect of understanding fundamental values entailed in subjective, intersubjective, and mass-mediated life. Jacques Lacan has discovered the structure of the unconscious to be that of language itself, and existential phenomenology holds that consciousness is language. Do these strata fit together? What phenomena allow for the integration of intention and performance? For Lacan and psychoanalysis, the signified is separated by a bar from the signifier (S/s), which represents the barrier separating consciousness from the unconscious. *"The structure of the unconscious is the structure of language,"*[24] says Lacan. Motivations arise from the unconscious structure of the self contributing to the porous constitution of the self. The self is decentered, ambiguous, unclear. Unconscious motivations affect awareness, and monadic consciousness is an illusion, according to Lacan. Psychoanalytic theory involves itself with an archaeology of the intentional self. Language can be seen structurally as a "witness" to times gone by; speech is a functioning of mental processes in the present, attempting to integrate experience. This plays an etiological part in striving to communicate.

Merleau-Ponty points to the constitutive process of the infant in its attempt to integrate its responses to its human environment.[25] An infant of two months laughs and smiles, not simply to express satisfaction but also to respond to those around it. This tells of a structural relation prior to the language he or she will learn. The child has only a diffuse sense of self. A sense of self must be developed through communication. A child directs himself toward others (taken as anything other than self) and confuses himself with them. Merleau-Ponty cites Paul Guillaume's study on imitation in children.[26] Here the classical approach is reversed. Traditionally, one supposes an adequation of self and consciousness, then one goes on to assume coexistence of other consciousnesses from the existence of oneself. To the contrary, psychoanalysis has long recognized that one actually forms one's self-representation from others. The child, as well as the adult, seeks from others integration and a sense of worth. The child sees himself as one among others, not as one above others. The interrogative is essential to personality formation, not as merely a logical or grammatical switch from the assertive but, actually, just as fundamental. The movement toward something in questioning is guided by language and ultimately is constructed in gestures and speech the child acquires from relations with others. Other people are "mirrors" for the child. He or she sees him- or herself in other's gestures, utterances, and expressions. The primordial direction of the recognition and formation of the self in a child is illustrated by the notion Guillaume related in the appearance of the child's own name in his or her speech development. The child refers to other people by name before it refers to its own name. The child uses its own name mainly, according to Guillaume, to designate its place beside others. The same holds true for the use of pronouns. Merleau-Ponty reports:

> The evolution of pronouns is equally tardy, marking the persistence of the confusion between self and other people. "I" is used long after "you" and "He" is replaced by the first name, which is not abandoned until near the end of the second year.[27]

Speech is behavior. Psychoanalysis holds that this kind of process also goes on in the adult. Meaning is maintained by reference to another meaning. Meaning arises from the binding of the signified and the signifier, which leaves the trace in what is referred to as "metonymy," that is, the connection or relationship in a dynamic sense between words in discourse, which give vent to meaning formation. This is, of course, a relationship of word to word and not of word to thing. It is an attempt, constantly partial, to fill the gaps of desire, which by definition and orientation are unlimited. The basis of communication can be seen as positive and negative.

But if, as Derrida claims, meaning is manifested by differing and defering, and the mind is differed-differing, the question arises about the nature or essence of what it is that is producing and projecting these negativities. Saussure's semiology cannot encompass this question. The question of essence is left unattended by differential techniques. What mediates consciousness and unconsciousness, desire and expression? We are in need of theory to blend the "I am able to" of the tacit *cogito* with actual expression. To rely on the body as the point of mediation to our relation of the object or of the other is too vague. The notion that transcendental subjectivity is intersubjectivity deserves our attention, and I think that by examining Chomsky's ideas concerning the acquisition of language we will be in a better position to more fully appreciate the implications of Merleau-Ponty's allegiance to Husserl's ideal of the intersubjective nature of language, communication, and even mass communication. One level, after all, builds on the prior levels.

Ironically for a philosophy of consciousness, Merleau-Ponty's contention that the results of perception and expression exceed their premises implies that there may be an organizing structure phenomenologically prior to consciousness. Upon considering the acquisition of language, this implication seems even more intriguing. Merleau-Ponty certainly is aware of the natural structures at work within our perceptual field. There are specific configurations which men and women favor, certain groupings present themselves as pronounced when introduced to perception, even though the phenomena in themselves are capable of various descriptions. "It is as if," Merleau-Ponty writes, "on the hither side of our judgment and our freedom, someone were assigning such and such a significance to such and such a given grouping."[28] Chomsky offers a phenomenologically sound theory of this assignation with regard to children's language capabilities.

An infant is capable of distinguishing between the phonemes P, T, and K. Since these distinctions are categorical and can be implemented before a baby has accumulated any lingual experiences, Chomsky argues it is reasonable to conclude this capacity comprises part of the infant's perceptual system—this system is not learned, but it comes prior to experience, it is innate.[29] The capacity to make these phonetic distinctions does not rest on a functional basis because the baby does not yet need to use these differentiations, and, of course, no one has taught the differences to him or her. Also, that which allows the child later to acquire vocabulary at the surprising rate of a dozen words a day must be in some sense innate. Chomsky locates these abilities in human nature, an essence common to humanity, which he refers to as the language faculty, a part of the mind/brain comprising a structure through which humans, in a sense, know what they experience.

Critical phenomenology should not limit itself to the examination of perception and discourse, our questioning of the field of communication must circumscribe the system it utilizes. Chomsky begins in a manner similar to Merleau-Ponty by critiquing behaviorism, and he recognizes the parallel efforts of the German gestalt psychologists. But, while noting Saussurian linguistics, he points out the inherent limitations invoked by a theory which, in his opinion, accounts for little more than that a sequence of signs manifested by the signifying and signifier. This conception relies too heavily on empiricist assumptions concerning association and abstraction, even if the product is difference. Reason is not Descartes' "universal instrument," but rather a specific biological system. This system exists as an aspect of the individual and not for something else. In this way, we can appreciate the desire to communicate, the desire for freedom, and the desire for aesthetic expressions as values in themselves and not as functions of something else. I find this valuation of the subject consistent with Levinas's grounding of ethics in an appreciation of the other through the lingual project. So, when Chomsky speaks about a language system, he refers to the system as it forms the individual. It is not yet some sort of societal phenomenon, but the language faculty provides the matrix in which the mediation of a shared community is founded and upheld.[30]

Chomsky's approach to the problem of language is to try to explain how a child develops his or her complex system of language in spite of a comparatively fragmented, limited experience of the structure and use of specific expressions. A baby has a very limited range of intersubjective experience to draw from. It is quite remarkable, Chomsky recounts, that "in a very short time he succeeds in 'constructing,' in internalizing the grammar of his language, developing knowledge that is very complex, that cannot be derived by induction or abstraction from what is given in experience."[31] There must exist, he concludes, an intentional structure, an intrinsic mental schematism, that can order the composition of the language faculty before experience and maturity; this intentional structure, or universal grammar, accounts for the acquisition of language and perhaps values as well. This language faculty is "structure dependent" and organizes the relational subject-object asymmetry one finds at work in perception and discourse. It follows that there will be other sorts of separate yet interactive systems at work, systems such as perception, or a faculty for numbers or structures of memory. The account of the lateral structure of cognition between left and right hemispheres seems consistent with Chomsky's account of these kinds of discrete structures at work within the mind/brain.

I think that Chomsky's work begins a reinvigoration of the subject, not as the principle by which to explain cultural phenomena, such as bureaucracy, mass media, or information systems, but rather as one stratum of phenomenological questioning into how meaning is generated, communicated, and understood. If each of us is different yet similar, then a basis for interest and appreciation can be staked out. The phenomenology of Levinas and Merleau-Ponty mark what I would like to designate as an appreciative sphere within the domain of critical phenomenology, while the critical emphases of Derrida and Foucault engender a deconstructive mode of thought. Of course there are disagreements. A major one is to be located in the various conceptions of rationality. For Levinas rationality is the process through which we guarantee the ethics made possible by language and actualized through expression. The desire for others is effected by the guarantee of justice, which speaks for the individual against the totalizing system. "Rationality is not a *problem*,"[32] Merleau-Ponty announces. Rationality inheres within the situation to be read through the configuration of foreground and horizon; it is at work within the logic of history, contingent, the reason within unreason. Rationality can be traced through perception and meditation in history. Even if history accrues much of its structure by accident or contingently, rationality makes possible understanding of the norms by which the structure of society is forged.

But rationality exactly is the problem. Derrida feels that reason is enforcement, entrapment by authority. Rationality is the justification for unfreedom, the logos and presence Derrida works so intently to refocus and critique. Foucault goes to great lengths in various studies of the prison, sexuality, madness, medicine, and politics to articulate the constraints foisted on the subject that have been undertaken in the name of reason. Yet, it will be helpful to reexamine the idea of constraint. Through the amalgamation of the two approaches, we hope to mediate a critical appreciation, one which can be detected in the critical and linguistic work of Chomsky. In terms consistent with Foucault, Chomsky relates that learning language is not so much something a child *does*; the acquisition of language is something that one is subjected to by virtue of simply being present. William Blake is right—the child's toys and the old man's reasons are the fruits of the two seasons. However, as in all circumstances of situation, the qualities of the environment matter greatly. If the child does not get proper care and attention, the results are, of course, less than optimal. Capacities can be encouraged or suppressed.

Faculties can be employed destructively. Here the notion of constraint takes on an interesting shift. Constraints are part of any frame of reference. A set of constraints determines to a great extent the nature of the cognitive system constituted by the mind/brain. This is so for the production of any intentional system, no matter whether it be developmental, organizational, intersubjective, or mass mediated. Constraint is productive, as Foucault notes, in the construction of any system. His interpretations trace out the development of limits through what we can see as the excessive organization of just about everything within society. But one may expand this notion of constraint to see that constraint allows for the production of any system of meaning within a culture; it accounts for the particular configuration of culture. Then we have come full circle back to Merleau-Ponty's notion of the sense of things. "Rationality is precisely measured by the experiences in which it is disclosed."[33] Experience is itself constrained within intersubjectivity. So, if communication is intentional, its effects are not always predictable, yet the notion of the subject deserves reconstruction.

FREEDOM OF CONSTRAINT

Chomsky's work in the philosophy of language is consistent with the existential phenomenology of Merleau-Ponty and Levinasian ethics, and his criticism of the political economy of the mass media[34] bears much in common with Foucault's critical theory of power/knowledge grids at work within society. Chomsky and Foucault debated one another on Dutch television in 1974, before Foucault had conceived of the power/knowledge couplet and prior to the evolution of Chomsky's more radical view of power structures and information systems. Nonetheless, the debate, reprinted in a book titled *Reflexive Water*,[35] furnishes a framework for our discussion of phenomenology and critical theory and establishes the contention that they are not at cross purposes, but are advancing perspectives on various levels of culture and experience. The moderator of the debate suggested the analogy of two thinkers tunneling through the same mountain, with different intellectual tools, toward a common goal, even as they themselves are unaware of the joint nature of the projects.

Chomsky's basic position consists of the attempt to approach the mystery of how a child acquires highly organized and articulated language abilities, which he or she seemingly derives from quite fragmented and limited personal experience. How can such a leap in complexity and capability occur? The child comes by detailed, particular, and vast knowledge on the basis of experiences which are already organized by a definitely structured, innate schematism, which Chomsky refers to as human nature, or a part of the configuration that constitutes human nature. In other words, Chomsky is grappling with the phenomenological problem of consciousness and how meaning is generated at the level of individual awareness.

Can Foucault's work be encompassed within the phenomenological camp? Foucault was a student of Merleau-Ponty's, and one will notice certain, most likely unconscious, connections: Merleau-Ponty predicts from "the course of things" that sooner or later irrational historical forms of organization might be eliminated. Foucault analyzes the "order of things" by which man constructs these grids of organization within human sciences. Merleau-Ponty at his death was working on a "genealogy of truth," and much of Foucault's efforts are aimed at such a genealogy, although with his own inflection. Merleau-Ponty urges us to look at our cultural environment, in part, by examining "the mental equipment or gear" of the 18th century. Foucault chooses to title the second chapter of his archaeology of the human sciences of the rationalist period in France, "The Prose of the World," which, of course, is the title of one of Merleau-Ponty's books. If phenomenology consists to a large degree in reducing background presuppositions of experience in order to elucidate the context in which the background silhouettes phenomena, this can be seen as not inconsistent with Foucault's efforts: for example, the reexamination of power and discipline he undertakes within the prison system allows him to bring to the fore the strategic advantages, the organizational evolution of discipline, which eventually spread throughout society's institutions under the guise of increased efficiency and reform. More important, the reforms furthered the conditions for surveillance and control. These motivations were at work within the background, and Foucault's analysis moved the productive dimension of power to the foreground. It is true that these processes are not largely dependent on individual planning and circumspection. But Merleau-Ponty recognizes as well that the will and means of expression correspond to historical forces and cultural institutions. Further, "When equilibrium is destroyed, the reorganizations which take place comprise, like those of language, an internal logic even though it may not be clearly thought out by anyone."[36] Here we see a foreshadowing of Foucault's structural intentionality without particular planners. Ihde notes that Foucault's analysis of a painting of a painting in "Las Meninas" owes much to phenomenological analysis, and The Order of Things itself is a history of perception.[37] So, one can locate internal parallels; Ihde goes so far as to refer to Foucault as doing "a kind of subterranean edifying phenomenology." Another author has referred to Foucault's as a semiotic phenomenology.[38] Foucault himself, however, tells us:

> If there is one approach that I do reject, however, it is that (one might call it , broadly speaking, the phenomenological approach) which attributes a constituent role to an act, which places its own point of view at the origin of all history—which, in short, leads to a transcendental consciousness.[39]

Even with Foucault's avowed rejection of Husserlian phenomenology, we will see in the next section that his later work on ethics is not incompatible with aspects of the ethics of desire.

His effort is aimed at reconstituting studies of the structure and development of knowledge away from the constituent subject, to arrive at a conception of the subject within a historical framework. Foucault calls this attempt genealogy. This is also the problem for existential phenomenology; Merleau-Ponty's adventures with the dialectic found a parallel struggle, attempting to place the subject within history. Both rely implicitly on the idea of the organization of structures, whether of intentionality, intentionality without a particular author, a human science, or the state. One can locate the intersection of phenomenological thought and Foucault's variation of that attitude in the different emphasis each places on the cardinal category: experience. It would seem that Merleau-Ponty approaches experience as intersubjectively modulated interaction within the framework of relations, that is, reality, by which all sensation, perception, and intellection cohere. This approach emphasizes intentionality and is similar, I believe, to Chomsky's idea involving the understanding with which humans, as human beings, are born. We could call this essence. A child's experience is organized according to a framework which, Chomsky asserts, is universal among cultures and includes recognition of intention, will, causality, and goals as part of his or her innate endowment.

In his approach to experience, Foucault emphasizes the communal contribution society orchestrates through its institutions and discursive practices and the types of discourses society accepts and gives the status of truth. This contribution is thoroughly historical and, while continuous over long periods, undergoes shifts, fragmentations, and reorientations within specific periods. Foucault understands experience as some sort of correlation among various disciplines or fields of knowledge, along with accompanying normative structures and particular formations of subjectivity, a system of organization forming a grid within a particular culture at any specific period in its development. From Foucault's comments, one gets the feeling that he developed these theories in part in reaction against his tradition, the discursive tradition we recognize as transcendental phenomenology, thereby realizing the very notions of fragmentation, discourse, and the order of things he puts forth. The generation before,

Merleau-Ponty developed his existential phenomenology in reaction to the then prevalent Cartesian and Kantian rationalism.[40]

Essential to this discussion is the idea of constraint, limitation, and structure evident on the phenomenological plane advanced by Chomsky and Merleau-Ponty, as well as on the cultural plane articulated by Foucault. Their intersection allows for the approach we describe as critical phenomenology. For without limitation and restriction one could not conceive any structure that could give rise to individual awareness, nor could one consider a culture in which institutions, apparatuses, and disciplines might do battle. Constraint is a necessary condition for freedom. One notes that Foucault does not account for the acquisition of language or the intentionality of the individual. When, during his debate with Chomsky, he was asked whether he had any sharp disagreements with Chomsky's formulation of the internal structure of individual awareness, Foucault responded that while he had reservations about using the term "human nature," because it seems more of an epistemological indicator rather than a scientific concept, he really had no major objections to Chomsky concerning internal form. In fact, he asserted their fundamental agreement, noting the necessity of responding to one's particular discipline, its prejudices, and distortions. Chomsky is struggling against the tradition of linguistic behaviorism, according to which the subject is treated as only the location wherein information combines with rules. Foucault categorizes his work in the history of thought as an effort, in part, to overcome the interrelated claims that every idea be attributed to someone and the attendant sovereignty of the subject in advancing original and important ideas in the history of knowledge. The primacy of these two claims has resulted in the marginalization of the consideration of systematic social practices or disciplines of constraint. So, Foucault's objectives and adversaries are, quite simply, different from Chomsky's. For Foucault, "[I]t's a matter of superimposing the theory of knowledge and the subject of knowledge on the history of knowledge."[41]

In that case, the relationship of the subject to truth is not, certainly, direct or, strictly speaking, original. Truth is an attribute or effect of knowledge: truth is produced. Foucault is concerned with undermining traditional theories of truth, theories which place their emphasis on the clarity of the knower or discoverer of true propositions. Truth is not a simple position taken by an individual; rather, the formation of truth is not "subject to the subject." The production of knowledge and truth, thus put, becomes a communal enterprise, what Merleau-Ponty refers to as a sedimentation, an intersubjective project. The production process is rule bound, with some individuals counting for more than others. Nonetheless, Foucault's conception has little to do with the correspon-

dence theory of truth, which, after all, accounts for only empirical verifications of observable fact. His real target, I think, is the hermeneutic conception of truth as *alētheia*, discovery or uncovering truth. Truth as illumination. If truth is produced, then it wasn't preexistent, waiting for
authentic being to shine its laser beam upon it. Knowledge is transformed by human interests, and so its status, or what is regarded as
truthful, undergoes mutation through history for strategic reasons.
Knowledge is discovered within discursive regimes, allowing for certain
kinds of statements to be articulated and accepted. We will see an example of how this works when we examine the epistemological indicator,
objectivity, and its deployment and strategic value for mass communication. According to Foucault, understanding is modified within an institutional grid of practice during a historically specific and strategically
circumscribed situation. Such is the order of things. When mass media,
for example, chose neutrality, professionalism, and objectivity, that constituted a new procedural and substantial network of rules and practices, allowing for the truth to be reported—some kinds of truth. Other
kinds of truths are disallowed if they violate the canons of accepted,
institutionalized reporting. Again, this conception of truth joins with the
notion of constraint to produce effects perhaps not intended, but systematic and generated according to definite structures; the scope of knowledge, then, is delimited by specific sets of conditions.

Foucault and Chomsky are very much concerned with the political ramifications of constraint on freedom and the production of information and knowledge. At this point the real debate between them
emerges. They do not disagree on the idea of limitation providing for
the production of discourse, or the subsequent fragmentation of knowledge within various fields of endeavor, or with the consequent need for
vigilance and contestation of the powers in charge of enforcing force
relations within society. But Foucault asserts that social conflict, with its
attendant network of relations, is not only a struggle over power, it is
fought out under the emblem of power. He does not find power to be a
medium, rather it works to secure force itself. The rules to the game
have been invented and deployed in such a fashion as to favor a positive
outcome for those forces that articulated notions such as freedom, justice, and dignity in the first place. The notion of justice is a creation of
the forces in charge of its dispensation—the struggle is weighted so
much in favor of the designers of values that the only meaningful contest situates adversity within a strategy concerned only with success. For
Foucault, the essence of life is concerned over the political functioning of
society; the only way to democratize a society, which Foucault argues is
democratic in name only, would be to wrench power relations in the
direction in which the population could effectively exercise power.

At the time of this dialogue in 1974, Chomsky seemed to be arguing that, although Western society is not truly a democracy, the situation is not so unprincipled as Foucault indicates. True, segments of society have been excluded from the debate over the real conditions under which all us live, yet the state, at least in the United States, provides, for example, a Bill of Rights, which is not simply or even essentially an expression of class oppression. To the contrary, Chomsky declares, it is an expression urging persons of conscience to defend the minority against state power. Of course, one must recognize the racism, poverty, and imperialism embedded in American society. It is in the very coexistence of liberty and domination where one locates the possibility for struggle. Toleration of minority views springs from the tension and balance of the various forces at work within society. The proper function of an "intellectual laborer" is to promote arguments to implement justice, especially by exposing power relations. It ought to be noted that in the 1980s, I think, Chomsky had become less optimistic about tipping the balance of power relations in any significant fashion. The nearly complete takeover by multinational corporations has rearranged the network, hopelessly undermining the opportunity for individual expression. The very apparatus for expressing one's views is controlled by those corporations with interest in limiting the diversity of views. The majority of mass media are controlled by a very small number of corporations. The elite media in the U.S., Chomsky now argues, preclude anyone with a truly adverse critique of policy from being widely heard, or worse, if he is heard, he will be portrayed as crazy or soft-headed. As of 1974, Chomsky claimed that law is the safeguard for justice. Not all of law, but much law represents particular, decent values, and existing systems of justice are not simply institutions of oppression. "[T]hey also embody a kind of groping towards the true humanly, valuable concepts of justice and decency and love and kindness and sympathy, which I think are real."[42]

Foucault does not speak in terms of justice, but in terms of power. Referring to Nietzsche, Foucault describes the very notion of justice as an idea formulated and implemented in society as a tactical term of political and economic interests; the concept may be used by any of the various interests, dominant or dominated, but, for Foucault, the sole effort of war is to win, not in the name of justice, but to win control. When discussing the problem of human nature, Chomsky and Foucault find themselves in agreement. But as far as Foucault can see, the concepts that make up the particular configuration of the culture are specific to that civilization. There is no historical justification for fundamental, unchangeable values in our society. It is at this point that we find Foucault the most distant from the percepts, not only of Chomsky, but also of Merleau-Ponty, Levinas, and Derrida, who argue that one simply cannot step outside one's native tradition, so the question is moot. Knowledge, Foucault thinks, systematically modifies itself according to internally generated rules, and values will follow along in consistent fashion. Conversely, justice is a concern for how the community integrates its citizens, from the existential point of view, which promotes the concept of rationality as that which allows individuals and groups to live among one another within a culture which employs discourse to extend conflict and consensus.

These various strands of critical phenomenology part at points, but come together in the realization that, as Foucault says, "the real political task in a society such as ours is to criticise the workings of institutions, which appear to be both neutral and independent."[43] But of course, they are not. By distributing information, institutions mediate power; they configure knowledge by guarding its gates. Such an institution is, naturally, exemplified by the mass media. The media order discourse in one very interesting fashion, according to a pervasive method, under the professional rubric of objectivity. The dissemination of information in postmodern society (information society as opposed to industrial society) is undertaken according to a strategy which comprises what Foucault has termed an epistemological indicator. The arrangement of news will be organized, articulated, and given status only as it fits the requirement of this norm and method.

EPISTEMOLOGY OF OBJECTIVITY

How would contemporary journalists approach the Kantian question: Can humanity use reason to overcome ignorance and domination? A traditional editor, even an exemplary editor such as A.M. Rosenthal, responds by referring to the method which guarantees fair play, neutrality, and regularity in news gathering. In a memo to staffers of the New York Times, then Managing Editor Rosenthal, reminding them that their business is facts, went on to trace out the character of the newspaper. "The belief that although total objectivity may be impossible because every story is written by a human being, the duty of every reporter and editor is to strive for as much objectivity as humanly possible."[44] Objectivity for journalists shares a trait with validity in argument; the form may not guarantee truth, in fact, truth is not a function of the form, but if the necessary steps are followed in a consistent fashion, the coherence of the presentation will be accepted. An objective story could be methodologically sound and false. When Senator Joseph McCarthy announced in 1950 that he had a list of 205 Communists shaping foreign policy in the State Department, he was lying. But reporters, following the objective method, relying on observation and verification by an authority, conveyed to the public information leading to one of the more shameful periods in American history. William Randolph Hearst Jr. knew, "he didn't have a damn thing on that list. Nothing."[45] Even journalists privy to that communication, who knew better, printed the story, anyway. The official statements of a U.S. senator are by definition acceptable facts. The method configures what is known with the status of who says something to create a practice by which the facts verify themselves in what has been referred to as a "web of facticity."[46] Practitioners of the method assume that the truth, no easy matter to get to, is fraught with pitfalls of bias and competing interests. One can, however, employ a method by which one can neutralize the various forces and in the process protect oneself, while effecting neutrality. In other words, let the reader decide. This professional mediation is achieved and information is structured, according to the objective method which allows for the normatively accepted construction of the story. "An across-the-board commitment is needed, a continuing commitment by reporters and editors to the character of the paper, to its belief in objectivity, to its principle of eliminating editorializing from the news columns,"[47] Rosenthal exhorted his staff. Even though the editor abandoned this norm when occasion suited him, he frequently encouraged accounts that "treated humans and institutions unfairly."[48]

The objectification of news as presented by the mass media works as an institutionalized technique throughout a system, forming patterns of presentations and uses, while also working as a process by which individuals disseminate meaning to large and diverse audiences who, from their position, are limited in ability to respond. Those employed in the profession are themselves normalized by this process; they are educated to accept this standardization of reporting which organizes their thinking, patterns their efforts, and results in a system of controlled distribution of news, the construction of social reality. Objectivity constitutes the contemporary problem of language in mass communication. Since, after all, it is a human being that speaks or writes, discourse is subjective; journalism is essentially, or authentically, a subjective practice. On one level, objectivity serves to mask the subjective frame that organizes the manifest presentation, and on another level, it disallows the individual reporter from presenting conclusions that he or she may have drawn from evidence and interview.

As Derrida has pointed out, reason, by dint of its impersonal, seemingly disinterested, character upholds and supports the tradition, the status quo, with its attendant inequalities and prejudices. So, too, does objectivity in American journalism serve to legitimate the official point of view. The method dictates what gets put on the page and screen, in what order and with what authority. Objectivity is law and order in journalism. As with all standards of control and constraint, it has brought regularity, accountability, fairness and balance, even justice to the practice of informing the public about society. However, it is also the case that this professional norm was historically developed for purposes amenable to standardization and profitability, or, to be more precise, conformity was institutionalized to ensure the successful expansion of the marketplace. Objectivity structures knowledge in the service of power: one can examine a genealogy of objectivity through its history and its application.

Objectivity is clearly a contemporary form of empiricism, and as such, is susceptible to a phenomenological critique of empiricism, behaviorism, and positivism. We will characterize objectivity according to its common characteristics and assumptions: the passive recording of facts, which are patently neutral and self-evident, standardized presentation of these facts by attributing expert sources, and, most important, the separation of fact from value. Journalists, then, will embody as best they can qualities of neutrality, disengagement, and balance. As professionals, journalists are recognized by function and role, not by beliefs and values. As recorders of events, media professionals deal with concrete facts. Making sense is ultimately up to the audience. But the audience arrives at meaning from the constellation of facts presented. How? If one sticks to the facts, meaning is not possible. All one is left with are the facts. Meaning is something constituted, to some degree, by a subject. But empiricism does away with subjects. The strict association of facts leads only to further associations. Nothing allows for understanding, which is a process of synthesis. Empiricism cannot account for the generation of meaning, the connection of a series of associations or facts. In other words, somewhere along the line, one must account for the process by which the subject advances interrelationships and draws conclusions, structured by values over a course of time. One notices, for example, that the professional standard of striving to separate facts from values is attributable to the value judgment that it is more desirable to gather neutral facts than to present sense. Here sense is meant to describe a process not only of meaning, but also of direction and intention.

Empiricism makes the subject into an object in an objective world (polarity is reduced to univocity). Finally, or methodologically, there is no subject, no space for intersubjective judgment. The epistemology is deficient. If the world and society have meaning for us, this meaning does not exist in events and objects themselves, but is constructed in dialogue between subjects and objects. This dialogue is structured socially and historically. Empiricism presumes the structure that the report of an event attempts to produce,that is, the dialectic of meaning and its horizon. Structures of meaning, such as our societal conceptions of liberty or equality under law, allow for the generation of specific situationally bound meanings to arise, which over time, may alter the structure of law, tradition, and everyday life. To the extent that empiricism disallows what it really must presume, it takes as derivative what originates meaning. Quite simply, empiricism and objectivity proceed mistakenly from the whole to its parts, ignoring the structure of behavior that gestalt psychology recognized as generating sense.

As Chomsky notes in a discussion of the curious qualities of behaviorism and science,[49] behaviorism is the theory that legislates against the creation of an interesting theory. Any conception that decrees that one must keep only to the data or the facts and not attempt to realign facts to come up with novel ideas is inherently conservative. Nothing will change, and the construction of meaning is procedurally outlawed. The idea in journalism or social science that historical development and cultural context is to be ignored severely restricts the interrogation of reality. To define a story solely by its facts would be parallel to defining physics by meter readings. The objective journalist's sources and facts will appear more real than the historical and qualitative physiognomy of society. This objective approach results in an impoverished attitude; it hides the cultural world from us by excluding perceptions, emotions, and values. The objective, empiricist epistemology shrinks from Merleau-Ponty's problem:

> We want to know how . . . consciousness can, in course of time, modify the structure of its surroundings; how, at every moment, its former experience is present to it in the form of a horizon which it can reopen—'if it chooses to take that horizon as a theme of knowledge'—in an act of recollection. . . .[50]

One ought to look at the structures of consciousness by examining the relationships of figure/background, foreground/horizon, fact/value, and text/context, according to which people generate sense and which are not reducible to the particular presentations in empirical situations. The empiricist tradition cuts us off from the world, with the consequence that its adherents impoverish those they wish to enrich.

The emergence of objectivity as a practice began with the transformation of American journalism in the 1830s in reaction to elite publications serving definite political allegiances, with an emphasis on narrative, to the penny press, with its self-professed political independence and informational, rather than narrative, approach to reporting.[51] It was at the turn of the century that the norms of objectivity came into play when the industry attempted to make the news product seem a more legitimate form of knowledge by claiming professional status for journalists. However, objectivity as a recognized norm followed in the wake of a series of specific practices, later rationalized into a professional method. Also contributing to the rise of objectivity, as we have characterized it, was the expansion of the public to include others besides white Protestant males, making public opinion more suspect, less amenable to "reason," and a more interesting object to study, and the commercialization and politicization of news sources as embodied in the rise of public relations after World War II. Yet, it took up until the 1930s for the term "objectivity" to reach common usage within the profession by journalists themselves. The professional newsperson is actively engaged in the construction of social reality, not its reproduction, by ordering social discourse and producing socially constituted meanings, literally presenting a "web of mutually self-validating facts."[52] This produced a system of norms, while manifestly promoting independence and objectivity, that systematically ensured the presentation of constricted, official versions of reality. Conflicts reported by the media are in reality most often policy disagreements framed by official sources and interested parties, without benefit of institutional, strategic explanation or analysis of possible cultural ramifications and are bereft of any description of historical context. The idea is to obey the economic imperative, which the objective method accommodates in the achievement of market domination by a very few competitors, tacitly agreeing to: "Standardize the product as much as possible so as to minimize the risk of losing a minimally acceptable share of the market, and compete for greater market share via production efficiencies and market techniques,"[53] writes Lance Bennett. In the 19th century, the wire services made access to standardized news a convention, and now a busy editor can subscribe to a service which will advise him or her of the news budget (list of stories from wire services) that the major papers are considering for page one, and, later, the budget of the actual stories that will appear on page one of the major metropolitan newspapers. So much for free competition in the marketplace of ideas. Now, the news is standardized by commission. It is a more thorny problem to explain a divergence in media coverage than the strategic conformity marshaled by mass media in a truly postmodern society.

Recalling the words of Deng Xiaoping, "Great democracy is avoidable, and this requires having small democracy." Media practitioners manufacture social consent by a homogeneous, if episodic and fragmentary, construction of social reality. If Chomsky is correct, and we are born with the creative mental equipment by which we organize our world on the basis of quite partial and, at birth, insufficient information, then perhaps there is an ethical question here, a moral concern that infatuation with objective method cannot adequately address. Merleau-Ponty notices:

> The advent of higher orders, to the extent that they are accomplished, eliminate the autonomy of the lower orders and give a new signification to the steps which constitute them. This is why we have spoken of a human order rather than of a mental or rational order.[54]

Mass communication is of a "higher" order because it is of the social order and what society talks about structures the autonomy, not only of the present generation, but of a society to come. With this in mind, we turn our attention to the ethics of the other. Where method has failed, perhaps appreciation might provide some insight. Merleau-Ponty's defense of Husserl bears repeating: Transcendental subjectivity is intersubjectivity.

The phenomenological theory of desire is founded on the notion of lack and the realization of the attempt in discourse to bind our notion of self and other in communication. Accordingly, one sees that mass communication affects not only how people look at the world and their community, but on how people view themselves as well. Mass media take the simultaneity of events and structure them for their audiences. The determining role of the mass media is one of producing truth through what Merleau-Ponty refers to as a process of sedimentation. As media help structure our world at almost every level through discourse, they call up our experience in specific and interpretive terms. The media form, to a large degree, our culture. Yet, as we have seen, culture depends upon values, and values depend upon ethical traditions, even more fundamentally than our more obvious reliance on facts and authority.

NOTES TO CHAPTER 3

1. M. Merleau-Ponty, *Phenomenology of Perception*, trans. C. Smith (New York: Humanities Press, 1962), p. 300.

2. M. Merleau-Ponty, *Consciousness and the Acquisition of Language*, trans. H. Silverman (Evanston, IL: Northwestern University Press, 1973), p. 9.

3. J. Derrida, *Speech and Phenomena, and Other Essays on Husserl's Theory of Signs*, trans. with intro. D.B. Allison. Preface by N. Garver. Preface cited here. (Evanston, IL: Northwestern University Press, 1973), p. xxxv.

4. Ibid., p. xxxv.

5. E. Husserl, *The Crisis of European Sciences and Transcendental Phenomenology*, trans. D. Carr (Evanston, IL: Northwestern University

Press, 1968), p. 168.

6. E. Levinas, in R. Kearny, *Dialogues with Contemporary Thinkers: The Phenomenological Heritage* (Manchester: Manchester University Press, 1984), p. 56.

7. M. Merleau-Ponty, *Signs*, trans. R.C. McCleary (Evanston, IL: Northwestern University Press, 1964), p. 90.

8. F. de Saussure, *Course in General Linguistics*, ed., C. Bally & A. Sechehaye with A. Reidlinger, trans. W. Baskin (New York: The Philosophical Library, 1959), p. 113.

9. See J. Schmidt, *Maurice Merleau-Ponty: Between Phenomenology and Structuralism* (New York, St. Martin's press, 1985) pp. 102-154. Saussure felt that one must place priority on system over speaking subject (langue over parole).

10. K.H. Whiteside, *Merleau-Ponty and the Foundation of an Existential Politics* (Princeton, NJ: Princeton University Press, 1988), p. 12.

11. See G. Madison, *The Hermeneutics of Postmodernity* (Bloomington: Indiana University Press, 1988), pp. 57-81.

12. D. Ihde, *Consequences of Phenomenology* (Albany: State University of New York Press, 1986), p. 192.

13. de Saussure, *Course in General Linguistics*, p. 120.

14. Merleau-Ponty, *Consciousness*, p. 96.

15. Derrida, *Speech and Phenomena*, p. 85.

16. Ibid., p. 129.

17. Ibid., p. 140.

18. M. Merleau-Ponty, *Sense and Non-Sense*, trans. with preface by H. & P. Dreyfus (Evanston, IL: Northwestern University Press, 1964), pp. 93-94.

19. Derrida, *Speech and Phenomena*, pp. 148-149.

20. Ibid., pp. 142-143.

21. Nature—art, law.

22. Derrida, *Speech and Phenomena*, pp. 148-149.

23. See J.M. Edie "Forward," in Merleau-Ponty, *Consciousness*, pp. xi-xxxii.

24. Ibid., p. 98.

25. Merleau-Ponty, *Consciousness*, p. 13.

26. P. Guillaume, *Imitation in Children*, trans. E.P. Halperin (Chicago: University of Chicago Press, 1971).

27. Merleau-Ponty, *Consciousness*, p. 38.

28. Merleau-Ponty, *Phenomenology of Percepton*, p. 440.

29. N. Chomsky, *Language and Responsibility*, trans. J. Viertel (New York: Pantheon Books, 1979), p. 52.

30. N. Chomsky, *Language and the Problems of Knowledge* (Cambridge: MIT Press, 1988), p. 63.

31. Chomsky, *Language and Responsibility*, p. 63.

32. Merleau-Ponty, *Phenomenology of Perception*, p. xx.

33. Ibid., p. xlx.

34. See E.S. Herman and N. Chomsky, *Manufacturing Consent: The Political Economy of the Mass Media* (New York: Pantheon, 1988).

35. "Human Nature: Justice versus Power," in F. Elders, *Reflexive Water: The Basic Concerns of Mankind* (London: Souvenir Press, 1974), pp. 135-197.

36. M. Merleau-Ponty, *In Praise of Philosophy and Other Essays*, trans. J. Wild, J.M. Edie & J. O'Neill (Evanston, IL: Northwestern University Press, 1988), p. 56.

37. D. Ihde, *Consequences of Phenomenology* (Albany: State University of New York Press, 1986), p. 193.

38. R.L. Lanigan, "Is Erving Goffman a Phenomenologist?" *Critical Studies In Mass Communication* (December 1988), p. 337.

39. M. Foucault, *The Order of Things: An Archaeology of the Human Sciences* (New York: Vintage, 1973), p. xiv.

40. See M. Merleau-Ponty, *The Structure of Behavior*, trans. A.L. Fisher, (Boston: Beacon Press, 1963), pp. 185-201.

41. Foucault, "Human Nature," p. 149.

42. Chomsky, "Huamn Nature," p. 185.

43. Foucault, "Human Nature," p. 171.

44. A.M. Rosenthal, quoted in J. Goulden, *Fit to Print: A.M. Rosenthal and His Times* (Secaucus: Lyle Stuart, 1988), p. 175.

45. W.R. Hearst, Jr., quoted in B. H. Bagdikian, *The Media Monoply*, 2nd ed. (Boston: Beacon Press, 1987), p. 44.

46. G. Tuchman, *Making News: A Study in the Construction of Reality* (New York: Free Press, 1978), p. 86.

47. Ibid., p. 176.

48. Goulden, *Fit to Print*, p. 177.

49. Chomsky, "Human Nature," pp. 165-167.

50. Merleau-Ponty, *Phenomenology of Perception*, p. 22.

51. See M. Schudson, *Discovering the News: A Social History of American Newspapers* (New York: Basic Books, 1978).

52. Tuchman, *Making News*, p. 95.

53. W.L. Bennett, *News: The Politics of Illusion*, 2nd ed. (New York: Longman, 1988), p. 17.

54. Merleau-Ponty, *The Structure of Behavior*, p. 180.

Ethics
of Difference

Since the breakdown of classical liberalism during the latter half of the 19th century, uncertainty has pulled at the seams of Western culture. Various forms of collectivism point to external circumstances and crises as manifesting contradictions, scarcities, and failures of sections of society in meeting our needs. Classical liberalism has put forth the belief that values and facts operate in their separate realms of human concern, with values manifesting themselves subjectively, almost as the peculiar and arbitrary choices of particular individuals, and facts presenting themselves objectively, illuminated by the clear light of truth and reason for all to acknowledge. From another point of view, transcendental philosophy anchors freedom and social reciprocity within horizons by which we locate dialogue. Each tradition offers insights, but, if collectivism locates the problem outside any individual's conscientious efforts, liberalism disallows any existential connection between individuality and community, and transcendental philosophy rarefies consciousness to the point where structures and vested interests go unquestioned. Existential phenomenology offers valuable insights, leading to Merleau-Ponty's suggestion that values structure not only our outlook on the world, but effect the structures of perception themselves. Critical theory points to specific problems that I think carry fundamentally ethical force. Foucault's analysis of specific elements of ethical formation in the process of self-formation allows for a specificity not accounted for by phenomenology. But questions about why choose one way of existing over another, or what kinds of values ought society to champion, cannot finally be measured by modes of subjectivity or fundamental historicity of humanity. We perhaps need to examine the conditions for responsibility that somehow ordain the values and morality of intersubjectivity. Emmanuel Levinas has come to think that we must go beyond essence to the possibilities of desire and recognition, which always overflow the conceptions the subject may have of another person; this surpassing of understanding locates a radical anarchy within our tradition, a movement not often appreciated, until Levinas. The conditions for sensibility are the possibilities for appreciation and enjoyment of what is other than oneself. That is the force of desire and the ethics prior to morality. Levinas describes the structure of ethical relations among people, a structure and process that precedes any particular system of norms and provides an outlook from which to question, critique, and even appreciate the practices of mass communication. For, if we are to announce and judge some ideas, norms, and outlooks as "better" for us than others, we really do "need" to apply some view to measurement. Justice and freedom, responsibility and enjoyment, truth and value are not adversarial for Levinas, but are modes of existence beyond being or existence. They constitute the possibilities that Levinas tells us are otherwise than being, the infinity of desire at work within the totality of culture. The central problem of contemporary theory, as Levinas sees it, is to overcome the subject-object structure which dominates us so at present. At some level, then, we all speak of freedom with the same voice. However, there has occurred a comprehensive disappointment, which Levinas locates in our unease over the dissolution of cultural optimism, and spreading out into all societies, whether the socialist republics of China and the disintegrated Soviet Union or the Western democracies of the United States and France. "Today's anxiety is more profound. It comes from the experience of revolutions that sink into bureaucracy and repression, and totalitarian violences that pass for revolutions,"[1] he writes.

SCHELER'S ETHICS OF VALUE

Since transcendental phenomenology is the precursor to the ongoing tradition of existential phenomenology and critical theory, we begin our description of ethics with its most advanced voice. Max Scheler supplies a traditional, comprehensive phenomenology of ethics, which, while ultimately insufficient, provides an opening for questioning value and exchange: communication. Scheler's efforts can be viewed as a critique of the Kantian sense of duty. Kant and Scheler hold that intentions, not their consequences, are the locus of ethical issues, although consequences are produced intentionally in retrospect. This appears to contradict much of contemporary social theory. Functionalism proclaims consequences to the social system as the key consideration. Intentions, according to functionalism, matter not to the system.

Scheler extends Kant's formal a priori to include nonformal moral judgments. Moral judgments present themselves qualitatively as intentions of essences. Good news is so judged because it is intuited as just that—good. By this Scheler means that through love and sympathy we gain insight into moral reality. By love Scheler means the capacity to draw together as in *Eros*, to assimilate and articulate higher value from lower value. This concerns the affective connation of another person. Any sympathy, quite simply, is respecting another individual as subjectivity, as a unique human being. Moral questions arise when some conflict occurs in the "correct" connation of such hierarchical values. Scheler's system thus forms a hierarchy—which leads to insurmountable confusions. One locates values on different levels, according to discrete spheres such as spiritual and cultural. The problem is that often these spheres are not at all discrete, but form a chiasm, intertwining perception and affection, or desire and need. Scheler writes:

> Even the simplest sensible feeling is never connected with one single sensation; but always represents, in relation to the contents of sensation, a new *quality* founded on a series and an order of the contents of sensation.[2]

But while he acknowledges the formulation of a new quality founded on a series, he does not spell out the conditions for the limit of that series. Is this merely a linear progression that wears itself out? Or, is a gestalt occasioned, opening new activities of a different order?

Scheler takes great care to outline three distinct phenomenological interconnections:

(1) the essences (and their interconnections) of the *qualities* and other thing contents . . . given in acts.
(2) the essences of *acts themselves* and their interconnections and relations of foundation . . .
(3) the essential interconnection between the essences of acts and those of things. . . .[3]

Scheler points to "the ultimate principle of phenomenology: namely, that there is an interconnection between the essence of an object and the essence of an intentional experiencing."[4] Such is the structure of describing interconnection for phenomenology—interconnection is not causality but perception of what informs the experience.

For ethics, this involves the ethos (variations in feeling values) of structuring preference. Ethics entails an assessment of these values. While people engage daily in this complex set of interconnections, Scheler refers to a central ambiguity:

> [T]he antinomy of which Aristotle was aware. Moral insight is necessary to lead a good life (to will and act in a good way). A good life is necessary to eradicate the sources of deception in moral insight so that we can eliminate the sophism of our interests that obstruct moral insights but also the ever present tendency to adjust our value-judgments. . . .The theoretical solution to this antinomy consists in the fact that all good *being, life,* willing and acting presuppose the *fact of moral insight* (but not an 'ethics').[5]

Authority cannot be the answer. Ethics, Scheler implies, entails the answer. However, hierarchical values form a structure wherein the highest realm commands. So, it appears Scheler differs from Kant's conception of the authority of duty only in degree. For Scheler, true perception of the situation commands the proper percept. It remains problematic as to how one "knows" that his or her connation is phenomenologically essential and, consequently, correct.

Values are thus to be "felt" in the act, not in the person's mind, or in language, or in the object of the act. This aspect marks an advance in ethical theory. Scheler distinguishes his phenomenological, interconnected, approach from both psychologism and nominalism, which, in turn, must be distinguished from one another. Psychologism is the doctrine that purports that moral beliefs occur or are "found" in the mind of the beholder. Nominalism tells us no; connations and moral beliefs are agreed-upon conventions, definitions of terms, and commonly held traditions of culture. No moral facts can exist apart. One sees in Scheler an integral modulation of the two extremes, a modulation that itself engenders new dimensions for ethical meaning. Scheler's approach is certainly not sterile or neutral. He does not reduce ethical life to a film one views, either. His ethics comprise two directions and many tiers. This connection between intentional feeling, desire, and what is felt gives birth to value. The theory does not locate essence in an area or core. Here Scheler presents a quite sophisticated attitude.

> This feeling is a goal-determined movement, although it is by no means an *activity* issuing forth from a center (nor is it a temporally extended movement). It is a punctual movement . . . . This feeling therefore has the same relation to its value-correlate as 'representing' has to its 'object,' namely, an intentional relation.[6]

In other words, a person intends values and their meaning to be for direct benefit and fulfillment and not in order to judge benefit and fulfillment. Responsibility becomes a function of a quality of an object or relation and a person or between persons. However, responsibility remains isolated, not shared. We can communicate to the extent that our subjective systems overlap or share similar features. This seems to be Chomsky's notion of the development of the language faculty, for example. That faculty is an essential feature of all people, but even within a homogeneous culture, individuals develop their systems of expression subjectively. Values, again, entail inclusive, not exclusive, thought patterns. Value is formulated, felt, received, and shared. One can separate a value from feeling that value; it becomes distinct. The absence of the feeling in presence does not cancel the value; this makes room for more subtle ethical distinctions with some claim to validity. Pleasure and pain, as such, can shift value. "Not only a joy in the base and a displeasure in the noble; there is also a base joy and a noble sadness."[7] Continually presented in the media, one finds noble pleasure and base displeasure, noble displeasure and base pleasure: reading a well-reported story about successful educational reform and watching a lurid account of greed, lust, and nastiness on a daytime soap opera, or watching an account of national political scandal and cover-up such as the Iran-Contra debacle and watching a lurid account of greed, lust, and nastiness on a prime-time soap opera. The subtleties, then, of values present themselves in experience. Scheler finds it incomprehensible that first there are value-free objects, neutrally given, to which value is added as ingredient through a second act or ordering.

Actions as well as values arise from what Merleau-Ponty calls the tacit *cogito*. He appears to have borrowed this concept, "I am able to," directly from Scheler. "It is because we have the *immediate* consciousness of `being able' to do something that we expect or shall do it."[8] The satisfaction one enjoys from this `being able to' is more deeply felt, more primordial than the many daily realizations of what one *was* able to do. The difference is more than temporal; it involves a will to power and a sense of the unique.

Here is a touchstone for those in the business or art of communication—from teachers to editors. Scheler teaches us that education is more, much more, than manipulating bits of information. The true structure of communication is in the increasing of consciousness. Herein lies the responsibility of communication: introducing the consciousness of "I am able to" into the personalities of students and audience. It is a unique and individual process one ought to encourage according to the characteristics and abilities of the interlocutor. Scheler concludes, "The interposition of a 'Can I' before every 'I will do this' is especially pathological."[9]

Flowing from the tacit *cogito* is a clearer conception of power. Power holds an inverse relation to force. The less force needed to accomplish a task or to acquire a response, the more powerful the individual or organization. This leads directly to Schopenhauer's, "everyone ought to do what he can," as a most solid, ethical principle. This principle is not fundamentally utilitarian. If it reaches the level of what's in it for me or compulsion, "ought" is absent from the maxim, and force begins to emerge. Conscience truly is the bearer of values, but personality underlies conscience. "The word *conscience* first appeared in the Latin language, where *conscientia* meant both 'with knowledge' and today's conscience."[10] Perhaps the concept of responsibility is indebted to the original polarity of *conscientia*. If so, communication has an obvious responsibility, shared with the one who is "with knowledge." Layers upon layers of responsibility manifest themselves in knowledge as well as conscience, which is not unitary or original, but eccentric and developed.

Speaking of intentionality and the tacit *cogito*, Scheler points to the example of the ethical deformation involved in capital punishment. Phenomenologically, one can suspend the act to question its implications. If the intention is to annihilate being, then the intention is perverse, morbid, and twisted, for punishment that extinguishes the punished patently perverts its intention. Even if this destruction takes place for the good and protection of society, it remains, ethically, murder. "'*Punishment*' presupposes that the life of the punished is good for him as a person whose existence is not affected by the removal of this good."[11] So, the essence must insist on conformity with the intention to qualify as phenomenologically sound. The interconnection must subsist within the act. The strictly causal thinking involved in ethically condoning capital punishment results from confusion or, more specifically, a misapprehension of levels of intentionality and meaning. Scheler shares Pascal's lament:

> Only in an age in which the confusion of hearts, the *desordre du coeur*, has reached the degree that it has in our own could the totality of our emotive life be considered a process of causally moved states which follow each other without meaning or ends, and only in such an age could our emotive life be denied `meaning' and intentional 'contents.'[12]

It is not so much our concepts of feeling such as love, justice, or sympathy which deserve analysis, but the *forms* our attitudes take; the methods we unfurl, the rules and values we hold high. Content is secondary to form for Scheler. Judgmental and linguistic forms cry for examination; investigation precluded by the forms themselves. If one denies even the terms phenomenon, intentionality, and meaning, how can methodologies be examined for their content? The latent ethics of exclusive behaviorism galvanize and weather-proof its structure against any admittance of these concepts into its ground.

While Scheler's ethics has so much to offer with regard to emotive-value appreciation and discernment, he cannot finally locate the concept of responsibility outside of duty—duty to the religious, the most high, the ineffable. Not all responsibility invokes religious consideration and not all theorists are religious. Michel Foucault has been categorized in many ways, but religious is certainly not one of them. It is to Foucault that we turn to look at the specific, mundane aspects of ethics.

FOUCAULT'S AESTHETICS OF EXISTENCE

How are we to compare Scheler's ultimate principle of phenomenology— the interconnection between the essence of an object and the structure of intentional experience—reflexivity, to Foucault's postmodern approach to problems of truth, knowledge, and power? As has been noted, Foucault has said that if there was any approach which he reacts against, it is the meaning bestowing, subject oriented one of phenomenology. However, it is my contention that the Foucault of *The Order of Things* is different from the Foucault of *The Use of Pleasure*. Or, rather, it is not so much that the originator of the discourse has changed, but that his concerns have expanded to encompass dimensions of experience not previously examined. Foucault had, it is true, concerned himself with the problem of subjectivity in his studies of madness and medicine, but he did not at that time concern himself with modes of subjectivity; he did not attempt to describe how the subject makes sense out of him or herself, or how one forms oneself from experiences, desires, feelings, and intentions.

Foucault recognizes in his work three explicit, if interrelated, aspects of experience: truth, power, and ethics. One can locate "a game of truth, relations of power, and forms of relation to oneself and others."[13] Yet, he stated in 1974 that he had no concern with philosophy, but by the time of *The Use of Pleasure*, his work on ethics, he refers to his studies as a "philosophical exercise" to enable him to think differently, to free himself from studies that needed revision, correction, and reconstitution. Playing the "game of truth," one undergoes changes. Philosophical activity, Foucault declares, is the critical effort that one expends upon oneself. Indeed, we notice a rather remarkable shift in the sorts of terms Foucault employs. He writes of themes such as austerity, wisdom, and sexuality, not only as expressions of sanction, but alternatively as practices of liberty. While not attempting to fit Foucault into a practice he explicitly rejected, I think that at least insofar as his ethics goes, he is no longer hostile to a phenomenology of ethics, an aesthetics of existence or what he calls techniques of self. In speaking of his method, Foucault talks about the phenomenon sexuality in terms of "bracketing its familiarity," analyzing games of truth and error which "constitute experience," and framing the question in ways that are far from the "horizons" with which he claims familiarity. "In short, it was a matter of seeing how an 'experience' came to be constituted in modern Western societies . . . accessible to very diverse fields of knowledge and linked to a system of rules and constraints."[14]

Experience, as Foucault employs the term, is not primarily the set of relations by which a particular person organizes reality, as it is for Merleau-Ponty. Foucault deploys the concept as a "correlation between fields of knowledge, types of normativity, and forms of subjectivity in a particular culture."[15] Nonetheless, he has come to rely on experience as the medium through which one describes the constitution of self, which is no less significant, and perhaps even all the more noteworthy, because it provides the organizing principle for structures of knowledge, fields of power, and relations of ethics. Foucauldian ethics refers to "the kind of relationship you ought to have with yourself, *rapport a soi*,"[16] which establishes morality. Further, in 1974, Foucault articulated his preference for politics over all else, yet 10 years later, he told an interviewer, "I would more or less agree with the idea that in fact what interests me is much more morals than politics, or, in any case, politics as an ethics."[17]

While we content ourselves with noting that a shift has occurred, this discontinuity allows for Foucault's inclusion in our discussion of ethics from a critical phenomenological point of departure. Paramount to this approach is to insist upon approaching ethics as a study worthy of itself, a form of human activity that constitutes a dimension of appreciation that recognizes the necessary conjunction of fact and value, while not basing ethical justifications on the empiricism of social science or the objectivism of instrumental, neutral reasoning. Ethics, for Foucault, is not then based upon or linked in any essential way to political, social, or economic structures. As we will see with Levinas, the ethical relation makes their just articulation even conceivable.

Foucault asks the classical Greek question, "How to live?" Although he does not answer for us—the purpose of ethics is to constitute one's relation with oneself and others *by* oneself—Foucault does analyze the various aspects of the ethical relationship. By this time, Foucault is speaking of an interpretation of self, a hermeneutics of self, the general contours of which can be isolated by the pronounced values of society. For the Greeks, it was largely a matter of virtue, and virtue carried with it a notion of self-mastery. Foucault writes,

> It was one of the most constant themes of Greek political thought
> that a city could be happy and well governed only if its leaders
> were virtuous; and inversely, that a good constitution and wise
> laws were decisive factors for the right conduct of magistrates and
> citizens.[18]

His attempt is to describe the Greek and Greco-Roman ethics—arts of
existence or techniques of self—to look at the intentional acts by which
the ancients gave themselves guidelines for conduct and self-examina-
tions that aided them in efforts of self-transformation. This was undertaken, Foucault suggests, in order to fashion morality in a double sense:
a set of guidelines and values according to which people mediate their
activities (code-oriented), and the actual behavior of these people relative to the recommended codes (ethics oriented). Any given society will
emphasize its own unique formulations of code-oriented activities and
ethics-oriented morality. Ancient Greek society emphasized an ethics
orientation over a fairly general code orientation. The value of such an
investigation is not, Foucault warns, to go back and adapt ancient practices to modern problems, even less so upon recognizing the oppressive
character that practices of virtue over women and slaves produced and
promulgated, but to instruct us in the development of a chapter in what
Foucault regarded as his aim, the development of a history of truth.

In Volume Two of *The History of Sexuality*, we are presented with
four considerations which allow us to organize and recognize the ethical
horizon, the context and background that trace out ethical relations to
oneself and others. At base, this is a relationship with the social world in
which it is embedded, as well as a relationship with oneself.

> The latter is not simply 'self-awareness' but self-formation as an 'eth-
> ical subject,' a process in which the individual delimits that part of
> himself that will form the object of his moral practice, defines his
> position relative to the precept he will follow, and decides on a cer-
> tain mode of being that well serve as his moral goal.[19]

I take this to be a description of the intentional structure of the ethical
relation. Employing a particular situation, I would briefly like to sketch
out how these considerations play into a discussion of contemporary
ethics and mass communication.

While a reporter for the *New York Times*, John L. Hess wrote a
series of almost 150 stories exposing a nursing home scandal in New
York, affecting 650 nursing homes housing 90,000 people. The stories
resulted in the indictment of 200 nursing home owners for, among other
things, subjecting helpless elderly people to "'squalid' sometimes inhu-

man conditions" for profit.[20] Since we are concerned with the ethics of the reporter, I will attempt to reformulate the value and rule considerations facing Hess. Foucault urges us to first consider what might be the "ethical substance," the essence, of the situation. What are the crucial aspects for Hess and his behavior, that is, his reporting the story. The essence lay in unfolding the account of institutional cruelty and greed. Hess says, "I didn't want to write just about people lying in their piss, dying of malnutrition . . . The key question was: Why wasn't the state enforcing the laws?" "There was money to be made, large amounts of money,"[21] he concludes.

What obligations was Hess forced to recognize, what rule or principle was he obliged to obey, in other words, what intentional structure ordered his investigation? Hess, like all journalists, must pay allegiance to the norm articulated under the banner of objectivity. For contemporary American journalism, a reporter manifests responsibility by following professional methods in gathering and presenting information. Responsibility is largely a matter of professionalism; one is ethical to the extent that one is professional. The "mode of subjection" is rationally articulated by remaining neutral, presenting both sides to any issue, and relying on experts and officials for sources of information not directly observed by the reporter. So, for the mainstream of journalism, the dominant belief is that one behaves ethically to the extent that one acts professionally and that means following the tenants of the rule of objectivity.[22] But Hess did not accept the dominant discourse; for him, objectivity is a "subversive thing in American journalism."[23] Hess subjected himself to an allegiance to decency and an ethic of social justice over professionalism and the protective shield of neutrality.

Hess put himself through a rigorous process of self-examination, of "self-forming activity," in the process of attempting to portray the scandal. For instance, during a 4-month period, Hess often worked 12-hour days, seven days a week, producing 34 stories on the nursing home issue. Hess felt his editors repaid him by blocking his stories and underplaying his efforts. "Those bastards at the *Times* are cutting my stories and burying them . . . "[24] In fact, Hess' efforts to uncover corruption in New York finally cost him his position. After almost 20 years on the paper, he quit. Reportedly, his editors considered him an embittered old crank for his charges that the *Times* didn't want to know what was going on; "it stuck its head in the ground while the city went to pieces."[25] In spite of his efforts to reform the nursing home industry, "the structure of the industry remained what it was, and the cast of characters is only slightly different,"[26] he admitted.

Hess' goal, his "telos," involved writing a series of stories, employing the rules of the game to the extent beneficial to his tactics of successfully changing the nursing home industry by exposing the illegal strategies employed and by urging the replacement of the for-profit structure of nursing homes with nonprofit institutions. He kept the issue active and in the news by mixing the sorts of stories he wrote, by sharing his information with competing publications, and by working with government investigators, a blatant violation of the objective method. As a reporter from the *Village Voice*, with whom Hess shared information and strategy put it, "Our mutual objective was exposure and reform."[27]

A Foucauldian approach necessitates turning oneself inside out into a veritable work of art. This was a common practice in Western culture until the 16th century, Foucault claims. With Descartes' criterion of self-evidence, the notion of transforming oneself to appreciate the truth fell away. Truth and value were disconnected with the advance of the scientific method. Kant endeavored to reinstate ethics, but only as a realm cut off from scientific rationality. So, the worst of men are equally able to recognize truth as the most ethically responsible. Foucault concludes, "Thus, I can be immoral and know the truth. I believe that this is an idea which, more or less explicitly, was rejected by all previous culture."[28]

LEVINAS' METAPHYSICS OF DESIRE

Scheler's concern with values maps the traditional approach to ethics as a discernible hierarchy. He realizes that logic, by itself, is inadequate to the task. Foucault's ethics of self is inadequate to explain the bond between individuals, that is, intersubjectivity. A further problem with Foucault's aesthetic approach is that it is an aesthetic approach. We have no adequate way to measure the standards a given individual chooses in order to make himself a work of art outside the possibilities a particular culture and specific historical period provide. To oversimplify, why is the work resulting in Edward R. Murrow more aesthetically successful or more morally valuable than the efforts at constitution which produced Joseph Goebbels? Levinas insists "that before culture and aesthetics, meaning is situated in the ethical, presupposed by all culture and meaning. Morality does not belong to culture: it enables one to judge it; it discovers the dimension of height."[29] He views the ethical relation as constitutive of humanity; the relation—founded on a lack—is by its nature asymmetrical. Desire presents itself in proximity to others and risks uncertain response in the trace of the Other. Desire speaks from the fact. There can be no further intention behind the fundamental desire for discourse. Desire founds a behind which is nothing and in which arises good will—authentic communication, shared meaning.

For Levinas, theory is primordially subtended as ethics. The reasoning through which ethics illustrates itself is dialectical, asymmetrical, and intertwined among individuals as receptive and neighborly (taken in the widest sense). "Communication" stems from the Latin *communicare*, to share as in intercourse. Americans are expert at shoving information at each other, but we seem to have foundered in the constitutive process in its primordial form—communication as sharing.

The media "inform" their audience, for example. The media impart "knowledge" of some particular fact or event; the media speak of something and, intentionally or not, appraise what they speak of. One must discern communication as affective (not to be taken as successful, but as making a difference of some sort). Levinas has made penetrating inroads to a radical and humane philosophy of sharing through language. If subjectivity is affectivity, then critical phenomenology urges pluralizing reason, recognizing various planes of rationality, because values are integral to our relationship to ourselves and our perceptual and lingual relationship to the world. Misguided values are no superficial matter. Therefore factors and innuendo are pregnant contributors to real understanding. Facts are either true or not true, but to arrive at such determinations in the social world, one must understand the reasons for situations and personal perspectives. Strictly speaking, there is no neutrality in communication. We are all situated and committed through our intentions. The question: "Who is speaking and why?" is an interrogative imperative for any critical phenomenological attempt at conceiving philosophy from, and as, communication. Quiddity, Levinas maintains, has all but suffocated identity, as a result of both philosophy and science. Today, one can ask Levinas' question with a straight face: "What does who mean?"

Levinas reminds us of an essential reduction:

> [T]he object of consciousness, while distinct from consciousness, is as it were a product of consciousness, being a `meaning' endowed by consciousness, the result of *Sinngebung* [an impression of meaning]. The object of representation is to be distinguished from the act of representation—this is the fundamental and most frequent affirmation of Husserl's phenomenology. . . .[30]

Such a conception is understood within a horizon, with a subject as situated in perception across lines of opinion and position. Communication is a metaphysical relation, and one's enjoyment in communication is a relation within a relation. This is elemental and is a resulting effort or accomplishment. Communication and perception are integral. Discourse teaches one to understand. One questions the message and the speaker, and, in turn, oneself is put into question and reevaluation. There is a synergy involved in communication which is an indefinite gestalt; it is not bounded; something else can be said. Something else must be said by someone for the maintenance of meaning. Hence, putting oneself in question according to the address of another founds the ethic within the ethical relation. It is an interweaving. Rationality is seen as a reduction of ignorance, insensitivity, and oppression in self-righteousness. Thus, we hope to avoid committing the genetic fallacy: A method derived from an artificial mode according to causality. Dialectical thought accepts reciprocal interactions rather than monadic entities.

Levinas emphasizes that the uniqueness of the individual does not arise from his or her subsumption in a genus or a species; individuality does not spring from a concept. Individuality of the "I" remains outside logical schema and is general, pertaining to many. When we attempt to integrate personality into a thematic closed system, we abstract and lose the concrete sense of selfhood. Selfhood is subjective; it does not lend itself to objectification or quantification. Dialectical interrogation accepts the fact that human relations and personality in language are open systems, not predetermined. To understand ourselves, we need to be understood by others; for another to understand us is to grasp comprehension of himself. The differences between oneself and the Other are not, Levinas points out, psychological states or properties, but they emanate from the nexus of the "I-Other" relation. This is an orientation, a direction from oneself toward the Other. "Speech is not instituted in a homogeneous or abstract medium, but in a world where it is necessary to aid and give."[31] This movement in discourse is transcendence and desire. Desire is a striving for exteriority which is founded on a lack. The lack is constitutive of humans, as we are all incomplete. Desire is felt and exercised in discourse, not in logical manipulation. All desire is a desire for meaning or response. It is always contextual but open ended. Desire is different in kind from need. A need assumes necessity, compulsion, and consumption, whereas desire is insatiable emotion, a request or petition for aid. Human lack is a fact or condition of deficiency. Truth resides in sharing and "association" (with others). Communication is rooted in commitment. The stimulation to wonder is correlative to one's desire of someone. We enter into relations with others in language, which assumes and embodies the ethical relation.

For Levinas,[32] the original phenomenon is the Other; the world becomes understandable through the discourse of the Other. The affirmation of communication comes not from oneself but from the Other. Discourse originates when he says yes. It is one's desire to learn which answers his affirmation. The presence of the Other offers the possibility of knowledge of one's reality in a multiplicity which forms no totality, as it is a temporal flowing on and on. This is the principle through which signification flows. Signification is a call or description from a distance; the Other is physically, absolutely separate from one; hence, communication is the metaphysical relation. One does not consume the Other; one relates with him or her. Communication is a creative attempt to integrate the world, others, and oneself through communication with the Other. "To conceive of separation as a fall or privation or provisional rupture of the totality is to know no other separation than that evinced by need."[33] As sense is never full, awareness brings light to new crevices in the world. This ferments other questions. The lines are visible (writing) and invisible (speech) presentation from a distance. The Same cannot be Other; one cannot define "him" or "her," but one can relate to "him" and "her." Discourse is the self-interrogation or questioning of the Other. Levinas tells us that this rudimentary function of language is teaching. Teaching produces exteriority, external relations. In authentic, multivalent communication, the first lesson, the functional lesson, is the ethical because real teaching, one that lends rationality, is ethical.

This attitude takes the social to be the primordial relation. The individual grasps the very concept of self from the social fabric, essentially presented through the language structure. The social is ultimate and beginning. As we saw in Chapter 1, we are born into a community, a language, a culture. One does not posit or in any way create this world: it is there (*dasein*). A phenomenological attitude does not accept statements such as the *cogito* to be underived. Community is the primordial relation. Mind, for example, is a punctuation of this relation. Mind is a social relation between self and environment. Language is contact with the non-touchable. The Other has attributes one grasps, of course. The Other's uniqueness and opacity are not my themes; they are her reality. Consequently, the Other is absolutely exterior. She expresses this exteriority in a current of signs offered, translated, and represented. One "enjoys" this discourse from the height of language as a teaching.

Interhuman relationships are economical insofar as they involve a give and take—asymmetrical, temporal, and open-ended discourse. Language places people and artifacts in commonality; the grid is partaken of energetically in multiplicity. Language itself is hypostatic; it supports us and our realities. Rational hypostasis is located at the individual level, and language is the metaphysical relation with the Other. "The generality of the word institutes a common world. The ethical event at the basis of generalization is the underlying intention of language,"[34] says Levinas. One remembers though, that the infinity of discourse never concretely forms a whole but fashions multiplicities.

> Being-for-the-Other must not suggest any finality and not imply the antecedent positing or valorization of any value. . . .The fact that

in existing for another I exist otherwise than for me is morality
itself . . . .Transcendence as such is consciousness.[35]

    This is Levinasian *common sense*. Commitment and responsibili-
ty are existential bases for the metaphysical relation, the elemental
ephemeral conveyed by the Other. One does not transcend the same in
consumption and possession. One goes beyond the self by remaining the
same but changing the sameness which is oneself. While Self and Other
are not in any sense identical, the relation is transitive in a philosophic
sense: One has an effect. The relation is not one of identity but of difference. The relation is an inequality of terms (not better than but different
from). One views alterity constituting meaning and felicity through language: asymmetry. Asymmetry accounts for freedom in the transcendence of the Other which allows and accommodates my transcendence
with the freedom of a discourse in community. Signification is directional and dynamic, coming to us across a distance. Communication is not
"being" but "becoming."
    Levinasian metaphysics is constituted according to four cate-
gories: separation, interiority, truth, and language (exteriority).
Existentially speaking, humans are separate from each other as entities,
and one's mental processes, cognitions, and interior mental life take
place within oneself. But for truth to insist, it must do so in language, in
the desire for the Other by her discourse. The relationship is infinite
because of the absolute alterity of the Other. The visible is a surface of
inexhaustible depth. The Other can envelop us in his uniqueness or her
porous being, in a teaching. Desire is realized in the paradox of expression because solicitation is an appeal for relationship, a continuous relation among persons, but this relationship itself is mediated by the self-
relation of the subject to the object, that is to say, the subject sees him- or
herself mirrored in this relation. This mediation deserves emphasis; to
view the Other as a manipulative object is a distortion of the ethical relation of which Levinas writes. The paradox of desire and expression lies
in the realization that desire is continuous but can be engaged only in a
discontinuous, asymmetrical process—expression. Thus it is a constant
beginning, or a recourse from a different perspective.
    However, we ought not view separation as a spatial blockade or
pitiable isolation. For Levinas, separation is to be taken as a temporal
position; it necessarily produces itself in difference and multiplicity, an
open system. It is metaphysical, the essence of freedom. Porous being
does not need to be filled but desires confirmation. Finite limitations
pass within the infinite possibilities present in discourse with the Other.
We are determined by the Other; he presents himself in representation.
The Same recognizes the Other, not in a causal or definitive sense, but

from a perspective in perception and listening. We cannot causally or completely determine the Other because he is an "overflowing" of any conceptions and perceptions—he is Other, radically Other. Here is dialectics: We understand what someone says to us, and we show the fact of understanding in gestures and in our turn. Understanding dawns on us. "Familiarity is an accomplishment, an en-ergy [in-work/effect] of separation," says Levinas.[36]

To exist within the life world of community in communication is, for Levinas, to "dwell;" this represents a personalization of Heidegger's *Dasein* (Being-there). It is not a logically equivalent term, but a "personification," which phenomenology and existential communication theory have lacked. People are not simply "thrown" into existence but are taught (for better or for worse) how to dwell within society through discourse. Man is not a pure or independent entity but returns to himself through dealings with the constellations of human efforts within a societal universe. The ethical relation inherent within the concept of "dwelling" and manifested by the Other is expectancy and welcome, *Sorge* (care) as intersubjectivity. To dwell, then, is not an anonymous existence, but a subjective process within a network already there before the world arises from Levinas' notion of infinity, inexhaustible Being, which can always become other, unbounded and indeterminate. "Why did he say that?" "What will she say next?" This is the interest which communication and all lingual art holds for the reader or listener. This interest, then, is an interest in the infinite multiplicity and diversity possible in the understanding that speech-discourse does not terminate with the "I" or the "Other" but is indefinite from the lingual relation. "The idea of infinity, which is not in its turn a representation of infinity, is the common source of activity and theory,"[37] Levinas says. Metaphysics is the relation between the "Same" and the "Other:" It is language.

Obviously, metaphysics can only operate to the extent that needs are met. Starving people, the sick or mentally deranged, are not going to be able to comply with their human constitution, as its very possibility has been denied to them. Need implies necessity, not choice. Choice is the node of ethics. "I will eat" has little to do with good or bad; it is equivalent to "I will live." Need demands satisfaction (food, sex, tools, clothing, etc.). But desire recognizes no fullness or satiety. Desire fundamentally is temporal, and its future is unspecified. Levinas feels that temporal desire is presupposed by need; need rests on desire. This occurs in labor—unfortunately all too often, alienated labor—doing that which one would not otherwise do. Thus, desire can be polluted through need. If the two important verbs are "to have" and "to be," the former has triumphed over the latter in our society, thus distorting metaphysics into trite, glib insincerity and grayness. To forget or deny the metaphysical is to lessen our own awareness. Levinas writes, "Consciousness and desire are not modalities of consciousness among others, but its conditions."[38] One must draw his own course according to his own sense of responsibility; one works his own path. This is the beginning of the relation originated from the Other in his or her language. Signification takes place from other people's understanding and relating the world to me; learning the Other is the end term from which meaning solidifies in discourse. To be free, we build a world where freedom is possible; in the language of the Other, we come to grasp our own signification, not by determining him but by appreciating his attributes. The attempt to make another in my image is an underlying compulsion of sadism. Control of the temporal process by terminating the movement of process is sadistic by definition.

Levinas outlines two primal modes of existence, the totalizing and the infinitizing. The way of totality is the striving for control, for power, the neurotic desire to make the Other like oneself. The emphasis is placed on systems building, and any who rebel against the system are rendered impotent, if possible. In sum, communication founds appreciation of the absolutely Other. Within the dialectic, there are two poles. Levinas says these poles may be labeled teaching and questioning. This is basically a Platonic conception. In discourse, language does not form symbols into systems; to the contrary, we decipher systems. We realize the desire to communicate with the Other through what Levinas terms the process of exteriority which manifests expression and interpretation. Learning is not maieutic; it comes about through appreciation in the face of the Other. One transcends self through the face or text of the Other. It is not consumption, but an interpretive lesson *ad infinitum*.

PROXIMITY AND RESPONSIBILITY

As ethics is lingual, and language mediates response, speakers are the sources of responsibility. Respondents make responsibility conceivable. Levinas urges the uniqueness of the individual. "I" and "we" are different levels of meanings, not ingredients in a recipe, yet the social is as factual as it is valuable. To mistake the social for merely a collection of individuals is the mistake of classical liberalism, leading to the decapitation of value from fact. For Levinas, one's identity is established and maintained through a relationship with another about something in a tentative approach. The tentative is evoked through the preconscious category of enjoyment. Enjoyment can, as all know, be thwarted. Vulnerability is a condition of responsibility. One does not at this level choose or not choose fundamental responsibility; one is responsibility. Of course, responsible people behave in irresponsible ways and hurt and pain occur. The responsible Other is so elected, yet there is no election. Levinas considers humanity to be a privileged group.

> But in the ontological adventure the world is an episode which, far from deserving to be called a fall has its own equilibrium, harmony and positive ontological function: the possibility of extracting one-self from anonymous being.[39]

Levinas' acknowledgment of personality is unique among current thought, which often seeks a skewed, unconscious, anonymous Being, disciplined subjects, deconstructed presence, professional agents, functional categories, or the statistical embodiments known as social science to explain "the current state of affairs." Levinas sees the human being breathing, eating, sleeping, loving, and thinking no matter where he casts his glance. Phenomenal can refer to light, food, love, femininity, position, totality, infinity, even home. Humanity is occasioned as much by ethics, domesticity, and sensibility as by economics, aggressivity, and the cerebral cortex. He writes:

> The statement, 'a house is an implement for inhabiting' is clearly false, and in any case does not account for the exceptional place that home plays in the life of a man belonging to sedentary civilization, the sovereignty it gives the so-called plain man.[40]

One leaves his or her dwelling; she situates and is situated, says and is spoken of, sees and is seen without being reduced to pure knowledge or information which, after all, is predicated on "self;" knowing does not constitute self. Levinas personalizes Husserl's notion of temporality. Rejoining Derrida, the present is not only a form for projecting hopes through events remembered, or evidenced by the dynamism of the trace; the present is also the condition for duration. It is not solely a fleeting unit. Any expression renders present the communicated as well as the communicator. This displays the possibility for responsibility. Responsibility implies someone to whom responsibility can be attributed. This locates one of the concerns brought about by experiencing culture through mass-mediated technologies. Anonymity reduces accountability. Personality and perspective provide depth to discourse.

Because communication realizes the ethical relation, the "I" (same) does not create or enact value. Meaning ushers forth from the ethical obligation of another (Other). Such obligation is not trivial, fortuitous, or incidental. Ethical obligation to another is essential. It establishes the situation. The Other is the nexus of social life. Groups do not emanate a steady flow; meaning and, hence, obligation pulsates in asymmetry. While the social presents the primary relation, separation does not just happen to the individual; it is essential. The world is horizonal; man finds himself in it, of it, to it, toward it.

Derrida appreciates this Levinasian ethic:

> It is true that Ethics, in Levinas's sense, is an Ethics without law and without concept, which maintains its nonviolent purity only before being determined as concepts and laws . . . .Levinas does not seek to propose laws or moral rules, does not seek to determine a morality, but rather the essence of the ethical relation in general.[41]

This is a relation without which moral concepts and laws would drift in a sea of ideological currents or freeze in authoritarian ice. The ethical relation depends upon articulation; one cannot assume it to be obvious. Appreciation takes practice. One locates no commandments within the texts of Levinas, no laws carved in stone as with Kant. The grammatical structure of the question delivers meaning and value. Freedom of speech is fundamental in such an appreciation of treatment. If one is not free in principle to ask, how can one receive a reply? If learning is not maieutic, curiosity must give vent to the exploration of what is other. Self-knowledge is precipitated through understanding at a very basic level—which is alter. The ethical relation does not then replace or surmount values or laws; it is their condition. Freedom removes limits for an infinity of other possible perspectives, exterior to one's own. Difference differentiates conception. Through the curvature of intersubjectivity, we may uncover what was once held divine—hidden from the view of men. James Joyce's parable of the "Ondt and the Gracehopper" tells of how the gracehopper stretches forth his langtennas in insectuous joyicity, while the "responsible," mirthless ondt keeps to his colonizing activities.[42] The difference, for Levinas, between violence and appreciation is the presence of identity through difference, personality, or the gaze of the other. The ethical significance of the face or identity is prior to any thought or conceptualization. Ethics does not ordain an order, it is anarchic, and the gracehopper's exposure to the Other opens up responsibility confounding the systems building activities of the ever-active ondt. One is located within a social fabric comprised of people who, by living in a community, articulate, through proximity, responsibility. Levinasian responsibility is so fundamental that it cannot be dodged, only practiced artfully or not.

Scheler holds that values exist in a virtual fashion as qualities independent of being felt or of the intended object. Levinas seems to think value becomes valuable in respect. As intentional, value is a "being," an end of a dynamic arc, fulfilled with the Other. Within the realm of ethics, the final term of value is found in the intended object as esteem through signification. Recognition founds the urging of desire. The intentional arc is desire; the desirable is, obviously, Other. Encounter with the Other (other person) is absolute, totally different from locating the Same (identification). Desire has direction and intention. Intentionality becomes respect. To reduce the Other to the Same is forgery and manipulation and institutes the breach of the ethical relation which can degenerate to violence.

Asymmetrical, one-for-the-other desire expresses the humane metaphysical responsibility ingrained in the situation. Appearance of the Other designates a diacritic rupture with coincidence. Difference locates the gaze of the Other. Derrida seems to agree with Levinas, "the other is the other only if his alterity is absolutely irreducible, that is infinitely irreducible; and the infinity of the Other can only be Infinity."[43]

The problem of the affinity of self and other becomes the difficulty of describing the moral conditions for conceptualization and law. This problematic is the driving force for Levinas' ethics. For instance, questioning is structurally primary in communication; yet one cannot begin to grasp the question until another, by joining the dialogue, tentatively attempts to resond. Responsibility is won from this labor. "Speech detaches itself from him who utters it, flies off. . . .But human labor and effort presuppose a commitment in which they are already involved,"[44] writes Levinas. Here freedom insists in guaranteeing its own work in effort through discourse. Discourse about something enhances reason which, in turn, strengthens freedom. Discourse about something introduces a third term. A third term always presents something, an event or relation as interest. One speaks with someone about something, a third term. Further, the third person institutes social structure and with it the possibilities of justice as well as enjoyment. According to Levinas:

> Social life in the world is communication or communion. To have a falling out with someone is to find out that one has nothing in common. It is through participation in something in common, in an idea, a common interest, a work, a meal, in a `third man' that contact is made.[45]

Personality (style) is traced ambiguously by and from the Other to one in an invitation to risk involvement by approaching the Other. This approach is channeled, for Levinas, through enjoyment. Sensibility is enjoyable. On more discrete levels of intuition, thought, speech, and writing, it is not always such a success that it may be called enjoyable.

Communication is formative, yet risky. Rejection, disgrace, and ignorance are all possibilities when approaching another. But communication traces out themes from the past that we share with another.

Derrida and Levinas share this theory of the trace for similar purposes. Their main difference in theory is one of temperament or style. Both attempt deconstruction of absolutist notions so embedded in Western culture that they go unquestioned. These assumptions have led society into serious problems—environmental, political, social, and psychological. Levinas actively deconstructs our notion of absolute subjectivity, which in turn supplies the concept of objectivity—supplying instead his notions about desire and the Other, and ethics as asymmetrical communication. Derrida works to deconstruct the concept of nonporous presence. He holds this as the cause of our abuse of authority, leading to a want of freedom and dignity. Derrida's theory of presence, then, is more critical but not, I believe, as radical, he writes:

> Here it is a question of knowing whether the trace permits us to think presence in its system, or whether the reverse order is the true one. It is doubtless the *true order*. But it is indeed the order of truth which is in question. Levinas's thought is maintained between these two positions.[46]

RADICAL ANARCHY

From this perspective, the ethical relation forms the prime term from which the order of truth is produced (or disfigured). Since any conception relies on polar opposition, mediation must be considered against the background of immediacy. It is not sufficient to argue that all is mediate and that there is no immediacy in perception, communication, mass communication, or cultural life. But, as we know, the senses interpret "sense data," information, for the brain, which in its turn organizes the already filtered and ordered "truth" in the act of perception, allowing us to interact with our environment. If that perception entails communicating with another person, who presumably is undertaking similar mediations, we are engaged in a process of mediation of mediation. If that perception and the consequent mediation occurs while watching television, events really become divorced from any sense of immediacy.

We are in the realm of the phenomenology of technology which Ihde sees as involving both a reduction and an expansion of perception and understanding.[47] One's experience of the face of the Other, in-depth perception of the person on TV is vastly reduced compared to face-to-face communication, while the reach and breadth of coverage on the national news, for example, is greatly expanded from what one could directly experience. What does this mean in terms of mass communication? Is mass communication a bastardization of the authentic dialogue situation? Are the media to be viewed by definition as hopelessly duplicitous and manipulative? Yes, if the question is framed in such a way that only direct interpersonal communication counts as somehow authentic. But that is a misapprehension, it seems to me. For we live in an "information age," and it seems a gigantic misstep to approach our present culture, and its attendant modes of communication, as hopelessly inauthentic.

The ethical relation shapes the prime term, from which mediation and dialectical thought devolve. This openness to the Other, for Levinas, forms the normative ground that gives rise to critical phenomenology. For ethics is a virtual, not a substantive, relation. Ethics is articulated through a "saying" and a "said," which, while by means of mass communication does remove the possibility of direct response, does not negate the possibilities of enjoyment of the differences of the Other, or the growth of responsibility as a pre-thematic appreciation of "one-for-the-other" that mass media are able to effect. So, while one foregos the immediacy of contact in the process of mass communication, the experience of pre-thematic immediacy which Levinas describes is not necessarily occluded by mass media. The cultural meaning imparted through the media may reveal a horizon and articulate a cultural field previously ignored or suppressed and, in so doing, describe the historical and contextual contours that give rise to it. Certainly this is not to imply that the media usually do what they could from an ethical perspective; they do not for reasons of profit and professionalism. But media people could do better, and sometimes they do well at sharing the experiences of others. At rare moments, the Other enters, disturbing the seamless continuity of media consumer-oriented programming, marking poignant, specific cultural experiences and historical contexts. Levinas says:

> The personal "order" to which a face obliges us is beyond being. *Beyond being is a third person* which is not definable by the oneself, by ipseity. It is the possibility of that third direction of radical *unrectitude.* . . .Through a trace the irreversible past takes on the profile of a "He."[48]

What is it and who is obliged by the face of the Other, beyond itself, and before reflection? The subject, for Levinas, is not the ego, the "I" of self-consciousness. Consciousness, discourse, and intentionality refer to a reduction of identity. Levinas refers to a self before reflection, on the "immediate" or on "this" side of reflexivity—a caring, vulnerable self which bears the responsibility of one-for-the-other. So, it is other than the pronoun "I", prior to self-identity, but it is not the unconscious or the tacit *cogito*, rather it is another plane contributing to self-formation of which one is finally, mediately, to some extent, aware. This self-identity, Levinas explains, is not the unity of mind and body, subjectivity and substance; it is a relation with others he calls neighborly—something, I think, akin to Merleau-Ponty's original "we" which upholds the identities of individuals through discourse. It is the violation of respect due another that institutes injustice for both Levinas and Merleau-Ponty. The Other supports the subject by a process of supplementation that works to exhibit the ethical relation preceding even the question of freedom, the underside of the perceptual field, what Levinas calls "beyond being." He refers to this structure or process as the difference that constitutes responsibility, the significance of signs, saying-said, communication. Reason, as the one-for-the-other, originary reasonableness, manifested at the level of state and law, draws its authority from the ethical relation and not the reverse. This conception offers an alternative to the reason of authority (that Derrida so relentlessly deconstructs), the difference between Levinasian infinity and systems totality. As it must, one flows into the other at various levels of practice, but the two movements can be recognized as counter to one another. Levinas asserts that this process comes between the communication and communicating fashioning the space and time requisite for distinguishing between truth and ideology. We see that, essentially, Levinas argues for a recognition of ethics upholding justice and morality, one which makes possible the conditions for specific ways of life, while at the same time articulating the commonality of humanity allowing for our enjoyment of individual difference, a difference that renders the Other absolutely other than oneself. "The reflection of cultural meaning leads to a pluralism which lacks a one-way sense."[49] But cultural meaning itself must rely on something other than the dynamics of various vested interests within culture. This is an implicit critique of the direction pointed to by the technological, instrumental sensibility, upheld by those who advance ever-increasing organization and totality.

Upon recognizing the veiled vision of the traditional, instrumental approach to ethics, Levinas wonders if it is possible for humanity to speak with a shared orientation, the ethical relation, and simultaneously to advance freedom. That appears to be his aim in doing ethics as communication theory. Because there is danger in urging a univocal approach, instead of settling for the vague marketplace-of-ideas concept or its postmodern equivalent, there is reverence for difference without identity. Going beyond, attempting to identify the characteristics of the invisible hand, to describe aspects of mankind as timeless has, on occasion, served to justify subjection and violence, as Foucault and Derrida forcefully argue. Levinas' "beyond being" is univocal only insofar as this implies an overflowing of every perception, communication, and understanding: Anarchy is the refusal to be totalized, assembled, and circulated as a product in a system of exchange. Anarchy is not apolitical. Chomsky, Foucault and Levinas proclaim themselves anarchists. Levinasian anarchy is radical. The radicalism springs from negation without affirmation, precluding the complete homogenization of the whole. Levinas would emphasize the subjective nature of radical anarchy. Such a radical commitment to anarchy can be seen, as an example, in playwright Arthur Miller refusing to cooperate with, to name names for, the House Un-American Activities Committee. Further, he refused the clandestine offer to have his hearing canceled if his wife, Marilyn Monroe, would only agree to be photographed shaking hands with the chairman of the committee. Because, Miller says:

> [T]hey had the power and were bound to make me concede that I did not by trying to force me to break an implicit understanding among human beings that you don't use their names to bring trouble on them, or cooperate in deforming the democratic doctrine of the sanctity of peaceful association.[50]

Miller's radical, anarchic refusal to cooperate, or co-opt, reaches to the essence of ethics. His defiance of the constituted instrumental order would not serve to change the situation in any substantial way; others like Elia Kazan named names and marshaled convincing reasons for doing so. Miller's ethical position was not based upon instrumental reason, in fact, it worked against his personal well-being. His refusal—actually, his affirmation—did not involve any profit or self-serving function, but was motivated nonetheless by a subjectivity prior to identity. His was an action for the world to come, for a future culture. It is precisely this responsibility and recognition of the intentional structure of moral relationships that prefigures the playwright's attitude and behavior, in his being put into question by those who negate the Other (Miller was in turn Other under the gaze of the committee), in his or her difference from the values of the time, that exemplifies Levinas' realization that the more one accepts responsibility, the more one is responsible. In turn, responsibility increases vulnerability. Anarchy, then, overflows even one's idea of freedom. This conception of ethics, or the good, is a responsibility for the freedom of others, and, as such, maintains a responsibility beyond, which overflows, personal choice. "It is also to find oneself able to judge civilizations on the basis of ethics,"[51] writes Levinas.

Taken in concert, one's responsibility for the Other and the vulnerability which this recognition of desire brings, constitutes subjectivity as the human condition. We see that beyond self-consciousness, or prior to the active existential subject, subsists a radical passivity that Levinas tells us underlies any particular theme or intention or sense of causality, an aptitude for caring and responsibility. This relationship with, and desire for, the Other is not a matter of calculation or analysis of data, in fact, Levinas recognizes in this intersubjectivity before representation the vulnerability of youth. It is youth, before the sedimenting of age, that unites this "groaning of the entrails" with enjoyment of difference. Returning to Miller's experience with HUAC, we can appreciate his reversal of the realist, empiricist tradition. He could have simply regarded the factual situation, objectively calculating the forces against him and weighing the data presented. Wasn't the meaning of the subpoena to appear and testify before the House clear in itself? Or does meaning come before data, forces, and facts? The situation, ethically, becomes meaningful because of the discourse and not on the basis of information given to thought. Miller's refusal to abridge the ethical relation in his communication to Congress gives evidence that the writer's understanding goes beyond the situation, the forces at work, or the facts to the essence of what is really at stake, the "implicit understanding among human beings," and "the sanctity of peaceful association" that were not mentioned by the honorable committee or honored by their strategy of control. Ethics is not technique. It is invested in signification toward the Other, which itself leads to equitable law and distributive justice.

Without Ethics prior to ethics, Levinas maintains that the transmission of information would not be possible. His idea of anarchy as essentially responsible comes together in subjectivity, that recognition prior to thematization; it is a sense of responsibility that enables one to appreciate the value of information. Levinas' conception of signification as one-for-the-other offers an alternative to the dominant functionalist tradition in Western culture: He presents this undercurrent as the "simplicity of an extreme complexity," a sense of mature infancy which allows any of us to communicate under the anxiety of failure, denial, and misunderstanding. The fulfillment of intention through signification is teleological. Meaningful communication does more than impart information; it anchors subjectivity through intersubjectivity, and mass communication contributes to this process at all levels. This interrelatedness lies behind the circulation of the knowledge it fashions in daily practice as an irreducible relationship with others. Like Newton's gravity, communication is action at a distance, somehow responsible for forming patterns and upholding the world, yet as itself, communication remains intangible. However, it is clear that signification as the act of saying is the condition for all communication and that this condition exposes the

speaker. This founds a realm of appreciation and not a model of representation; the "plot" involved in communication is not a mode of
thought at this level; communication is simply not reducible to the circulation of information because it relies on the "saying" of the "said."
Levinas concludes:

> [T]he one-for-the-other subtends society, which begins with the
> entry of the third man. In it my response to any problem, that is,
> my responsibility, poses problems, if one is not to abandon one-
> self to violence. It then calls for comparison, measure, knowing,
> laws, institutions—justice. But it is important for the very equity
> of justice that it contain the signification that had dictated it.[52]

It can be that the disruption or violation of the ethical relation,
the sense of insult, injury, even death that constitutes so much of what's
considered newsworthy, awakens sensibility. The incantation of violation supplements one's submerged sense of the dignity and vulnerability of others. Television is ideally suited to portray the emotive aspects of
human experience for the collective sensibility. The experiences of individuals stand, not only for themselves, but can sensitize the audience to
the living tissues of history and events which distill our values. For
many years *60 Minutes* has portrayed elements of American life, presenting to us the experiences of the Other, the person different from oneself,
sometimes as the Other to be judged, other times as another to appreciate or empathize with, and occasionally as the Other, not "us" thank
God. On one particular occasion the third man was a woman.

In the segment, "The Forgotten Veterans," Morley Safer, in a
voice over the picture, narrated the experience of Mrs. Susan Orlowski
as she received the telegram informing her of the death of her son in
Vietnam. She had no son in Vietnam. She had a daughter, an Army
nurse. This story within the space of a few minutes successfully communicated our experience of Vietnam at the personal level of four nurses
who served, witnesses to the carnage and brutality inflicted on previously innocent young men, and again alerted us to the arrogance, danger,
and tragedy inherent in turning from the face of the Other.

Many of the nurses stationed in Vietnam had no prior professional experience past nursing school; they had to decide who to try to
save and who would be let alone to die. Nurse Jackie Rhodes explains to
Morley Safer:

> Well, we had wall-to-wall bodies. We had bodies. We had to step
> over bodies and decide whether we were going to work on this
> guy, or whether we were going to leave this guy and try to take

care of this guy, and the wounds—we just looked at the wounds to decide who was salvageable, and who wasn't.

Rhodes describes her impressions of a boy whose "foot was under his chin, and one of his arms was behind . . . he was in pieces, in this bag." All the nurses interviewed were brutalized by their experiences of working on the brutalized themselves. One nurse admitted that she thinks of Vietnam every single day of her life, another nurse lost her husband. The searing experience of telling boys that they would be all right when the nurses knew that often they wouldn't serves to focus on and personify the feelings of many in the audience who have personal experiences of that time and maybe to provide a lesson to those who don't.

The faces of the nurses recounting their experiences were vivid, their vulnerability experienced by those watching, buoyed by the subjective vulnerabilities of the audience. These nurses were making sense by remaking sense; a cultural catharsis energizing the aptitude Levinas remarks, depends upon our sensibility toward the Other. The pain reflected in the faces and words of the nurses awakens our recognition of the experience of the absolutely Other that is beyond oneself and before reflection, the proximity communicated through vulnerability. Linda Schwartz was an Air Force nurse, granted leave, who decided to surprise her family with a visit home to participate in her younger sister's graduation from college in Ohio.

> And my dad came out on the porch, and he said, "What are you doing here? And I said, "I came home for my sister's graduation." And he said, "There isn't going to be any graduation." And I thought, why? And he said, "There's been something happened at Kent State yesterday that maybe you should know about." And I was all in my uniform, and I came into the kitchen, and there was my sister, Janet. And she got up and said, "Warmonger."

Diane Evans recalls returning home from Vietnam and the occasion when she and her father took the family truck into town to the feed store. Upon arriving, Evans remembers her father explaining to a friend of his, whom he had known all his life, that his 21-year-old daughter Diane had just returned home from Vietnam.

> And she wouldn't look at me. She would not look at me. And she wouldn't say anything. And my dad is feeling very embarrassed, and I want to crawl into a hole and disappear. And we get in the truck and we drive home, and I said, "Dad, don't ever tell anybody I was in Vietnam. Just don't talk about it."

While this sort of reporting, or story telling, makes us sensitive to the experiences of the Other, do the media generally attempt to get at the reasons or values by which we arrive at the kinds of situations that devalue the lives of many and threaten us all? Let's move from the experience of Vietnam to the America of Ronald Reagan and George Bush. I think it worthwhile to dwell on a commencement speech delivered to the graduating students of Brandeis University, 1989. In this address, novelist E.L. Doctorow employed the theory of value originated by Sherwood Anderson in his introduction to Winesburg, Ohio—the theory of grotesques—to illustrate what can happen to an individual as well as to a whole culture that takes on one truth to the exclusion of others. Any truth clutched too tightly becomes a lie and its bearer distorts him or herself, finally, into a grotesque. The truth of self-reliance, a beautiful truth, underlay the administration of Ronald Reagan. Reagan's conviction of the absolute worth of individualism and self-reliance turned him and our culture into grotesques. This obsession has caused us to shun values of community, moral responsibility, and the interdependence we share with one another. Doctorow explains:

> And so he [Reagan] was moved at various times in his Administration to take away school lunches from needy children and tuition loans from students, and to deny legal services to poor people and psychological counseling to Vietnam veterans, and Social Security payments to handicapped people. You see how it works—this theory?[53]

If memory serves, his account is right, the 1960s did not find countless homeless wandering and begging in the streets, the instances of corporate fraud did not seem so blatant or pervasive, nor did racism appear such a problem on campuses. The phenomenon of disregard for the Other has spawned progeny, nurtured by individualist values and resulting in outcomes one could predict, following a Levinasian analysis, might befall a society that disregards the interconnection of its citizens. The devaluation of morality decried by Doctorow finds its analogue in the coverage of the superficial aspects of news events in the media as singular or at best contemporaneous with others like it. Are these failures of character interconnected? Could the media portray them so? The media positively wallow in what Doctorow calls the "gangsterdom of spirit." Doctorow is right—there has occurred a deconstruction of spirit in the United States. The dismantling of the social safety net has been witnessed by the young who know firsthand no other society. The media should move beyond the objective method and the correlative interest in the lucrative status quo to report the connections between fact, policy, and value. (The power-knowledge practices circumscribing journalists will be discused in chapter 7.) Media provide the power base for the "experts" and they serve to authorize corruption in the government by not exposing it. The national scandals of the late 1980s at the Pentagon, the debacle of savings and loan institutions and at the Department of Housing and Urban Development are indicative of a crisis in values, values that determine facts just as much as facts speak for themselves. These are editorial concerns. When the drug czar says, "Drugs obliterate morals, values, character, our relations with each other and our relation to God,"[54] reporters ought to recognize and communicate the more important notion that morals, values, and our relations with each other have allowed for the proliferation of drugs at all levels of society. As the federal prosecutor during the trial of a cocaine financier told his jury, "You have to understand the modern gang. The modern gang wears a business suit. The modern gang doesn't rob banks, it buys banks. It doesn't take money from people. It gives them something they want."[55] The media have a moral obligation to represent Jefferson Morley's sad observation—the drug economy is not an aberration of our consumer economy but its outcome. We desparately need to know, we have a right to know, about the workings of power and the machinations of social strategists. This could become a subject for those working in the mass media, unless, of course, as we will be seeing in our discussion of Foucault, the systems of mass communication themselves form a part of the strategy of power and knowledge, which configure and constrain society, blinding and deafening us to the teachings of thinkers such as Levinas.

NOTES TO CHAPTER 4

1. E. Levinas, *Collected Philosophical Papers*, trans. A. Lingis (Dordrecht: Mirtinus Nijhoff, 1987) p. 143.

2. M. Scheler, Formalism in Ethics and Non-Formal Ethics of Values, trans. M.S. Fring, R. L. Funk (Evanston, IL: Northwestern University Press, 1973), p. 333.

3. Ibid., pp. 72-73.

4. Ibid., p. 261.

5. Ibid., p. 327.

6. Ibid., pp. 257-258.

7. Ibid., p. 250.

8. Ibid., p. 232.

9. Ibid., p. 234.

10. Ibid., p. 323.

11. Ibid., p. 313.

12. Ibid., p. 262.

13. M. Foucault, "Politics and Ethics: An Interview," in P. Rabinow (Ed.), *The Foucault Reader* (New York: Pantheon, 1984), p. 387.

14. M. Foucault, *The Use of Pleasure, Volume 2 of The History of Sexuality*, trans. R. Hurley (New York: Pantheon Books, 1985), p. 4.

15. Ibid., p. 4.

16. M. Foucault, "On the Genealogy of Ethics: An Overview of Work in Progress," in H.L. Dreyfus and P. Rabinow, *Michel Foucault: Beyond Structuralism and Hermeneutics*, 2nd Ed. (Chicago: University of Chicago Press, 1983), p. 238.

17. Foucault, "Politics and Ethics," p. 375.

18. M. Foucault, *The Care of the Self: Volume 3 of The History of Sexuality*, trans. R. Hurley (New York: Pantheon, 1986), p. 88.

19. Foucault, *The History of Sexuality, Volume 2*, p. 28.

20. R. Miraldi, "Objectivity and the New Muckraking: John L. Hess and the Nursing Home Scandal," *Journalism Monographs*, 115, August 1989, p. 2.

21. Hess quoted in Miraldi, "Objectivity and the New Muckraking," p. 4.

22. See R.D. Mills, "Newspaper Ethics: A Qualitative Study," *Journalism Quarterly*, 60, Winter 1983, pp. 589-594, 602

23. Hess, quoted in Miraldi, "Objectivity and the New Muckraking," p. 16.

24. Ibid., p. 6.

25. Hess, quoted in J.C. Goulden, *Fit to Print: A.M. Rosenthal and His Times* (Secaucus: Lyle Stuart, 1988), p. 234.

26. Hess, quoted in Miraldi, "Objectivity and the New Muckraking," p. 14.

27. J. Newfield, quoted in Miraldi, "Objectivity and the New Muckrakers," p. 6.

28. Foucault, "On the Genealogy of Ethics," p. 252.

29. Levinas, *Collected Philosophical Papers*, p. 100.

30. Emmanuel Levinas, *Totality and Infinity, An Essay on Exteriority*, trans. A. Lingis (Pittsburgh, PA: Duquesne University Press, 1969), p. 123.

31. Ibid., p. 123.

32. Other is capitalized when referring to Levinas' generalized sense.

33. Levinas, *Totality and Infinity*, p. 102.

34. Ibid., p. 173.

35. Ibid., p. 261.

36. Ibid., p. 155.

37. Ibid., p. 27.

38. Ibid., p. 101.

39. E. Levinas, *Existence and Existents*, trans. A. Lingis (The Hague: Martinus Nijhoff, 1978), p. 45.

40. Ibid., p. 43.

41. J. Derrida, *Writing and Difference*, trans. with intro. A. Bass (Chicago: University of Chicago Press, 1978), p. 111.

42. J. Joyce, *Finnegans Wake* (New York: The Viking Press, 1939).

43. Derrida, *Writing and Difference*, p. 104.

44. Levinas, *Existence and Existents*, p. 31.

45. Ibid., p. 41.

46. Derrida, *Writing and Difference*, p. 108.

47. See D. Ihde, *Technics and Praxis* (Dordrecht: Reidel, 1979).

48. Levinas, *Collected Philosophical Papers*, pp. 103-4.

49. Ibid., p. 90.

50. A. Miller, *Timebends: A Life* (New York: Grove Press, 1987), p. 412.

51. Levinas, *Collected Philosophical Papers*, p. 101.

52. E. Levinas, *Otherwse than Being*, trans. A. Lingis (The Hague: Martinus Nijoff, 1981), p. 193, fn 33.

53. E. L. Doctorow, "A Gangsterdom of the Spirit," *The Nation*, October 2, 1989, p. 252.

54. W. Bennett, quoted in J. Morley, "Contradictions in Cocaine Capitalism," *The Nation*, October 2, 1989, p. 346.

55. R. Merkle, quoted in J. Morley, "Contradictions of Cocaine Capitalism," p. 346.

Process and Practice

Maurice Merleau-Ponty thinks that values form an irreducible aspect of perceiving the world. Perception shapes notions of truth. As perception is a process, it is incomplete. Truth, by extension, also is incomplete. Freedom, from the phenomenological point of view, resides in our ability to rearrange and transform aspects of existence within experiential fields, so that truth, freedom, and perception are essentially interrelated processes that take on meaning in everyday practice.

Insofar as Merleau-Ponty subjects facts and values to mediation at levels of perception and expression, he rejects the idea of objective, final, ordained truth. The production of truth relies upon multiple perspectives and cannot be objectified. As perception is global in character, interactions take place simultaneously on various planes of experience. Fundamentally, for Merleau-Ponty, people display an interrogative attitude. But the process of trying to make sense of the world is mediated by tradition and authority, by culture and mass mediated representations of reality. I attempt to question how critical theory deconstructs various arrangements of power and knowledge from a phenomenological perspective. In what ways does the text emerge from the context? By looking at the cultural journalism of Bill Moyers, I conclude that mass media can help in constituting alternative structures by which to view our culture and the dangers posed by increasingly seamless corporate media representations of the world.

ONTOLOGY OF THE FLESH

Sooner or later, the concern with mass communication theory leads to questioning ontological assumptions underlying one's method of examining the multifaceted process of communication. As previously noted, the phenomenological approach is structurally triadic; dialogue takes place between persons about something or someone. This dialogue, admittedly, is mediated within mass communication. One speaks, another listens. Even so, how are these polar phenomena constituted? What are the conditions? How does man appear in the world as simultaneously rooted yet somehow transcendent of these very roots? The conditions for human existence are spoken and written about in different terms within various cultural traditions. How a culture discusses the ontological conditions of awareness and communication influences the way that culture sees life.

Merleau-Ponty, in his later years, took up this question concerning the ontological status of the world, of the being-in-the-world. Idealism admits coherence of the world only in accordance with overlays of the mind, while realism simply disdains any unifying ontological considerations. Presaging Foucault's reversal of the dynamics of power, Merleau-Ponty claims that sense is not to be gleaned from crimping one's neck, scanning the heavens; man is the bearer of meaning from below. Man embodies the unfolding of meaning in the world. Our questioning of the world is not merely a reversal or inversion of the indicative—it is an original manner of knowing something—affirmation in the most encompassing sense.

Within the network of intentionality we perceive the sensible and conceptual worlds. Nothing is simply, nakedly "there." Objects and people present themselves according to and by conditions of perceiver-perceived and environment. Events transpire across, not in, space. Events and objects organize perceptual and expressive planes. The sensible, the real, coheres not because of internal relations of identity; it is coherent because it is real. Merleau-Ponty says the same is true of the imaginary: The imaginary is improbable because it is imaginary, not imaginary because of improbability. This understanding of the real meets its limits within description. To completely define surpasses his method. Anticipating Derrida's conception of difference, Merleau-Ponty asserts that deferment takes the place of definition—always, there is more. But perceptions can be broken up; they are mutable. Horizons of the world trace out our perceptual constructions as well as the ways in which we think. For Merleau-Ponty, the first positivity is those conditions, the horizonal structures that shape our perceptions within which intentionality works. This cannot be derived. One suspends this positivity only to find its surety unshakable. To negate perception would be to negate experience, and life's condition is experience "of."

On the level of thought and speech, this means that the thinker-speaker already is implicated in what is thought and spoken. The problem is expressed in the intentionality of the one who poses it. The presence of a problem is another aspect of the situation which the individual embodies. Every relation covers and shades several others among interdependent meshings of perception. Merleau-Ponty's theory of perception saves him from relativism. Points of view issue from individuals with definite, not relative or absolute, perspectives. These points of view, while definite, are reversible, but this reversibility does not degenerate into relativity in Derrida's sense that nothing is sure. That we learn and express ourselves mediately is not to imply sense is lost. Rather, mediation allows for palpation of that which is presented to us. Phenomena gain meaning through examination.

This reversibility works vertically as well as laterally. One level of gesture and expression may provide context or serve as text in relation to another level. Picasso's "Guernica" presents or symbolizes human agony and destruction. The viewer jumps from one level to another, each prior level feeding into another. A television newscast of horrors taking place in Central America provides a text of suffering for which the situation serves as context; the situation is yet another text for a broader cultural context and historical process. But in an important sense, the texts of Picasso's "Guernica" and the television broadcast are the same—inhumanity and human misery. When one sees the pleas and perceives the cries on the faces of victims, a reversal takes place, and one responds to the pleas; one perceives a passivity coming upon oneself.

Perceiving, hearing, feeling, and seeing occur at a different level than discourse or discourse about discourse. Theoretical questioning must turn back upon the process of interrogation and wonder: What is it to ask or respond? Bertrand Russell and Alfred North Whitehead refer to this progression of levels of meaning as logical typing. Gregory Bateson terms raising the levels of text to context, communication about communication, as meta-communication. Merleau-Ponty points to the phenomenological discussion of fields. Areas, spheres, faculties of sensibility and expressivity form fields. Therefore, it is erroneous to assert, as do some linguistic analysts, that philosophy can be only speaking about language. Asserting, in effect, that everything takes place (for people) within the lingual realm, that language is completely self-referential, is to assert that terms like "world" and "person" refer only to semantic and conceptual differentials. The world shrinks to man's construction of it. Such reasoning is solipsistic. Semiotics comes close to returning to the philosophy of George Berkeley in its exclusion of the existential realm.

It ignores and implicitly denies the life world. In the attempt to construct orderly appearances, the world gets left behind in favor of a particular theory. This brings about a crisis in the humanities and social sciences. The truth of the perceptual field is sacrificed for the surety of the linguistic field. In fact, the perception assures and founds the discourse, yet language and perception maintain one another. Merleau-Ponty attempts to focus the problem when he reminds us that when we speak of the world, it is to intend a brute, wild existence.

> Not that language takes possession of life and reserves it for itself: what would there be to say if there existed nothing but things said? It is the error of semantic philosophies to close up language as if it spoke only to itself: language lived-spoken. . . .[1]

He concludes language is a regional problem. It is not an ontological foundation of the world but a field of endeavor and gesture. Invisible speech folds back upon the discourse among visible speakers. This process partakes of Merleau-Ponty's ontology. *Logos* forms the theme of philosophy and communication theory, but this *logos* has a pre-lingual dimension which doubles over on to the realm of the word.

There exists what Merleau-Ponty calls a "flesh" of the world. One's body and self are made from the same element (stuff) as the world; the flesh and the world are one. Merleau-Ponty attempts to transcend rationalistic dualism with an ontology of the flesh. When a person perceives something, the world fundamentally sees itself. Subject and object are no longer mutually exclusive or part and whole; they become reversible moments, marked by punctuation, focus, and emphasis. The flesh upholds the relationship at the most fundamental level: the very conditions for something becoming what it is.

Rationality, for Merleau-Ponty, becomes a crossing of conditions for identity and difference, a chiasm of the visible and the invisible effected by the flesh of the world. This notion supports his conception of human reality as intersubjectivity. Merleau-Ponty asks,

> If my left hand can touch my right hand while it palpates the tangibles, can touch it touching, can turn its palpation back upon it, why, when touching the hand of another, would I not touch in it the same power to espouse the things that I have touched in my own?[2]

This is a difficult, profound, and elegant notion. Grasping this fundamental connection of Self and Other according to the flesh really amounts to a unique vision of the world. Merleau-Ponty's thought is original; we do not customarily think of reality in terms of the primacy of relationship; we usually consider objects first. It becomes necessary in following Merleau-Ponty's expression to mediate one's analytic understanding with an element of the appreciation and enjoyment one brings to poetry and literature. Like the truly gifted poet or novelist, the philosopher presents an original view, marked by signs and styles to which we are not accustomed.

Merleau-Ponty attempts to transform social psychology's "black box" of consciousness into an expression of "carnal appreciation" and reversibility of the sensing and sensed. The world is "really" an interweaving among organisms and their landscapes. Merleau-Ponty wonders if cooperative, combined action among individuals is not as basic as the synergy we recognize at work within the individual organism. The world and the individual exist within one another. One must not methodically exclude reciprocity or interiority. Merleau-Ponty refers to the body as the "sack" in which one is enclosed. The sack is made from the same elemental flesh as the world. All of our senses work as a part of the same existence. Sensibility breeds perspective through the reciprocal chiasm of near and far. He writes:

> The distance which brings proximity and the nearness whereby we differentiate, the look and the body . . . the thickness of flesh between seer and the thing is constitutive for the thing of its visibility, as for the seer of his corporeity; it is not an obstacle between them, it is their means of communication.[3]

Perception originates from reversibility and the crossing over of perceiver and perceived. The same process works for speech and writing; signification takes place according to the reversible desire for the Other. The phenomenon of reversibility sustains mute perception and expression, manifested by a sublimation of the flesh.

The flesh is the elemental in the sense used by pre-Socratic philosophers. It forms conditions to determine processes of existence or being. This elemental flesh surrounds things and forms their proper sphere. The flesh is Merleau-Ponty's primordial principle, the source of polarity. The translator of *The Visible and the Invisible*, Alphonso Lingis, interprets the flesh as "the light that is not something seen but is that by which, or according to which one sees: what inaugurates vision of things is the elemental alliance with the visible light."[4] The flesh is not matter or mind but generality joining space-time, person-idea, and quality-object. Merleau-Ponty calls it the inauguration of where and when, facticity as the possibility of facts and their meaning about something. Flesh is not a union of contradictories (mind-body) but the emblem of modulation, the dehiscence of subject-object polarity. Merleau-Ponty thinks we must question the world to better comprehend how it opens up to us that which is different. The ways of questioning allow for certain pathways of response; multiplicity increases meaning.

Merleau-Ponty's conception of consciousness differs from both Husserl's and Derrida's, although it is more closely related to Husserl's. Merleau-Ponty takes consciousness as a central theme; it is formed in a world already there. Consciousness is upheld by elemental flesh and so awareness is not ontologically primary, as for Husserl. It is itself founded on the unconscious or preconscious. Yet, in opposition to Derrida's position, Merleau-Ponty says, "Our first truth—which prejudges nothing and cannot be contested—will be that there is presence, that 'something' is there, and that 'someone' is there."[5]

The alternatives of realism and rationalism allow for a fundamental confusion of how expression works. Based upon a relational ontology, we see that Merleau-Ponty views communication and mass communication as interpretation rather than representation. In fact, he refers to the theory that there exists in reporting a direct correlation of event and report as the "objectivist illusion." Two-dimensional expression, whether a child's drawing, the CBS Evening News, or the New York Times, Merleau-Ponty writes, assumes that "given some object or spectacle, representation would consist in reporting it and making a sort of equivalent of it on paper in such a way that, in principle, every element of the spectacle is indicated unequivocally and without impingement."[6] This is folly, he thinks. The two-dimensional perspective can claim no privileged conformity with the object or event; expression really is creation. Objective reporting, for example, claims to set down for an audience what is considered recoverable invariants from any perspective. This "information" is then objectively, that is, neutrally, passed along. The discourse is assumed to be valid for everyone. This freezes the life-world perspective. Yet, it claims not to, adopting a deconstruction presented as representation. This practice performs a theological function. It structures the truth for the audience of that which occurred in the audience's absence: omniscience as omnipresence. Merleau-Ponty writes:

> It gives subjectivity an axiomatic satisfaction through the deformation which it introduces into appearance. But since this deformation is systematic and occurs according to the same index in every part of the scene, it transports me amidst the very things and shows them to me as God sees them.[7]

But, Merleau-Ponty argues, this presentation (not representation) is a tracing of a field which ought to admit its testimonial nature. One questions the horizonal constellations of events as more than representing information. Two-dimensional perspective (depths and horizons not 3-D), obviously, is quite limited in comparison to the extended three-dimensional life world. There is certainly nothing malevolent about two-dimensional presentation, but it ought to be recognized for what it is. Communication in the media is founded and interpretive. It is partial and stylized. The difficulty arises when the two-dimensional realm of expression is taken for the text instead of as a framework for a text: when we forget that the medium involves a recipe. The constellation of signifiers carries the audience toward a meaning that did not exist prior to itself. The purpose is to admit a perspective. We ought to place a high value on as many windows for interpretation as possible, not to so value multiplicity because the marketplace guides truth to triumph, but because only through sedimentation of rich and varied presentations does a worthwhile portrait of an event arise.

Phenomenologically, communication is seen as a highly complex interaction which cannot be reduced to stimulus-response diagrams or analytically isolated categories. The subject-object dichotomy, from which many theorists orient modes of communication, is mistaken. One communicates only to others as subjects. We do not represent events objectively to ciphers but to people. We intentionally express interpretations of occurrences to persons similar but separate from ourselves.

To do this, a writer must bracket ongoing, straightforward events, to arrange perceptions and thoughts in a style that communicates essential aspects of experience. Such a reduction is not reductionist; it is necessary. Flux must be fixed to recognize patterns and produce meanings. But, bracketing must be recognized as a method for examining phenomena and not as a capturing of the life-world events themselves. This realization of perspective is an ethical consideration. Communicating through the media makes differences discrete to an audience. This sharing of differences, known as news, carries within it tacit suppositions concerning bias and values. The media are never neutral. To proclaim those in the media neutral intermediaries of a functionally noncommittal message is dishonest. Speech and writing work along lines of differences; to make one fact stand out really serves to cover a related but unstated alternative way of expressing a situation. Experience from perspective cuts off possibilities as expression unfolds realities. Punctuation of events is an inescapable process of communication. But this punctuation ought not be cause for consternation. Punctuation, as conditional for understanding, calls for recognition within the media. Emphasis and pause, perspective, and implicitly held values allow for style to emerge. Attention to style can render expression more forceful and effective. The processes of writing and editing, which produce a story, can anesthetize, hinder or spark audience reactions. If journalists strive for the gray dimension of agency-style writing, in which personality is not detectable and one story could be cut anywhere from the bottom up without making much difference, then culture suffers. The medium cheapens not only its product, but undermines the awareness of its audience. Apathy does not have to be a byproduct of the media. Clarity and appreciation for the experiences of others can be conveyed through various media to audiences that do care what happens to others. Care is an attitude which calls for nurture and practice. Disregard can lead to abuse, and abusive communication is one-dimensional communication. Mediation fertilizes the medium from which meaningful discourse and concomitant audience attention develops.

Being-in-the-world displays dimensions of meaning. Mass communication holds responsibility for shaping many dimensions from the mundane, peripheral, and amusing to the most extraordinary, essential, and serious aspects of humanity. We cannot care if we do not know, yet we will not know if we do not care. Mass communication can foster sensitive relations among people of the same society and across diverse cultures, or it can engender hatred, ignorance, confusion, and even stupefaction. But choices must be identified if we are to make differences, differences which can be seen by audiences as beneficial, rather than differences feared and guarded against. Choices *will* be made by those involved with the media.

PHILOSOPHY AS HYPERBOLE

Taking up the threads of Derrida's deconstruction, I will attempt to discuss his work from the phenomenological perspective of Merleau-Ponty. Since Derrida criticizes transcendental phenomenology so vigorously, we may gain some insight by reversing the interpretation to a phenomenological commentary on deconstruction. Derrida sees the phenomenological tradition as a bastion of the Western metaphysical tradition—logocentrism—*logos* presented as Reason. This attempt to understand the world as meaningful matrix, this desire for mastery of reality in Derrida's thought, must be deconstructed to interpret what is fundamentally theological—an appeal to authority. In the beginning was the Word.

Derrida considers phenomenology guilty of understating process, alterity, *differánce* (to differ and to defer), the unconscious for effect, identity, presence, and intentionality. The concept of intentionality opened up a new direction of philosophical interest and permitted the experience of constitution to illuminate productive experience as active and passive. Derrida holds that the common ground of activity and passivity was the root, the very possibility of meaning in Husserl's thought, that is, the transcendental ego. "Reason, Husserl says, is the *logos* which is produced in history . . . It is speech as auto-affection: hearing oneself speak. It emerges from itself in order to take hold of itself, in the 'living present' of its self-presence," reports Derrida.[8] Thus, by Derrida's standard, transcendental phenomenology stands condemned. Husserl has taken the stand against himself. Merleau-Ponty joins in Husserl's conception of presence. He writes:

> There is no truth that can be conceived only outside the field of presence, outside the limits of some situation or some structure. We are able to sublimate this situation to make it appear a particular case in a family of situations, but we cannot cut the roots which implant us in a situation.[9]

Apparently, the problem hinges around whether the concept "presence" is ipso facto an appeal to authority which, taken to its extreme, is God. Derrida has transformed a tendency into an absolute. While it is true that from acorns do great oaks grow, one ought not confuse the plant with its development (substance and process). Phenomenology is a way of describing the world. Nevertheless, Derrida proclaims the Western conception of presence and, consequently, rationality as oppressive; sense can be overbearing. He realizes, however, a complication inherent in his onslaught: The enemy refuses to acknowledge the threat. "Since the revolution against reason, from the moment it is articulated, can operate only *within* reason, it always has the language of a department of internal affairs, a disturbance."[10] Accordingly, he argues that hope for deconstructing the metaphysics of presence lies within a dialogue between that finite structure and hyperbole. The reassurance of meaning can be broken only by going beyond what is routinely accepted as reasonable and radically questioning our fundamental assumptions and accepted theoretical frameworks.

Derrida uses hyperbole as method. He claims that although emancipation from the fetters of transcendental phenomenology and philosophy in general must be attempted, we must not forget our historical debt to philosophy. He champions resistance, not complete disavowal, which, he admits, would be meaningless.[11] The movement of difference, according to the paradigm of the primacy of writing over speech, affords the opportunity for the deconstruction of tradition. Placing thought under "erasure," Derrida says, frees up interpretation. His deconstruction often appears whimsical. Because he criticizes reduction and intentionality, his interpretations may seem to lead him fortuitously in any direction without apparent structure. Derrida's play of forces neither completes a circuit nor acknowledges any field of experience as complete. His strategy is to indicate phenomena beyond the tradition, or even to turn the tradition against itself. Phenomenologically, intentionality structures communication. Derrida claims never to have disavowed the notion of intentionality; he does not break with the tradition of affording a place to the conception of intentionality. He does question the overbearing emphasis on intentionality—events and communications are not so lucid or transparent as we have been led to think. Attributing fullness, self-contained meaning, identical to itself and hence completely actualized, is a goal that the theory of intentionality cannot achieve. It often happens that communication of messages takes a completely untoward tack. The intention of the communicator is not the meaning interpreted by the perceiver. An event should be conceived of as an opening, then, it limits what it originates. We have arrived at that critical idea of freedom of constraint. This condition founds the communication process, as well as, Derrida thinks, the structure of intentionality. The weakness of transcendental phenomenology is exactly the plenitude Husserl seems to attribute to intentionality. To go beyond transcendental phenomenology would be to recognize identity and difference as part of the same process; this would be to allow for the possibility of intending ideas without claiming pure truth or ideal conceptions. One wonders why Derrida remains silent on Merleau-Ponty's conceptions of the flesh or even the dialectic of negative and positive tendencies at work within the historical process and expression. The finitude opened by expression, the infinity of possibilities latent in dialogue, are clearly ideas with an origin in the phenomenology of Merleau-Ponty and Levinas. Derrida recognizes an essential pluralism introduced by the very structure of an event; "Above all, this essential absence of intending the actuality of utterance, this structural unconsciousness, if you like, prohibits any saturation of the context."[12] The essence of this sentiment itself can be found in Merleau-Ponty's thought. The process of differentiation at work within the figure-ground couplet certainly relies upon unconscious processes. The chiasm of the visible and invisible is another way of talking about the trace and *differánce*. Yet, Derrida does supplement phenomenology by extending concepts of understanding, rationality, intentionality, horizon, and the tacit *cogito* beyond their somewhat positive and aesthetic emphases. He emphasizes the critical nature of theory: The essence of intentionality is *differánce*. Expression, in its essential structure, is removed from its source and opened up to and by others, and further, its removal is a process in advance of itself. Communication is experiment more than agreement. In this spirit, I think, Derrida confronts the phenomenological tradition with a reversal. Value carries with it a hierarchy. Deconstruction attempts to reverse the assumptions that values are positive, sense is full, contexts are clear.

That people intend goals is not the problem, that people achieve ends is obvious, but that the fulfillment of intentions as a sure bet or even as a completely understood activity from conception is an illusion serving to perpetuate the myth of the wisdom of authority.

From Derrida's point of view, figure and form serve to sweep real differences to the margins of the dialogue through metaphors of unifying structures. This making of metaphors, moreover, is not innocent. Metaphor fixes our conceptions and jells our attitudes and ideas about the text by framing an authoritative context. Once more, thought struggles vainly ensnared in conceptions of presence: equilibrium, form, figure, and symmetry. Derrida calls for a new economy of terms that escape the metaphysical conception of presence.

There is an implicit politics at work within the process of mediation of contexts which is not obvious. Deconstruction is an attempt to question common positive assumptions about the nature of the Western traditions of law, value, fact, and intention. Objectivity is a concept essential to the conservation of the tradition. It belongs to a conception of the possibility of laying out a version of reality which constitutes the Truth, the objective, neutral history of the Western world. But as Derrida points out, objectivity is rooted within a fabric of conventions that call upon a context we refer to as objective, meaning as stabilization. So the attempt would be to assert the infinity of recontextualization as a limitless process, thereby focusing on the particular and the discrete. One attempts to decenter what is attended to while recognizing that context is open, nontotalizing process. The critical strategy is to place phenomenology in a context within a network of differences, that is to say, that difference and the other are not reducible to identity and the same. But isn't this a reworking of *essentially* phenomenological values? I think it is. Levinas points out the infinite value of the teachings of the other and the desire to learn by the same. Derrida here advances the phenomenological understanding of the primacy of infinity over totality, of the lifeworld approach over positivism. Derrida argues that, no, his conception of the trace "perturbs every logic of opposition, every dialectic. It delimits what it limits."[13] Here we have philosophy as hyperbole. We need hyperbole in an increasingly impersonal world. It is a good strategy. Derrida never, he tells us, denies the possibility of truth, only its finality. Since values are limited and unstable, "the essential and irreducible *possibility* of *mis*understanding or of '*infelicity*' must be taken into account in the description of those values said to be positive."[14]

Merleau-Ponty advanced an antecedent conception of Derrida's trace. The history of language forms the trace for today's expression. Members of a linguistic community appeal to each other and through dialogue the chaos of difference is presented along lines of intentional discourse. Language, for Merleau-Ponty, is deconstructed in the sense that simultaneous events support our efforts to make sense with one another. Unexpected descriptions and replies, in turn, serve to add to the communal linguistic body. Cultural history recoups expressive acts from the logos in the present as brute facticity (the condition for facts to be recognizable). Presence is the "being there" which is not constituted so much as taken up. Merleau-Ponty describes the process of sedimentation:

> The operation of meaning has its own internal side of which the flow of words is only a wake, an indication of only its cross-points. But established significations contain the new signification only as a trace or a horizon . . . From the past knowledge to the new signification there are a response to and an acquiescence in past knowledge.[15]

Thoughts and wisdom of the past do not present the ancient culture itself, but writers allow access for us who are so distant from the ancients. Our language and our sensibilities about life are not created from nothing. They have history and archaeology. Signs evoke more than an endless procession of differences insofar as thoughts have a texture within discourse. One gets a "feel" for an author's style, for a thinker's grace. Language is capable of referring to the past and anticipating the future while moving synchronically to the sides among differences. These differences produce a mobility of thoughts at a higher level of meaning. This transition takes place within presence to something or someone.

Conceptions of presence lie at the center of Derrida's critical attempt. Presence constitutes the unique center governing the classical notion of structure. The conception of a centered structure represents coherent construction. Derrida wants to deconstruct this illusory coherence. Centralized structure, formally coherent expression, founds conditions for knowledge in traditional philosophy and science. Ironically, Derrida finds desire within frustration of that desire. Utter difference allows no recognition. Now, Levinas sees not frustration, but only incompleteness of the individual based on a lack—desire. Merleau-Ponty focuses on the porous condition, the slippage of meaning as the desire for a decentered coherence. Derrida, though, finds centered structure built upon fundamental immobility, sure of itself, beyond the realm of "play." This freezing of the force of life (of what this force consists, Derrida does not say) is itself built from the archaeology of presence. Presence refuses play. Certainly, as we have seen, this is not the concept of presence as phenomenologically presented. Derrida presses his critique:

And again on the basis of what we call the center (and which, because it can be either inside or outside can also indifferently be called the origin or end, *archē* or *telos*), repetitions, substitutions, transformations, and permutations are always taken from a history of meaning—that is, in a world, a history—whose origin may always be reawakened for whose end may always be anticipated in the form of presence.[16]

Again his hyperbole is a method. Derrida speaks of the metaphor of philosophy: darkness and light. He sees light as responsible for blinding us to the subtleties of darkness. Merleau-Ponty posits a play of light and darkness, object and shadow. The flesh of the world is made visible by invisible conditions. The metaphor itself disallows dissolution. We live on a sphere shadowed, encased by darkness and freshened by light; of course, man will describe his world according to conditions and manifestations of his existence in it. We can no more express thought without presence as life without breath.

Merleau-Ponty presents a conception of difference not as complete but according to something. He writes:

It is more accurate to say that I see according to it, or with it, that I *see* it . . . The word "image" is in bad repute because we have thoughtlessly believed that a design was a tracing, a second thing . . . and that the mental image was such a design . . .[17]

Perception occurs within the world, as part of the world. The world is not duplicated in perceiving it; that is the misperception of rationalism. Perception is the manner in which man dwells in the world; as such, it is unique and limited. Discourse connects us based upon our perceptions of events and situations. Perception blends and extends our ordering, signifying of the world, founding an institution—oneself. Merleau-Ponty calls for a shift from the fixation of a narrow, scientifically construed causality to a more humane and embracing rationality, employing reasons instead of causes. One traces or maps reasons connecting examples of what the phenomena present through description. Merleau-Ponty offers the concept of essence:

Of course, when Galileo succeeded in bringing under one signification the factors of uniform acceleration and deceleration . . . these phenomena became variants of a simple dynamic. Then it appears to us that he had fixed an *essence* of which the examples are only examples.[18]

However, it is the case that the essential signification appears only through empirical events which it unifies. This centers the structure. This center is realized through a tracing within signification. Structure is necessary to discover meaning. We suspend structural considerations and conclusions to trace new expressions from different perspectives. While structures shift, a return to them is the mode by which the signifier signifies—along pathways. One advances by intentionally sketching in meanings, expressing sensible relations in a cultural environment where others do likewise. We decentralize perspectives and events to rearrange meaning while invoking a style unique to individuals.

EXPRESSIVE FIELDS

Certainly, Merleau-Ponty and Derrida share common interests, yet in some respects their works do differ. Merleau-Ponty follows and furthers the tradition of phenomenology, while Derrida attacks transcendental phenomenology in his critique of the Western metaphysical conception of "presence." Both, however, exhibit concern for the insufficiency of the ontology of Western thought. Derrida strives to burst this tradition from within. Merleau-Ponty attempts to furnish a new grounding for the processes of intentionality, perception, consciousness, language, and history.

Merleau-Ponty labors to illustrate that the organization of perception and language are similar and interconnected. This, in sharp contrast to, for instance, contemporary semiotics, locates man in the world of beings and objects which are historically realized and situated. We must, he thinks, remain faithful to prelinguistic experience to understand the foundations of meaning. Such an orientation apparently is unfashionable today. But, if sense is not found in things themselves, as contemporary thought surely proves, neither is sense completely ethereal. Meaning emerges through communication with things, events, and others. Truth is produced by the sedimentation of this plurality of perspectives, differences, agreements, and values. Semiotics leaves itself open to the charge of idealism; sense is free floating within the chain of signifiers within discourse. Meaning, as the other side of the signifier, leaves us with idealities; the opalescence generated by signification calls for an existential ground in the world. For, if truth is inseparable from the operation which speaks it, we must recall that the "operation" is embodied by an incarnate subject. Hence, for Merleau-Ponty, the object of phenomenology is rationality, but rationality as rooted in existence, not in ideal concepts owing their existence to "signifiers" or "interpretants."

What fixes Merleau-Ponty's notion of the primacy of the worlds is, quite simply, perception. He says:

> And if perception always reaffirms the preexistence of the world, it is precisely *because it* is an event, because the subject who perceives is already at grips with being through the perceptual fields, the "senses." More generally, the subject of perception is a body made to explore the world. . . .In a single stroke the immediate data of perception signify well beyond their own context, finding an inordinate echo in the perceiving subject.[19]

This constitutes the perspective from which we communicate by embodying the ideality of language. The other also is internal to one's field of perception from an intersubjective horizon. There can be no absolute or exterior observer. From fields of perception and expression, all is connected; expression and visibility unite people, really, not ideally. One's field of perception presents the stage for a drama always in progress, through the body which opens upon other fields and horizons of the world. So, Merleau-Ponty conceives the person as both process and substance, subject and object, a reversible union of perceiver-perceived, speaker and listener. Along with psychoanalytic thought, and advancing the gestalt notion of perception, he approaches the concept of self as a derivative, decentered identity. No one is fully conscious. The self or subject is not, then, a completely self-constituting unity reacting with poles of experience. One creates and deconstructs in the most simple, everyday transactions—a dialectics of unity in identity and difference is continually put into play.

The phenomenological world emerges from a pre-existing, natural, or "brute" world, prior to the intentional structure of subject-perceived world. Analytically one can distinguish three levels or planes of meaning: ontological, perceptual, and expressive. These planes influence and condition each other. Being and appearing are related, but in what ways? As we have seen, the problem occupies Merleau-Ponty's final efforts. The ontological level (how we exist in the world) forms the conditions for the perceptual and evocative planes of existence. As consciousness never is a self-identical relation, the structure of the life world, the reciprocity of subject and object—intersubjectivity—interplay to form a unique sense of what Merleau-Ponty means for man to "exist." Consciousness is the meaning of the world as perceived; the world is meaningful for consciousness. A system fashions itself upon multiple perspectives. Merleau-Ponty writes:

> Perspective is much more than a secret technique for imitating a reality given as such to all men. It is the very realization and invention of a world dominated and possessed through and through in an instantaneous system, which spontaneous vision at least sketches, trying vainly to hold together all the things which clamor for its whole attention.[20]

This realization of transitory attention invokes style. The way we apprehend, comprehend, and express ourselves functions uniquely, inaugurating a style through desire-able expression. Perception itself already stylizes life. The organization of what Merleau-Ponty calls the habitual body temporally sediments past perspectives into familiar form and style. Merleau-Ponty speaks of this process of appropriation as a legacy at levels of perception as well as expression. Style, in turn, energizes the life world through the institution of values, a textual configuration from which we make sense. Accident and reason unite. Perception forms the bedrock of Merleau-Ponty's thought. He employs ontology to locate and guarantee perception.

Seen this way, language is not the sole human reality. Merleau-Ponty's phenomenology evokes language as *one* object of thought—one realm of awareness, among others. The senses, for example, have their own proper objects, and these interweave to form others. We see within a tactile environment; we feel in a visible world. The limits of language are of a perceptual nature. Language must refer to something other than itself, or language would have little survival value. The living present enters through speech about something or someone. "In the end language must signify something and not always be language about language. But signification and the sign belong to the perceptual order, not to the order of absolute spirit."[21] Speech takes place in the present; it is limited and involves a gestalt of the expressed and not expressed, content and form. So, function could be said to follow form. Merleau-Ponty argues signification takes place according to the order of perception and not the reverse. Since difference is qualitative, one never at any given instant perceives the actual points, only the results through the movement of difference. For example, when exactly does the color of a sunset shift from gold to marigold? If language traces only by difference, it does so based upon the differences allowing for perception. At the biological level, our sense organs apprehend only differences and these in turn are mediated and organized into temporal events. It is only at this level that perception occurs.[22]

Returning for a moment to the relation of part to whole, Merleau-Ponty sides with Aristotle: It is the whole that possesses meaning, not the part. The distinction takes place in language, through speech, from a perspective. Isolated morphemes have no more meaning than single phonemes. Only when joined in a significative chain does one link the sequence to sense. Clarity is of the perceptual order, and culture is a determining factor. Culture is a depth of sedimented perceptions. Perception is not a copy of the world, not an imprint on virgin, translucent wax.

Semiotics sentences meaning to life in language. Alternatively, analysis ignores the significance of perception. Analytic thought mistakenly places organizing power, meaning, in thought. "In its blindness to the perceived world, analytic thought breaks the perceptual transition from one place to another and from one perspective to another and then looks to the mind for the guarantee of a unity that is already given in perception."[23] This approach walls up man within his own skull. Conversely, a purely linguistic approach removes man from the world. Both expropriate the world of perception, leaving artificial constructs in place of the lived world. Both approaches stem from a system attempting to make sense absolute and complete, or to totalize truth. Rationalism claims to re-present the world "out there." This type of expression proclaims nothing new to already complete reality. Thought is transmitted through the message.

Communication makes the appearance of the sign identical with signification to another person. This is the model traditionally employed by mass communication: sender, receiver, and message. The lead, for example, of a news story is assumed to mirror the event and transmit this event to the reader's mind via print or through broadcast. That is, after all, what objective reporting claims: It holds up a mirror to society. The audience merely absorbs the transmission according to a stock of accepted meaning relations. We know the essential comes first, and the incidental toward the end. One cannot help but think that this method may not merely mirror the event as it unfolds.

Phenomenologically, in accordance with perceptual understanding, perception does not transpire solely in the mind. Rationalism is mistaken when it ensnares reality between our ears and mirrors it behind our eyes. Perception occurs within the life world, and, moreover, is not yet a function of thought. Perception is distinct from rational thought about perception. It transpires at a more fundamental level of experience. Perceiving (operational consciousness) is not yet the personality of which one is self-conscious. Operational consciousness is anonymous; it is not yet "I." This perceiving awareness experiences the phenomenal body as living in the world, as a part of the structure of the world and not as an isolated object in the world. This establishes existentially the intentional structure of consciousness, of subjectivity as intersubjectivity. The phenomenal body and the perceived world are polar aspects of the flesh of the world.[24] Approached from this perspective, the individual is not packed away from the world, nor removed from participation. Man's perceptual relation with the life world constitutes an internal relation as part of a system. Merleau-Ponty refers to perceptual awareness of the body, an awareness that structures our world, as the "I can" or "I am able," not yet the "I think" of the *cogito*—but its foundation. With Levinas, Merleau-Ponty locates presence in the world as a "here," standing not in opposition, but rather, amid the world and its inhabitants. Perceptual qualities become existential and are seen as differences, not as ideas or chunks of evidence.

One's perceptual awareness of body and world are anchored by one's body; a relation is fashioned. It would be a mistake to construe this difference between "I can" and "I think" analytically. It is only through expression at the level of self-consciousness or "I think" that any consideration of "I can" becomes thematic. The point is that "I think" is not pure; it is founded and porous. Since perceptual consciousness is not yet self-consciousness, it is realizable only from a cognitive situation. Truth must arise from "I think," but truth's foundations are laid within "I can." Truth is reflected in the mediation of perceptual awareness and thought. Truth, even eternal truth, does not then come from above; it must first be acquired and, consequently, endure through time. Truth is sedimented meaning, and in this sense truth is made while at the same time being received. The world and meaning do not admit separation. Culture is pervasive and "traditional" insofar as it provides frame and perspective.

Merleau-Ponty insists that all abstract thought, including the natural and human sciences, is based upon this system of perception and expression within the life world. Truth cannot be transparent adequation. Situated amid the world, writes Merleau-Ponty, "The awareness of truth advances like a crab, turned toward its point of departure, toward *whose* signification it expresses."[25] He applies the example of algorithm to make his case. The method or algorithm, at any moment, remains nothing more than an ensemble open on a horizon which presents the possibility of reconstruction. Structures are equivocal; they yield to alteration, interpretation, and application. New relations make difference; they do not entrap or contain identity.

Again, looking at the example of a news story, one sees an algorithm at work. The structure of the story expresses the application of a specialized method of solving a certain kind of problem. The problem is to transform what the writer considers the essentials of an event from life-world testimony of the reporter witnessing the event to its two-dimensional, economic presentation in print, exercising maximum efficiency in presenting information. When the structure of a story is changed, a new configuration arises. Another story, a follow-up, implies the original piece. The synthesis results from the development of knowledge and not preconditioned objectivity. The situation is open to question; the interrogative decenters the event or the report within a given structure or format. "There is no signification which is not surrounded by an horizon of naive beliefs and is thus not in need of other clarifications. There is no expressive operation that exhausts its object,"[26] says Merleau-Ponty. The algorithm can provide truth only through repeating the method in an original signification, employing new relations within the folds of events. It is the new signification, the shifting of the algorithmic expression, which produces meaning. In this regard, the algorithm, the formula, is secondary to the expression. A well-written piece leaves traces or reminders of its transformations, somewhat unintentional, or *more* than the writer intended. "[T]ruth is not an adequation but anticipation, repetition, and slippage of meaning. . . .The thing thought is not the thing perceived. Knowledge is not perception; speech is not one gesture among all other gestures."[27] Discourse evokes one's mode of truth. At another level, perception and body found the mode of being-in-the-world. What works sediments an integral, processional accumulation of truth called for, but originally undecided. Thus, there are steps which, in spite of occasional occlusion, make familiar original intentions in writing and speech.

Man transcends himself and the situation through this interconnection of perception and speech, an intertextuality partaking of metaphysical structure. Merleau-Ponty's metaphysics, although compatible with Levinas', differs to the extent that Merleau-Ponty grounds his metaphysics in perception and explains his phenomenology of perception and language by an ontology of the "flesh." Carnal generality folds back upon itself by exhibition of the same kinds of natural feelings and experiences of the world. "Metaphysics—the coming to light of something—is not localized at the level of knowledge: it begins with the opening out upon 'another,' and is to be found everywhere. . . ."[28] This coming to light begins with the opening up of Levinas' desire; the gaze is questioned in the lingual relationship which founds, for Levinas and Merleau-Ponty, ethics. I see a similar appreciation in the work of journalist Bill Moyers. Language presents metaphysical significance in speech and opens toward a multiplicity of other relations: economic, political, professional, recreational, and so on. The linguistic field must therefore open toward horizons which trail off indeterminately or vaguely, much like one's field of perception. Never having only a certain number of countable signs at one's disposal, the individual's field remains open and surpassable. The principle of distinction always allows for further elucidations and shifts.

Both semiotics and analytic thought endanger what they attempt to comprehend. One must not completely reduce thought to language, or expression to physiological structures of the brain. The experience of sense must be described and explained by mapping out bonds of the described phenomena. Thought is the obverse of expression. It is neither primary, as Husserl urges, nor is it derivative, as Derrida argues. Further, this ambivalence applies to the relation of speaker-listener and writer-reader. Discourse is equally in the listener as in the speaker, if the listener successfully follows the expression. Communication, after all, means communal undertaking, and mass communication mediates further what amounts to a cultural conversation. Neither pole is primary. Speech renews the mediation of the Same and the Other. The cultural word formed in society is invoked, not verified. Merleau-Ponty writes:

> Rationality, or the agreement of minds, does not require that we all reach the same idea by the same road, or that significations be enclosed in definitions. It requires only that every experience contain points of catch for all other ideas and that "ideas" have a configuration. This double requirement is the postulation of the world.[29]

Merleau-Ponty conceives of rationality as the promotion of freedom and human dignity. He contributes a phenomenological structure for fleshing out productive rationality.

The phenomenology of Levinas and Merleau-Ponty joins with the critical theory of Foucault and Derrida to fashion a critical phenomenology. They form moments of the dialectic. Critical theory offers insights into the workings of the tradition and power-knowledge strategies by which cultural contexts are produced, controlled, and insured. The discipline of the social sciences and the authority of the humanities have infiltrated areas of daily existence, especially well illustrated in mass communication, and have disguised the unreason at work in reason's name. Critical theory's revitalization of pluralism and its refocusing on the particular offers theoretical openings beyond the closed contexts presented by those who keep the tradition. Yet, we find the concepts of essence and presence, rationality and understanding to articulate what also is valuable in Western culture. Merleau-Ponty's aesthetic approach to theory allows us, by appreciating the contributions of phenomenology, to recognize the value of the antithetic perspectives articulated by Derrida and Foucault. Yet critique alone is insufficient to anchor values, stimulate healthful strategies, or preserve the worthwhile traditions of a society.

Levinasian desire provides the affirmation beyond rationalism or idealism, positivism or skepticism, capitalism or Marxism by which to discover the reason in unreason. Levinas truly is the radical thinker, the anarchist devoted to exploding dominating power relations. Beyond accounting for any concrete situation, he tells us that we are here together, and that appreciation of difference is the necessary condition of accepting oneself. The world is an infinite arena in which the possibilities are limited by our abilities to appreciate what others have to say. Critical phenomenology, then, is made up of differential and integral moments. In the realm of mass communication, Bill Moyers applies a phenomenological approach, basing his efforts, I think, on an implicit recognition that perception and dialogue are fundamental moments. If we are to appreciate American culture, we must venture to criticize that which weakens, shames, or endangers the values that vitalize it. Our society does have a tradition driven by values such as the appreciation of the other; authentic individualism of the sort which allows the other his or her identity; freedom understood as the mediation of will and value; and justice conceived as fairness curbing arbitrary power, which necessitates reliance on the rule of law.

CULTURAL JOURNALISM

James Madison wrote the free speech and press clause of the First Amendment of the Bill of Rights to institutionalize the right of the people to govern themselves. Yet, it is painfully obvious that the people don't govern themselves. Madison recognized the reciprocity of knowledge and power. He feared power that is arbitrary and exercised by those who know over those who do not. All too often the press, which was granted Constitutional protection to inform, works as an agency of power, disseminating the opinions of experts. In Henry Kissinger's terms, experts are those who are capable of articulating the interests of the powerful. The press realizes the experts' strategies by communicating interests from perspectives designed to convey the impression that all is well, or at least manageable, because the interests of those who know are consistent with the majority of the population. Regularly, this is not the case.

Existential phenomenology develops the insight that critical theory refines and applies: Perception is nine-tenths of the law. Within our cultural dialogue, certain perspectives are communicated by the media that are intended to perpetuate hierarchies of authority among dominant institutions. This institutional intentionality transcends, of course, the strategies of any given individual or even any specific group of persons to take shape through history and to deploy particular positions as circumstances dictate. This is recognized by the powers that be. According to one Reagan White House advertising manager, "You can change perceptions, that's what communication is all about." Nevertheless, as Derrida has argued, values are oppositional. One perspective dominates another within the social system. Systems, as Merleau-Ponty points out, whether at the levels of perception, consciousness, or culture, are essentially hierarchical. That is precisely why critics must deconstruct particular configurations. Currently, freedom of information and the consequent restriction of people's access to the media marketplace of ideas is imperiled by government secrecy.

Fortunately, the press is not yet monolithic and its power is still fragmentary. Voices of difference do make themselves heard. Formerly a correspondent and documentaries editor for CBS, Bill Moyers grew disenchanted with the corporate media perspective and quit. Working with PBS, Moyers' documentaries and interviews embody a vital, if minor, current within a largely complacent sea of journalism; his is a journalism in the service of culture. Moyers enters into dialogue with cultural advocates, those people who would mediate through criticism and alternative perspectives particular malformations perpetuated by the minority upon the majority. He focuses on aspects of what he considers democratic values by critiquing the status quo. He speaks about unnoticed values influencing visible, factual situations. By unpacking meaning more thoroughly than others in broadcast journalism, he succeeds in articulating interconnections between fact and value, choices and alternatives, while investigating perspectives ignored by others.

Moyers seems to recognize implicitly the notion put forward by Merleau-Ponty that perception forms the ground for all subsequent meaning, whether of personal or political situations; historical as well as contemporary problems must be recognized as problematic before anything further can be attempted. It is fashionable today to renounce foundations, to act like the positivists of yesterday. Bertrand Russell advanced the notion that philosophy should bother only with what can be proven or demonstrated without doubt and renounced as mere idealism that which does not lend itself to surety. Richard Rorty tells us that philosophy, and one assumes that includes political and cultural theory, cannot claim to provide a foundation. In fact, philosophy must jettison its historical claims to ground anything and instead focus on edifying its audience. Edification replaces reliance on principle. To engage in theory would be a process of edification. One need not, in fact one cannot, justify actions on the basis of any foundation. On one level, existential phenomenology claims to advance understanding and appreciation of various dimensions of human existence by relying on the foundational structure of perception. At another level, phenomenology claims that truth is a process of sedimentation. This process is foundational as well. In other words, tradition, for example, the American legal tradition, rests on certain foundations: the Declaration of Independence, the Constitution, certain specific phenomena trace out the essential structure of society. This in turn determines the bounds of acceptable policy and behavior for later generations. A historical tradition develops along certain lines from foundations. Derrida`s point, however, is well taken that there is a moment of arbitrariness in human endeavors, and therefore no context is absolute. What in fact did the signers of the Declaration depend upon to announce independence? The American people? But the American people did not exist as an entity before the Declaration. And even if somehow they had, they did not legitimate the signers by any vote. So, in the sense of first or sufficient cause, Rorty is correct. But in practice some conditions serve as ends in themselves. Freedom, justice, equality, and life would appear to need no pragmatic purpose by which to justify their continuation. They are sufficient to themselves. They rest on no other ground. They form the foundation for a democratic society, and theory ought to recognize that this entails more than edification. Freedom, justice, equality, and life are themselves the justifications for acceptable philosophical, cultural, political, critical, and aesthetic pursuits.

Drawing out the text from context, foreground from background, involves perceptual activity. Moyers undertakes to describe situations by shifting our perceptions of context—largely presupposed or unarticulated framing of a given situation—and he unpacks, through questioning and interview, the background assumptions which constitute our contemporary experience. Drawing out the context from behind the experience forms an essential strategy of phenomenology and cultural journalism. Because our perception of meaning resides in the movement of phenomena from background to foreground, shifting one's perspective of the event, the audience's grasp of the intentional structure of the issues develops along these perceptual lines, bringing out new relations as the program develops. Moyers inserts new perspectives into his presentation of events by relying on the traditional, accepted values of our culture. To the extent the culture has forsaken its own moorings, Moyers' program on the secret government or the illusions bound up with the public mind and media representations of reality begin to seem radical. He returns us to the roots of our culture.

Critical phenomenology and cultural journalism fight the prereflective option of accepting the way things are as natural. Cultural journalism offers the possibility to shift socially accepted meanings on to a critical, interrogative plane. The freedom of constraint particularly is in evidence as Moyers works to direct audience attention past ongoing consumption to critical reflection. If the government employs a policy of secrecy and George Bush can joke that his views on secrecy are classified, if the pattern of deception spreads to journalists who chortle at his comment, if these secret policies result in the perpetuation of campaigns of terror abroad, promoting bondage, injustice, inequality, and death, then democracy in the United States is at risk.

Decisions depend upon the methods by which they are made. This recognition motivated the architects of the Constitution. To champion equality under the law, for example, depends not only on Constitutional protection, but adherence to the morality of equality. "The worst excesses of the American experience have come in defiance of this moral spirit—from slavery to lynching, from the Trail of Tears to Wounded Knee, from the Palmer raids to Joseph McCarthy's witch-hunts, from the rebellion of the Southern states to the war in Vietnam,"[30] Moyers warns in an afterword in the publication of his PBS broadcast, *The Secret Government, The Constitution in Crisis,* which aired in 1987 and again in 1989. A secret government has been under construction now for 40 years in defiance of law and morality.

During the Iran-Contra Hearings of 1987, Lt. Colonel Oliver North told Congress that he saw nothing wrong with taking the Ayatollah of Iran's funds and applying them to support the Contras against Nicaragua. Many of the millions watching him on television perceived a hero. Why? Partially because a picture of a man in a military uniform displaying confidence, pride and superiority becomes the message he communicates, overriding the actual words he utters. When Moyers frames his presentation of North in front of advocates of democratic values, the meaning is completely different. Moyers tells the audience that Oliver North had been the secret government's chronic liar, furthering a pattern of deception that cost many lives in pursuit of the violent, illegal overthrow of a government the United States legally recognized, while selling arms to aid and abet an acknowledged enemy of the U.S.

> Moyers: All this was being done to advance the President's policies, but it wasn't enough. To get around the law, the White House enlisted the services of something called "The Enterprise."

The Enterprise was designed to turn a profit. Controlled by a retired general and an Iranian arms merchant, the Enterprise sold arms to the Contras at a huge markup, raking in profits of 200 percent. When asked by a senator if profiteering was an acceptable practice for a government sanctioned organization designed to aid those from whom they were profiting, General Richard Secord said he thought the Enterprise could have two purposes.

> Moyers: While profits were being made, lives were being lost. Iran has used missiles supplied by the Enterprise to fight its war against Iraq. That war has already lasted more than seven years, as many as a million people killed or wounded.

> And in Nicaragua the Contras use weapons from the Enterprise against civilians. It's a terrorist war they're fighting; old men, women, children are caught in the middle or killed deliberately, as the Contras use violence against peasants to pressure their government. Thousands have died.

Moyers is charging the secret government with putting in place a technology of control by which to commit crimes against democracy. He describes a strategy designed over the years to thwart the will of Congress. Historically, the structure was made possible with the passage of the National Security Act of 1947, giving birth to the National Security Council, the CIA, and helping to create the current national security state. Juxtaposing the situations of 1973 and 1987, he compares testimony illustrating the secret government's contempt for law and truth.

Moyers: There was contempt for the law.

Sen. Herman E. Talmadge, (D) Georgia [Watergate Hearings, 21973]: If the President could authorize a covert break-in, and you don't know exactly where that power would be limited—you don't think it could include murder or other crimes beyond covert break-ins, do you?

John Erlichman, Assistant to the President: Oh, I don't—I don't know where the line is, Senator.

Sen. George J. Mitchell, (D) Maine [Iran-Contra Hearings, 1987]: During your discussions with Mr. Casey, Mr. McFarland and Mr. Poindexter about the plan, did a question ever arise among you as to whether what was being proposed was legal?

Col. North: Oh, no, I don't think it was—I mean, first of all, we operated from the premise that everything we did do was legal.

Moyers: And there was contempt for the truth.

Sam Dash, Senate Chief Counsel [Watergate Hearings, 1973]: Mr. Mitchell, do you draw a distinction between not volunteering and lying?

John Mitchell, Former U.S. Attorney General: Well, it depends entirely on the subject matter, Mr. Dash.

Mr. Dash: Well, you're asked a direct question, and you don't vol-
unteer a direct answer you might say you're not volunteering, but
actually you are lying on those respects, aren't you?

Mr. Mitchell: Well, I think we'd have to find out what the specifics
are of what particular occasion and what case.

Sen. David Boren, (D) Oklahoma [Iran-Contra Hearings, 1987]:
Could you explain to me the difference that you think there is
between knowing that you've left a false impression or a wrong
impression and lying, to use an old-fashioned term?

Elliot T. Abrams, Assistant Secretary of State: Yeah, I think lying,
we—we really mean—I mean—a deliberate effort to mislead people—uh—uh—to a deliberate effort to leave them with a misleading impression. What I hoped to do was to avoid the question and
duck the question, as I explained.

The apparatus of the secret government is still very much intact, and this
allows the White House to control what others know and, as Moyers points
out, that's power, the power to subvert society while claiming to support it.
National security is given precedence over the freedom of citizens to be
informed and understand what government is doing in their name.

Interviewing Noam Chomsky, Moyers observes that while we
see continually more of our elected officials on television, we know progressively less of what they do.[31] That is because, Chomsky explains,
they see themselves as farsighted creatures employing a specialized
class of experts who, from this perspective, view part of their job as find-
ing means to marginalize the population.

Moyers: Marginalizing?

Chomsky: Reducing them to apathy and obedience, allowing them
to participate in the political system, but as consumers, not as
true participants.

A concern for the needs of others and for the care of a fragile environment make up a part of human nature, they make possible the continuity of generations. If these deeply embedded, inherent human values are
going to be able to flourish it is essential, Chomsky maintains, that people be able to discover what they think and believe. That in turn

depends upon some sort of arena for diversity. Understanding primarily depends on honesty, and not on the sophisticated knowledge of the experts. Corporate journalism reflects the interests of those in charge of media institutions, involving their audiences in endless webs of seamless deceit. Chomsky explains to Moyers that the primary function of mass media is to mobilize support for the special interests dominating the government and the private sector.

This practice is marked by the advance of a curious coup. The interests of the people have come to be regarded as the "special" interests government must guard against. The interests of the poor, the old, women, labor, youth, ethnic minorities, and farmers make up just about the entire population. Corporations are never identified as comprising a special interest because they represent the national interest. The people, the special interests, must be marginalized. This revolution of reality largely is carried forth in the media through the manufacture of consent, comprising what Walter Lippmann referred to as a revolution in the art of democracy.

> Moyers: A lot of people complain that the media are unpatriotic, disloyal, too liberal.

> Chomsky: That's an interesting complaint because if you take the actual incidents and cases, what you find is that the media are remarkably subservient to power. There are some people for whom subservience isn't enough, you actually have to grovel. They're the ones who call the media unpatriotic.

> Moyers: You're saying that the primary function of the mass media is to mobilize public support for the interests that dominate the government and the private sector. But that's not how the media see it. We claim that our news judgments rest on unbiased, objective criteria.

> Chomsky: The chairman of the board also sees what he's doing as service to humanity.

It seems Moyers is skeptical of Chomsky's position. But in the 1989 documentary, *Illusions of News*,[32] Moyers agrees with television correspondent Sam Donaldson that a picture is worth a thousand facts. Video images are the discourse of politics. Men and women in the news business determine what is taken for reality. Television offers the audience an official version of reality as producers collude with the White House to script productions, and the ratings determine the news. The market orientation is of news as entertainment, news as collusion.

> Moyers: In the competition between the ear and the eye, your judgment is . . .

> Michael Deaver, former Reagan Advisor: The eye wins every time. The producers have to say, "Okay, we're gonna use it." And we sit back after it is on that night and say, "Ha, Hah! We did it again." We thought of ourselves, when we got into the national campaigns, as producers. We tried to create the most entertaining, visually attractive scene to fill that box.

Moyers reports that the pictures become the whole story. Reporters are told by news executives not to make critical comments about the president unless they are covered over by a wallpaper of pleasant pictures. That is to say, producers and executives know that the critical verbal message will not, under these circumstances, register in the minds of the audience. One television reporter, Brit Hume, attempted to report that presidential candidate George Bush was making a ludicrous simile, linking the condition of the flag manufacturing business with the condition of the country. Picture candidate Bush at a flag factory. "My friends, flag sales are doing well, America is doing well." There is a huge American flag looming behind him. Bush is kissing people. Cut to a man and a woman wearing large red, white, and blue hats, waving, of course, American flags. Cut to their small child, counting coins, dressed as Uncle Sam. The reporter's attempt to criticize an obvious public relations stunt backfires. The message is "America and the flag are flying high."

What if the networks were to refuse to run a photo opportunity because it is empty, because it is not true, it has no relationship to reality, Moyers asks Martin Koughman, former CBS news producer. "It's much easier to be a packager than a real reporter," Koughman replies. In television, there is a conspiracy among some reporters, producers, and politicians to "wallpaper" the news. "You basically have to use staged events, because the fact that it's a staged event, nevertheless, it is an event and you have to use it," says the president of NBC News, Michael Gartner.

> Moyers: Well, what should we do?

Deaver: If I had tried to do what I thought was the right way to go about it, we would have lost the campaign. People would have been bored to tears. In a democracy that's interested in where their leaders are going to stand, on what issues, that would have been the right thing to do. But this country isn't interested in it. They don't want it. They want feel good and fuzz and not to be upset about all of this. They just want to sit in their living rooms and be entertained.

Even if, as Moyers admits, Deaver has it right, illusions of news pay off, journalism is still a necessary calling because without it, "we're at the mercy of politicians whose sole aim is to win, and those corporations whose aim is profit only." Perhaps Deaver's expert perspective is only partially correct. Perhaps Chomsky's view of the average human exhibiting exquisite creativity in the most ordinary communicative acts is a more healthy perspective. We really do care about others, about the nature and values our culture chooses to perpetuate. And Moyers is right, "Sharing is the essence of teaching. It is, I have come to believe, the essence of civilization. The impulse to share turns politics from the mere pursuit of power and makes of journalism a public service."[33]

NOTES TO CHAPTER 5

1. M. Merleau-Ponty, *The Visible and the Invisible*, trans. A. Lingis (Evanston, IL: Northwestern University Press, 1968), pp. 125-126.

2. Ibid., p. 141.

3. Ibid., p. 135.

4. A. Lingis, "Translator's Preface," *The Visible and the Invisible*, p. 1v.

5. Merleau-Ponty, *The Visible and the Invisible*, p. 160.

6. M. Merleau-Ponty, *The Prose of the World*, ed. C. Lefort, trans. J. O'Neill (Evanston, IL: Northwestern University Press, 1973), p. 148.

7. Ibid., p. 149.

8. J. Derrida, *Writing and Difference*, trans. A. Bass (Chicago: University of Chicago Press, 1978), p. 166.

9. Merleau-Ponty, *The Prose of the World*, p. 107.

10. Derrida, *Writing and Difference*, p. 37.

11. Ibid., p. 28.

12. J. Derrida, *Limited Inc*, trans. S. Weber and J. Mehlman (Evanston, IL: Northwestern University Press, 1988), p. 18.

13. Ibid., p. 137.

14. Ibid., p. 147.

15. Merleau-Ponty, *The Prose of the World*, p. 132.

16. Derrida, *Writing and Difference*, p. 278.

17. M. Merleau-Ponty, *The Primacy of Perception*, trans. J. Edie (Evanston, IL: Northwestern University Press, 1964), p. 164.

18. Merleau-Ponty, *The Prose of the World*, p. 105.

19. Ibid., p. 123.

20. Ibid., 53.

21. Ibid., fn., p. 37.

22. See G. Bateson, *Mind and Nature: A Necessary Unity* (New York: E.P. Dutton, 1979), p. 79.

23. Merleau-Ponty, *The Prose of the World*, p. 82.

24. See G.B. Madison, *The Phenomenology of Merleau-Ponty, A Search for the Limits of Consciousness* (Athens: Ohio University Press, 1981), p. 27.

25. Merleau-Ponty, *The Prose of the World*, p. 128.

26. Ibid., p. 127.

27. Ibid., p. 129.

28. M. Merleau-Ponty, *Phenomenology of Perception*, trans. C. Smith (New York: Humanities Press, 1962), p. 168.

29. Ibid., p. 143.

30. B. Moyers, *The Secret Government, The Constitution in Crisis* (Washington, DC: Seven Locks Press, 1988), p. 108.

31. B. Moyers, *A World of Ideas with Bill Moyers: A Conversation with Noam Chomsky*, broadcast on PBS in 1988. Published in book form, *A World of Ideas* (New York: Doubleday, 1989).

32. B. Moyers, *The Public Mind: Image and Reality in America, Illusions of News*, broadcast on PBS in 1989.

33. Moyers, *A World of Ideas*, p. vii.

The Political Dimension

Central to the political concerns of critical phenomenology are notions of power, knowledge, freedom, and discipline. One's understanding of politics encompasses questions of how power is produced and circulated within cultural settings, in which ways and on what levels are relationships between choice and control traced out, and, correlatively, how are order and conflict mediated in this information age? In particular, I will discuss Michel Foucault's critical theory both for its value in analyzing media in Western society and for insights it may provide into the expanding realm of electronically based surveillance over the individual through the now ubiquitous dissemination of personal information. Mass media order society's discourses by structuring the thresholds of thought, knowledge, and communication. Institutions strategically, if unintentionally, collude with corporate and governmental interests in the pursuit of policies that maximize control over populations, as well as individual members of society. Television and computers, in our analysis, mold subjectivity over time and across space. But this is achieved *productively*, rather than by coercion or subterfuge.

HEGEMONY, POWER, AND THE MEDIA

Foucault's studies concerning the role of power in society, and its productive function, offer cultural studies an opportunity to extend its theo-

141

retical boundaries, to encompass more ground than by remaining solely within an ideological approach. Foucault's thought contains perspectives, interpretations, and theoretical openings to enrich the study of culture. The idea that power is productive as well as coercive, situational as well as pervasive, adds a crucial dimension to Foucault's contribution. He draws out a theory of power that, I believe, lies dormant in cultural studies. For purposes of comparison, I cite the work of Stuart Hall, which I think represents the cultural studies approach fairly comprehensively.

While Hall and Foucault by no means trace the same territory—Hall is quite critical of Foucault—it seems their approaches are not mutually exclusive, either. They share similar concerns, but address those concerns on different theoretical planes. Those planes intersect, I think, at the point where each addresses the problems of domination, the structuring of norms in society, and hegemony. Hall emphasizes the centrality of ideology. Foucault leaves ideology alone. The reciprocal relation between power and knowledge situates Foucault's thought. Foucault does not primarily concern himself, however, with the blocs of ideas by which individuals constitute and make sense of their lives. He is concerned with power, its evocation, relational nature, and situational character. Because he denies the Cartesian subject, yet does not accept the structuralist position of a self-perpetuating totality, he painstakingly searches out alternatives. Foucault examines the workings of power through local, "micro-processes" at work within discursive formations, producing regimes of truth that pervade society. Neither does Foucault agree with the proposition: power represses, truth liberates. So, he advances a conception of social discipline as a productive, complex social function. Configurations of relations structure the social world as much as, perhaps more than, formations of ideas.

After situating Foucault in relation to cultural studies, I attempt to describe Foucault's conceptions of power, including his rejection of "the repressive hypothesis," and its replacement with normalization and discipline. I try to mark out the import of Foucault's thought for analyzing media. Obviously, the media shape public discourse, and one can argue they do so in accord with Foucault's conception of power-knowledge. Further, the media affect the formations of discourse, and, consequently, the public whose interests they profess to advance. Cultivation analysis provides empirical verification, I think, of some of Foucault's key concerns. Television presents carefully structured, strategically shaded versions of social life. It thereby aids in the production, as well as the reproduction, of social discipline by enculturating viewers to values and norms useful to the development of "docile" individuals and to the maintenance of hegemony in society.

Hegemony

Hall and the Centre for Contemporary Cultural Studies recognize that power works within the structure of society and not as a property some individuals hold. Power manifests interest which is ideologically garbed as a practice. This involves a system of ideas which provides frameworks by which men and women interpret experience. One deciphers the world in ideological terms. Experience is institutionalized concordant to specific codes of meaning constructed according to generalized interests of the dominant social groups. Following Gramsci, Hall refuses the strict homogenization of class; the organization of dominant social groups or the dominant culture is more complex, more heterogeneous than the classic Marxist conception of class. Hall thereby distinguishes culture from ideology. "Dominant and subordinate classes will have distinct cultures. But when one culture *experiences* itself in terms prescribed by the dominant culture, then the dominant culture has also become the basis of a dominant ideology"[1].

These codes of meaning appear transparent. They are so ingrained in everyday use that their meanings are obvious to all, natural and largely unquestioned. One simply "knows" what is meant by such institutionalized terms as "free speech" or "democracy." Hall refers to the practice of employing particular discourses as ideological not so much because the language is consciously, intentionally distorted. Rather, the message is delineated by limited matrices from which transformations might be generated. One selects alternatives from those available. Speakers and writers themselves may be unaware that the significations they employ are taken from an ideological network contributed by the dominant social groups or culture.[2] Consequently, communication theory must concern itself with the conceptualization of ideology within the social formation, especially with regard to mass media. Otherwise power relations may go unnoticed. The politics of signification take place largely through the media. Our legal-political system, projected through the media, constricts communication, resulting in acceptable views by trusted sources through strategic manipulation of power relations. At the very least this is accomplished by agenda setting, restricting possibilities and alternatives, and legitimizing some perspectives while relegating others to the realm of idealism or casting ideological suspicion on them.

The Contemporary Culture Studies Group has put forward a critical paradigm. Since ideological concerns work within the sign system, one must examine the mechanics, production, and transformations of ideological discourses. "The critical point for us is that, in any theory which seeks to explain both the monopoly of power and diffusion of consent, the question of the place and role of ideology becomes absolutely pivotal,"[3] writes Hall. Ideology organizes social experience. This organization serves political purposes—signification formulates socially advantageous outlooks and perspectives that uphold hegemony. Hegemony, Hall says, is the *"process* by which a historical bloc of social forces is constructed and the ascendancy of that bloc secured."[4] While the dynamics of the social situation may be quite Byzantine, the state of affairs upheld by the diverse structures and articulations serves a dominant cultural order. The dominant culture contains all the more narrow and specific interest groups within its guiding light. And ideology forms the terrain on which the ever shifting hegemony is maintained by the dominant groups leading and guiding society.

Again, this process is made to appear as the natural way of things, as the spontaneous unfolding of events. The hegemonic order guides subordinate interpretations by subsuming them under the more general rubric of the dominant culture. The resulting obfuscation comes about by strategically interlocking elements of the dominant group and rearranging social, political, and cultural fields of discourse so that they appear to be in the general interest of all. By directing the various means of production, semantic and economic, the hegemonic leadership lays out social reality for the subordinate cultures. The inscription of the social universe confirms the political legitimation of the State and forms the hegemonic enterprise.[5] Hegemony is maintained by setting a national agenda that purports to map a course for society as a whole. At the same time it legitimates the dominant culture.

Foucault suggests that there is another way of analyzing society. One ought to view power as relational, not as univocal. Power imbues the social system. Individuals are as much constituted by power as they are wielders or subjects of power. Both Foucault and Hall declare the struggle to be between social groups, while Foucault argues further that it may indeed be a struggle of all against all. The struggle, therefore, is among forces that call out for analysis and interpretation at many levels, even the intrapersonal. Power does not work only as repression, but displays multiform productive aspects as well.[6]

In order to examine the capillary activities of power relations, Foucault argues that a skeptical, detached attitude serves best. Thus, while one conducts an analysis, the truth of discursive relations is not of primary import. This aspect of his method concerns Hall.[7] Foucault remains agnostic with regard to formations of class struggle. The significance of social disciplines, class struggles, and ideologically motivated discourses lies not in their veracity but their verisimilitude. Regimes of truth organize society.

Foucault is a pluralist, and therein lies the rub. His critical pluralism avoids totality. Cultural studies emphasizes holism: culture structures society, and a social formation is a "structure in dominance." One finds totality located at the heart of the approach. Foucault, if he did not deny holism, certainly questioned its theoretical primacy. But I would argue that implicit in Foucault's thought is a tacit acknowledgment of society as a unity articulated by cultural apparatuses, disciplined by social sciences, and regulated by administration. After all, as power works from the bottom, upwards, it circulates within networks that, no matter how diverse, form some sort of configuration within a society. Yet Foucault is an original, critical thinker, and he regularly questions the accepted conclusions of those who preceded him. He does not accept the analysis of critical theory on the development of prisons, nor does he agree with what he termed the repressive hypothesis, especially with those who argue that the truth will free us.

Hall chides Foucault for his emphasis on difference over unity and for his establishing the plurality of discourses within society. Hall contends that Foucault's analyses push beyond even the possibility of conceiving society as a "unity in difference."[8] But I think Foucault chose to examine social relations from a pluralist position because he became convinced that holistic attempts were inadequate. Foucault's interest in diversity lies in his conviction that theory and practice could be approached in unique ways, from fresh perspectives. Indeed, analysis has to become more particular, as opposed to universal, in light of the excessive expectations of much of the critical tradition. As mentioned previously, Hall attacks Foucault's lack of a theory of totality. Foucault may have decided on "eloquent silence" rather than reiterating the litany of the State. His conception of the micro-processes of power is an original attempt to take us out of comfortable and reassuring categories of social thought.

Hall characterizes the State as involving:

> [A] range of political discourses and social practices which are concerned at different sites with the transmission and transformation of power—some of those practices having little to do with the political domain as such, being concerned with other domains which are nevertheless articulated to the State, for example, familial life, civil society, gender and economic relations.[9]

That being the situation, what is the necessity of placing the State at the center of one's analysis? It certainly provides a ground for holism, but such a description does not seem requisite for critical analysis or cultural studies to the exclusion of other conceptions. Althusser[10] collapses the social to State apparatuses, and Anderson[11] presents the difficulties

Gramsci encountered in his writing on hegemony based on the State/civil distinction. Foucault attempts to outflank this problem by reformulating the problem of hegemony outside this approach. Foucault locates social discipline and regulation as practices evoking power-knowledge relations within society. There seems to me no necessity to postulate the State as the locus for condensing various social practices. This is especially so in liberal democracies in which the problem of civil society and government serves to obfuscate so much. For instance, business privatizes public concerns affecting all of us, such as the claim by those who own vast property to do what they will, without duly considering a community, or those who own the media to exclude positions they consider unworthy.

Hall claims that Foucault refuses the concept of "articulation." He is certainly correct that Foucault does not explicitly address linking diverse elements to a general theory of ideology. Hall says, "I still talk about ideology, whereas Foucault talks about the discursive which has no ideological dimension to it".[12] Foucault's analyses take place on a different, yet not, as mentioned earlier, incompatible plane. Foucault feels that ideology is concerned with the consciousness of the subject. He is interested in pursuing the effects and relations of the process on the developing subject. Power does not simply seize upon one's mind because a person is not a pregiven entity. Foucault's position is, "The individual, with his identity and characteristics, is the product of a relation of power exercised over bodies, multiplicities, movements, desires, forces".[13] Further, Foucault's studies could themselves be interpreted as linking elements of the social sciences, demographics, political practices, discursive formations, and nondiscursive tactics of, for example, surveillance, in ways previously overlooked. Foucault does not refuse the notion of articulation; he simply does not situate it on ideological terrain. Hall stresses that knowledge is produced by practice. Foucault adds that social practices alternatively structure knowledge.

Power

What is the relation of power to knowledge? How does discourse transmit power through knowledge, or knowledge transform discourse? Foucault meticulously recasts these questions in an effort to examine individuals in society—as subjects fashioned by strategies of power, knowledge, and discourse. Knowledge is not primarily a product of understanding. Inextricably imbued with power, knowing is perhaps power's corporeality. Power, localized as forms of discursive practice, organizes activity. Power is made for cutting.[14] Relationships endure, yet shift: power, knowledge, and discourse form individuals as well as society. One must look to locate signification within a context of a theory of power and not a theory of power interpreted through signification. While Foucault researched the evolution of madness, medicine, the archaeology of human sciences, disciplines, and sexuality, he did not write about mass communication. Yet, his method appears applicable to communication study, and much of what he thinks relates to cultural studies and mass media. Foucault deals with our world as it unfolds, not as a representation of a historic logic or lodged within subterranean levels of meaning, but at the surface, the material struggle of power relations transforming cultural apparatuses. He strives to analyze a period or a discipline by taking what was said, not what flowed underneath, and to decipher the process, according to power-knowledge relationships. Power forms an individual. "Thus it is not power, but the subject, which is the general theme of my research."[15]

Developing from, and reacting to, the phenomenological tradition, Foucault rebelled against the primacy of the intentional subject—individual consciousness as the meaning bestowing pole of rationality. The individual does not constitute discursive practices; the subject develops consistent with status and role. But this development involves struggle and is not to be considered as a natural process or teleological progression. Insofar as it is power that affects signification, one cannot locate personalities behind developments because power is as much structure as process, diffuse and affective. Power infuses society at all levels, dominant as well as subordinate groups. Foucault argues that power works its way intentionally but anonymously. Because it is systematic and self-generative, it radiates forcefully throughout a culture. The concern, then, is how to discuss power while remaining faithful to power's relational tendencies to emerge, displace, educate, abuse, appropriate, and control without making of it either a formula or a transcendental scheme.

If power is local, it nonetheless transforms populations and societies. If power does not contain an essence by which to be recognized, its positivities mark events. So coercion, manipulation, and domination are not the sole provinces of power, yet Foucault certainly does not deny the realities of class domination. Domination waits as a possibility for those who win or lose; even masked as liberty because it is the struggle of men and women that gives rise to various values.[16] One simply ought not reduce this complexity to one interest group which dominates the others. The field is more complex. The question of power is not, finally, one of justice, but of tactic and strategy. Behavior and attitude, signification and discipline, learning and community life are informed by power-knowledge relations. Foucault reports his experience of studying the penal system as pivotal for his understanding of the pragmatic deployments of power. The purpose of prison is to transform individuals, no more so than other social disciplinary institutions. "The prison was meant to be an instrument, comparable with—and not less perfect than—the school, the barracks or the hospital acting with precision upon its individual subjects."[17] As power inheres in economic, sexual, medical, informational, and other relationships, it forms diverse networks which the theorist interconnects. Such a mapping of discursive practices treats events as unique, acute manifestations of force relations, not as a rational continuation of a tradition or ideological practice. Foucault attempted his examinations to point to differences—a curative undertaking or a series of interpretations from unique perspectives. But he agrees with Merleau-Ponty that knowledge is perspectival. Foucault arranges his thought around three axes: domains of knowledge, systems of rules, and models for relations to the self. These axes form trajectories from corresponding fundaments of experience involving discourses of truth, power, and relations of self to others. The fundaments transform one another as they work their paths within political, epistemological, and ethical modes of experience. Foucault attempts to incorporate not only the dynamics of domination, but classification and subjectification as well.

Foucault increasingly comes to see Western democracies as the historical products of the technologies of power inscribed in experience, based on value and utility, regulation and orchestration. His conception of the dynamics of power, coupled with his effort not to fall into the traditions either of liberal-pluralist positivism or Marxist ideology, leads him to think of power from a nominalist perspective. Power works as concept, a way of thinking about human activity—not the activity itself, yet not outside life either. His stance seems compatible in this regard to both the pragmatic and phenomenological approaches; what we can think and say about events and phenomena are not these things themselves, yet thoughts and statements about them that remain consistent with and alter human experience. Foucault clears a space for a productive consideration of power.

Repressive Hypothesis

What Foucault labels the repressive hypothesis constitutes human reality in a negative, constrained fashion. Dominant social groups lead subservient ones into distorted approximations of authentic life. Ideology is posited as the tool or weapon employed against the service of truth; if truth were available to man, then liberation and freedom could develop and flourish, but power wrapped in ideology masks people's real interests with the interests of the few who hold the reins of power. Thus truth is buried or concealed by those with vested interests and the power to obfuscate reality. Power represses the truth and these concepts remain exclusive of one another; truth liberates and power suppresses, so power represses truth through the creation of an ideological system whereby the world comes to be seen through a single, naturalized system of meanings. Again, Foucault does not deny the reality of hegemony, the uses of ideology, or the juridical-discursive uses of power, since knowledge masks the uses to which power is put. "It is both much more and much less than ideology. It is the production of effective instruments for the formation and accumulation of knowledge—methods of observation, techniques of registration, procedures for investigation and research, apparatuses of control,"[18] he says. So power is a way of speaking about a complete societal situation located historically, as exercised through discursive practices which serve fundamentally, and at the local levels, to structure reality and produce relations of interaction and knowledge. This relation is reciprocal, and knowledge expands as well as constrains the apparatuses and institutions of society, but not purely or even primarily consistent with an ideological scaffolding. The teleological march of history or the repression of freedom through falsehood effectively maintains a myth relied upon by the tradition to further its own existence. The development of meaning and its impediment call for analysis and reconsideration. "Progress" makes for the continuation of the conditions that ensnare one further in the grid of power-knowledge. The real problem lies not in the idea that humanity progresses, but in what fashion events have unfolded and by what social practices understandings have come about? The present is not necessarily an advance or an improvement over past arrangements of power relations, and the future contains no guarantees. Foucault abandoned deep structure, the truth encrusted in falsehood, in favor of an immanent conception of power relations. Economies of discourse and technologies of the self transform interests at the micro-levels and structure social and political dynamics. One ought not look solely toward a system of representation as the determination of hegemony. Foucault argues that the individual is not a natural essence in the Cartesian tradition; he or she is in some sense produced by the interworkings of power relations and social development.[19] Cognitive development is, at least partially, socially structured. It does not simply develop according to the nature of man. Discursive practices, tactics, and strategies influence development in a coherent and particular fashion, yet again, no one plans such developments. If truth is power, the repressive hypothesis leads one astray insofar as it focuses on order rather than "a natural order of disorder."[20]

Contemporary thought offers the repressive hypothesis as a strategy of subterfuge. Mass communication, for instance, produce symbolic products through signification. A product is constructed: Choices are made to employ this articulation rather than another account. Cultural theory takes the position that this selection, or repression of alternative views, has helped determine the development of post-industrial society. Through practices of selection, combination, and organization the media present symbolic representations that further the development of a state of affairs along a particular track. Whether one speaks of labor union problems or nuclear strategies, the problem is cast in a social mold, a semantic contest that excludes or represses alternate presentations and interpretations. But truth is power—power and knowledge. One can argue not that the media repress interests other than the dominant, useful views, but that the effective strategy works to contain minority interests as regional views, that is, as acceptable minority positions, or affordable costs for sustaining democracy in the marketplace. Power increases by its exercise, and the media work surveillance at different levels. Perhaps surveillance is not carried on primarily as purposeful; it works as a by-product of editorial functions, advertising, marketing schemes, readership surveys, polls, law suits, and other multifarious capillary interactions among agencies and subjects. Foucault does not uncover a single, latent, or an original domination, but a series of interpretations examined at the local levels. Stealthy shifts of unique events are manipulated according to systems of transformations and guided by normalization processes—power produces knowledge through directing desire. The incorporation of the processes and channels of mass communication interact with other forces within society to forge a network of the lines of power, normalization, and discipline.

Since power operates on many levels, Foucault holds that a discipline must be regarded as "a complex social function,"[21] not solely as effect, ideology, or area. Foucault makes the technology of power the principle for both the "humanization" of consumerism and the knowledge of the subject. The principle is embodied at a site, the body of the historical subject. Bio-power is reflected in media operations and maneuvers, structuring and educating individuals to facilitate the order of things, the social composition of interests. Power relations, not power itself, form the field of analysis. "It becomes necessary also to distinguish power relations from relationships of communication which transmit information by means of a language, a system of signs, or any other symbolic medium,"[22] Foucault writes. Because individualization and totalization occur simultaneously, the domains may be analyzed in keeping with their distinctive movements. The spatial organization of the workplace, the discourse of a discipline and its capacities enfold on one another and reciprocate to fuse systems of cultural apparatus. These moments or aspects of experience should not be homogenized or subsumed under a rubric of language, ideology, economics, or law. They overlap and support one another in an ongoing process involving each of the moments. Power then is not *the* phenomenon; it exists only insofar as it actualizes events or combines to form "capacity-communication-power blocks."

Normalization

Generally, it has been acknowledged that one of Foucault's major contributions to critical thought has been an increased methodological sophistication. Foucault begins with a hypothesis, an objective, such as prisons are linked to a more global project of social transformation, that is, control. He states this objective as the interest in controlling abnormal people. From this Foucault examines the tactics which arose to deal with the objective: What strategies, individual practices, and relations of forces realigned directing the struggle? At another level, a certain kind of discourse evolved to meet the situation, a coherence evolved, normalization took place, values and morals emerged to treat or structure the tactics. Hence, one unearths the production of truth, which at the global level works through more generalized programs within cultural apparatuses and institutions. Society advocates certain programs and policies, and support mechanisms arise with which to better channel the normalization processes. All of these kinds of relations interact with one another. Ideology is present, of course, but it is not the determining category for Foucault.

Following our example, psychiatry was developed in the prisons, while penal controls were adopted by psychiatric practitioners. This brought in the legal establishment, medical, and other experts to formulate and convey discursive practices and administrative processes. All of this developed to deal with degeneracy. From another perspective, degeneracy, Foucault argues, was a process whereby society instituted a network of surveillances over the population. The prison model of informants, prostitutes, and social surveillance regenerated within the society itself. This regeneration fed into what Foucault terms a grand strategy.[23] These processes are masked by the multifarious presentations and reciprocalities of power relations at work within differing dimensions and levels of social practices. From the penal instance, the increasing social organization and control of individuals within a social setting developed a grand strategy, conceivably *the* grand strategy, yet a strategy without an author. Upon analysis such a strategy appears rational and coherent, but no one planned it. All the mechanisms of society produce these tactics through power relations, beginning with micro-relations and working circuitously through macro-relations. One unearths a historical construct, not a biological or mechanical entity, that is, power relations produce truth through historic situations.

One can speak of a social body, yet it is not the Leviathan or the generalized will of the people. Foucault emphasizes, "I believe the great fantasy is the idea of a social body constituted by the universality of wills. Now the phenomenon of the social body is the effect not of a consensus but of the materiality of power operating on the very bodies of individuals."[24] Foucault approaches power relations from an alternative perspective. From one vantage point he examines the social, human sciences employing the power-knowledge paradigm, but he adds to that an interrogation of the body, the subject—bio-power.[25] Historically, theorists have centered their analyses on the nature of right or sovereignty; power works through law as sanctions. The propagation of the body of restrictions imposed limits to behavior and acceptable attitudes by imposing punishments or penalties on those who violated the law, thereby setting examples for others. The limit to the right of the sovereign was the death penalty,[26] the ultimate negation. Foucault declares that around the 18th century a very different cluster of relations began to form. Attitudes had shifted and positive strategies came to displace the monopoly of the negative system of the sovereign; state power, the power to inflict death, reversed direction and invested social structures with the power to mold subjects—a subject may be viewed in two ways, as an individual and as a body acted upon. Bio-power is itself a polarized relation of forces clustering around norms, manifesting at one pole a mechanics of the docile subject and at the other an institutionalization of social apparatuses to regulate a whole population. The disciplines symbolized the productive pole, while the regulatory focused on control. The two poles endowed society at all levels. The materiality of techniques of power guaranteed the maintenance of productive relations as well as the health and well being of the society. Educational structures, communication-information systems, and the armed forces formed subjects on the disciplinary plane, while health programs, disease control, and census activities began to monitor and regulate the population.

Bio-power exerts control over life by infusing everyday existence with power relations, ordering, directing, producing, and controlling activities, that is, structuring alternatives. Bio-power progresses positively garbed as progress, improved conditions for the subject and society; this strategy was not authored by an intentional, meaning bestowing identity any more than the tactics examined through power-knowledge. Nevertheless, bio-power works by motivating the management of life through the polar activities of disciplines and regulatory controls. This technology of power is in no way ideal: It is material. In the patterns established, bio-power continues its inclusion into ever-organizing domains of activity. These relations take over responsibility for the subject and modify personal space and alternatives accordingly. Relations of power-knowledge are what serve to isolate, order, and segregate individuals. These micro-processes secure and continue the ongoing legitimation of domination. Hegemony is produced and sustained through force relations, often unnoticed, investing the body of the subject and his or her life and values. Foucault thinks that normalization has taken precedence over the coercive legal apparatus. Consequently, a subjective and cultural myopia has developed. "For millennia, man remained what he was for Aristotle: a living animal with the additional capacity for a political existence; modern man is an animal whose politics places his existence as living being in question."[27]

Discipline

Foucault wrote histories of various social disciplines in the attempt to understand the present situation. His middle studies are especially relevant for those interested in political signification, cultural studies, and mass communication. These studies of technologies of the self attempt to describe how discursive practices, power-knowledge, and bio-power have given rise to our current condition: the increasing organization of life through the normalization of multifarious aspects of social, professional, familial, and mental life.

The social disciplines work; they work more efficiently, if differently, than commonly understood. Their aim, according to Foucault, is not to understand human beings (in that capacity they are justly criticized) but to control them. His argument in *The History of Sexuality* runs counter to the repressive hypothesis; far from being repressed, talk about sexuality was an obsession throughout the 19th century. In *Discipline and Punish*, Foucault examines the strategical method of surveillance which he conjointly posited as the basis for military, medical, industrial, and educational disciplines. Returning to Bentham for a model of the social disciplines he finds in the *Panopticon* the grammar of the human sciences:

> Bentham's preface to Panopticon opens with a list of the benefits to be obtained from the 'inspection-house': 'Morals reformed—health preserved—industry invigorated—instruction diffused—public burthens lightened—Economy seated, as it were, upon a rock—the gordian knot of the Pool-Laws not cut, but untied—all by a simple idea in architecture!'[28]

The all-seeing, controlling model of the *Panopticon* formed the bedrock for the social disciplines. Through the panoptical process, observation illuminates—all becomes visible, accessible and, finally, organized into a manageable network. Society transforms itself into a vast field of perceptions and ordering processes pervading all walks of life. The progressive control manifested in society and presented in and by the media—for good or ill—results from the discursive strategies practiced by individual disciplines. Mass communication theory or cultural studies, however recently constituted, manifests the same sorts of influences in society as psychiatry, criminology, medicine, or political science. Power-knowledge channels discourse so some speak, others listen; experts act, laymen submit; media inform, audiences listen and watch. Power and influence, while related, are not, as the liberal-pluralists assumed, identical or interchangeable. Yet this reduction of power and influence, from the Foucauldian perspective, is successful. It masks the power of the media as merely indirect. The media appear to support and extend pluralism or, alternatively, to constrain freedom.

The media perform an orthopedic service for society; if they strengthen the structure of post-industrial society, they must also correct deformities and stimulate the public to participate in meeting the economic requirements of society. Foucault does not think that the consensus of wills arises from a social body, but that power-knowledge results from strategic, social, political, and economic power investing each individual throughout society:

> One would be concerned with the "body politic," as a set of material elements and techniques that serve as weapons, relays, communication routes and supports for the power and knowledge relations that invest human bodies and subjugate them by turning them into objects of knowledge.[29]

Do the media facilitate Western democracy? Or do the media ensure the status quo, constricting, if not the topics, the kinds of perspectives that will be considered, given any subject of discourse? Will new technology break, qualitatively, with the threads of development from the past? Foucault seems to have taken a view similar to the structuralist notion of meaning as it works in language as well as history. Foucault juxtaposes continuity with discontinuity. We can see the development of media shifting as technology becomes more encompassing, however, a definite structure can be presented. In *The Order of Things*, Foucault analyzes shifts and developments in life sciences, language, and economics. Tensions were played out and shifts surfaced as man's conception of the world and himself evolved. But shifts and discontinuities took place at local levels before they were recognized as global breaks with the past. Foucault does not accept the notion that a great invention or great thinker was responsible, but that a process finally played itself out and a new strategy emerged, taking the discourse along different lines. As

Dreyfus and Rabinow suggest, the continuity of forms might be another way of approaching the concept of power.

Mass Media

As previously mentioned, Foucault says very little about mass media and modern society. But his work lends itself to the study of information systems and their influences and effects on the current situations in which we find ourselves enmeshed, by which we construct meaning, and from which we recognize our lived reality. Public discourse is formed, to a significant extent, by discourse as presented in the media. One medium, television, seems to be affecting our very notions, not only of public discourse, but of subjectivity itself.

The mass communication systems in the Western democracies link public discourse with governmental strategies by tacitly encouraging and explicitly disseminating information within what Chomsky calls the "bounds of thinkable thought."[30] Media managers, of course, dedicate their resources to, among other concerns, the preservation of the social formation, if for no other reason than that the status quo ensures the smooth proliferation of economic and professional activities. Because the government does not have the capacity to secure popular obedience through force, the state relies upon the media to produce a discourse, which from the outset does not threaten governmental strategy, but limits criticism of foreign and domestic policies to tactical concerns. These limitations are not announced to participants. They work all the better by remaining tacit. Within public discourse, Chomsky locates a "framework for possible thought" to which he attributes the genius of Western democracies, that is to say, their ability to control thought by normalizing public discourse. To be admitted to the debate within mainstream media, one must not violate the fundamental principle that the government is fundamentally benevolent. Violation of this doctrine would disqualify the culprit as surely as Vladimir Danchev's denouncing the Soviet invasion of Afghanistan. Obviously, the government could not intern a network news anchor for denouncing the American foreign policy in Grenada as an "invasion," but he certainly would not repeat the accusation, or more to the point, a newsperson for any mainstream medium would not step outside the bounds of possible thought from the start. Chomsky notes that he has not been successful in locating any reference in mainstream scholarship or journalism to an "invasion" of South Vietnam. He has found references to the tactically unsound and unwise defense of South Vietnam, but nothing in the mainstream press even mentioning the immorality of the conflict.

The problem with what Bagdikian has labeled the "private ministry of information and culture" is that it continually becomes more powerful by reducing the number of its ministers. In 1983, Bagdikian reported that 50 corporations controlled the majority of American media,[31] which in turn interlocked with major industries and several prominent banks. By 1987, that number had dwindled to 27 corporations. As daily journalism provides the database for Western societies, and shapes and defines the truth, the culture's dialogue admits fewer and fewer possible disagreements with those who now control the media.

Journalists most often speak the same language as their sources, those in control. They speak the discourse of power and knowledge produced by those in charge of nuclear arms and massive toxic waste dumps. The public discourse is thus inscribed within the discursive formation of a discipline, the bounds of thinkable thought. Strategic arms "control" provides an illustration. Gitlin points to an ever widening gap between public power and public knowledge.[32] In fact, this gap is produced by the structure and semantics of the dialogue. The experts employ terms that not only muddy the issues, but also formulate the alternatives. A major portion of the American public may have earnestly supported a nuclear freeze, yet the technocrats in control of the strategic situation did not represent this point of view. Consequently, the nuclear freeze was not reported as viable by the correspondents who quote the experts, who are often the sole sources for their stories. On the other hand, the steady formation of the issue along certain preordained bounds strengthens the fusion of public ignorance and public impotence. Gitlin cites a 1985 poll in which only 19% of the people asked realized that the United States does not have a "no first-use-policy" concerning the deployment of nuclear weapons.

Clearly, as Foucault points out, the dissemination of information shapes social awareness and produces knowledge. Schiller[33] advocates politicizing further these information biases inherent in the media and government. We suffer from an "information malady" in the culture industry, compounded, Schiller notes, by billion-dollar acquisitions and network takeovers. He offers the tactic of including the information malady as a political issue in upcoming national elections. The federal government, especially the executive branch and its agencies, has developed a disinformation mechanism, which fabricates scenarios often uncritically relayed by the media. The reasons for the American bombing of Libya serve as a case in point.

Even more critical, Neil Postman advances the notion that society has undergone a media, and consequently an epistemological, shift. We have undergone a technical transformation, which realigns the forces of communication-capacity-power from print to television, in which truth is "drowned in a sea of irrelevancy." Postman's position is that public discourse is polluted to the extent citizens depend on television. Television, he argues, can only reduce public discourse to absurdity, triviality, and, finally, nonsense. One can take issue with the notion that public discourse could be nonsense. Discourse is produced along lines that serve to mask the true functioning of power. Public discourse is produced and structured by political and cultural technologies, institutional and social agencies. So, the remarkable phenomenon by which television disciplines individuals and regulates segments of the population is not primarily trivialization, but discursive formations and presentations of information without context which distribute current affairs in particular patterns that *appear* trivial. That is dangerous. That is how, as Postman says, we are "amusing ourselves to death." The media perform functions that alter our conceptions of knowledge and truth. In Western societies, truth is largely articulated through media. The media take and resonate conceptions of justice, fairness, and credibility. The media structure the public discourse by creating forms of truth telling, for example, television promotes image and instancy that shape perception and knowledge. "Serious television is a contradiction in terms,"[34] says Postman. Television employs the voice of entertainment, and its discourse carries the terminology of show business. For example, network newscasts are often presented in 8-minute packages with each story broken up into a discrete package of 45 to 90 seconds. At any rate, right after one hears and sees a murder scene, an international crisis, or the weather forecast, the announcer says, "Now . . . this." "Now . . . this," indicates "what one has just seen has no relevance to what one is about to hear or see, or possibly to anything one is ever likely to hear or see,"[35] he says. Discontinuity disguises import and disconnects thought, which nevertheless reforms attitudes and perceptions.

Cultivation Analysis

Foucault tells us that power relations vitalize agencies by working on the bodies of individuals, rendering persons docile while regulating populations (normalizing audiences, in the case of television). Institutions guide cultural discourses along trajectories. They work on an individual's desires and identity, assumptions of status, and political convictions. On a different level, the structure of democratic society determines, to some extent, the format of institutional ensembles such as mass media. But the development of this political technology in turn shapes and alters the democratic relations that engendered those communication systems. Gerbner and Gross conceptualize television as an institution, a centralized information system, which, through ritualized drama (news as well as entertainment) patterns our symbolic environment. In fact, stabilizing social patterns form television's major contribution. Television "cultivates" common perspectives.[36] Television extends the legitimacy of the social formation by the presentation of power and authority through ritual. Television presents rules of power through programs which portray what befalls people who violate those rules, thereby exploiting individual fears and maintaining power structures by dramatizing the fate of miscreants and victims. Ritualization serves most importantly to "enculturate," not to entertain or inform, viewers. The institutionalized function of television serves as an agency to establish norms and values.

Gerbner et al. remind us that as natural as the televised portrayal of the world may sometimes seem, it is a normalized view.[37] Television reproduces "consumer values and social power." Further, the medium cultivates a quite restrictive view of women and minorities through the distribution in programs of values and life-chances. Power maintains this distribution.[38] Gerbner employs a conception of power similar to Weber's, but if one shifts the emphasis from ability and influence to process and production, then it is not incompatible with the normative and heuristic conception of power Foucault advances. Cultivation analysis questions the distribution of power, rather than amounts or numbers of exchanges. The patterns of power relations presented on television impose greater burdens on some rather than others. Portrayals of dramatic situations distribute power relations through ritualization in particular formations. This disciplines viewers to the lessons of television life, which the viewer cultivates, to varying degrees, toward real life. This does not occur, however, only on the conscious level, but the viewer's body is acted upon by the power invested in ritual. It also works on the viewer's sense of self. To continue the Foucauldian interpretation, power works over the subject's body and structures norms, fears, and desires. Networks work to complete the circuit by monitoring select samples for successful productions through ratings.

Gerbner and Postman seem to share similar views concerning the essentially dramatic form of all programming, but, while Postman thinks television trivializes weighty matters, Gerbner sees the process as a pivotal strategy of social stability and control. Entertainment pleases us, while fusing dominant attitudes and prejudices. The discursive patterns imparted over a long period of time help shape an individual's knowledge of what is normal, right, and real. They assert, "Entertainment is the most broadly effective educational fare in any culture,"[39] and educational fare cultivates the predispositions that affect future choices and values.[40]

Cultivation analysts have uncovered two telling aspects of television programming: discipline resulting among heavy viewers from the widespread portrayal of violence and the gravitational pull toward the "mainstream" of the socio-political spectrum occasioned by heavy viewing. The former tends to isolate a person, and the latter normalizes him or her. "We may all live in a dangerous world, but young people . . . the less educated, women and heavy viewers within all these groups sense greater danger than light viewers in the same groups,"[41] they point out. It can be argued that fearful people are less secure, and hence more dependent, than confident individuals and that democratic forms are weakened to the extent that large segments of the population are made fearful and docile. Insecurity breeds dependence on and acquiescence to social and political authority. These feelings are regularly aroused and manipulated to legitimate the need for more police, more forceful police, and the converse constriction of freedom to maintain life and limb.

Dependence on authority is buttressed by a vastly expanded television presentation (over real life) of the role of law enforcement at the expense of other segments of society. "The typical viewer of an average week's prime-time programs sees realistic and often intimate (but usually not true-to-life) representations of the life and work of 30 police officers, 7 lawyers, and 3 judges, but only very few blue-collar workers."[42] Moreover, during prime time, crime is presented at ten times the rate it occurs in the real world. Women, elderly, young, and minorities are much more likely to be portrayed as victims rather than perpetrators in violent situations. This "warped demography" within television programming cultivates norms and values among viewers about real life. Prime-time power hierarchies of victimization cultivate mirror-image structures of fears about real life victimization within demographic groups. Among heavy viewers, "those minority group viewers who see themselves more often on the losing end of violent encounters on television are more apprehensive of their own victimization than are light viewers in the same groups."[43] Heavy viewers are those who watch four or more hours daily, and light viewers are those who watch less than two hours daily.

Values and opinions of heavy viewers differ consistently from the views of light viewers in the same demographic categories. Conceptions of reality are cultivated by television's presentation of values and norms. For instance, light viewers among lower socioeconomic groups are more likely to refer to themselves as working class than are heavy viewers. Heavy viewers from the same groups tend to classify themselves as middle class. The obverse holds, too. Higher socioeconomic-group heavy viewers tend more than light viewers to refer to themselves as working class. Interestingly, heavy viewers are more likely than light viewers to call themselves moderate, but they hold positions that are "unmistakably" conservative on civil rights, minorities, and personal rights.

Cultivation analysis is an empirical research strategy to record slow but pervasive cultural shifts, much as Foucault's studies of disciplines and social histories document the development of strategies of social control. To be sure, Gerbner's reliance on statistical and survey research data is not as encompassing or theoretically informed, but it surely serves to indicate the value of Foucault's approach for cultural studies in mass communication. We turn now from the study of television to look at the dissemination of personal information through a network of electronic databases designed to enhance recordkeeping on the "domestic" population.

SURVEILLANCE, PRIVACY, AND INFORMATION

Back when the various states and the FBI were in the process of first computerizing their records on criminal offenders, the Los Angeles Times reported a sobering, if prescient, anecdote. Alan Winslow wrote a letter to the governor of Massachusetts recounting the experience of how his brother, a deputy sheriff, while on dispatch duty one night, ran the names of his family through the National Crime Information Center (NCIC). "Ten out of 11 of us were listed," Winslow writes. The deputy's mother was listed. It seems that years before she had attended a noisy sorority party while she was in college, and neighbors had called the police to complain. The deputy's stepfather merited a listing in the database after reporting to the local police that he had received a bad check.[44] There was no evidence of criminal conduct or conviction of any family member.

Twelve years later, a headline in the *New York Times* ran, "FBI Says 12,000 Faulty Reports On Suspects Are Issued Each Day."[45] This estimate of inaccurate or faulty reports was compiled by the FBI *itself* in a series of internal audits of 12 states. The flawed information was provided to the FBI's National Crime Information Center by over 60,000 state and local law-enforcement agencies. At this time, the center was accessed by law enforcement officers approximately 400,000 times daily. The head of the FBI's auditing services said that about "6 percent of the 211,196 warrant entries and 4.5 percent of the 126,253 stolen vehicle entries being transmitted throughout the network each day had serious flaws."[46] Further, it appears that checking procedures for ensuring the accuracy of data often are not followed.[47]

Postmodernism offers, I believe, a theoretical advance over the traditional pluralist notions of the marketplace and power as coercion. I think that the productive conception of power offers a way to rethink problems of information invading privacy, public versus private, and information fracturing knowledge. Shifting relations within social discourse map out new terrains of meaning and control. Through the myth of privacy, surveillance powers are left in the thicket of social beliefs to pursue their goals uncontested by public recognition of the strategic situations played out to constrict further the individuals under surveillance. It is not my intention to attempt a critique of Foucault's work; I am attempting to apply some of his ideas to a contemporary problem for critical phenomenology. While society proclaims a goal of social equality, Foucault's conceptual couplet, power-knowledge, is helpful in describing how that professed goal is deflected, manipulated, and redirected to compliment a strategy of governmental and corporate control.

Closely associated with an assault of efficiency on truth and justice is the technical appropriation of knowledge by information. One finds very powerful aggregates of power interested in exchanging information for efficiency and profit. But there are growing numbers of voices concerned with this ever-increasing growth of mechanisms for social control. It is imperative to recognize that information is collected at the local level and is passed along through networks created through increased circulation and not from systems put in place from above. I attempt to come at the problem of electronic data-base surveillance from several perspectives. Information technologies have provided surveillance techniques for normalizing our lives—on the job, at home, in our business and social dealings—never dreamed of by Bentham's panopticon. Information has largely replaced the control tower. It allows for new configurations of our social universe. Jean Francois Lyotard's analysis is helpful in sorting out in what ways discourse strategies work over our concepts of how we see rationality, ourselves, and our relations with others. Even the traditional concept of "mind" is under challenge by what Theodore Roszak has referred to as the information processing model of the mind.

Information has usurped what traditionally has been regarded as knowledge. As Foucault shows in his studies of madness, medicine, the prison, and sexuality, power relations are functions of what society accepts as knowledge. Following Foucault, Lyotard treats power and knowledge as aspects of social formation, or areas of specialization. Who decides what is knowledge and what is to be decided? The technical discourse promoting efficiency places the dialogue in a context that naturalizes conflicts brought about strategically, that is, through essentially political decisions. Management efficiency, for example, is a strategy purposefully developed along a trajectory which can, however, be deflected. Linguistic clusters form meaning patterns; discursive formations and political strategies can be analyzed and redirected. Domestic policy tactics do not have to proscribe civil liberties if individuals decide against the endless growth of social control mechanisms. Management efficiency is not necessarily the primary condition of social life. If power governs exchange, in this case the exchange of information, then those with interests in protecting privacy must promote tactics, productive mechanisms produced by discourse in which subjects see themselves as individuals *and* as objects of knowledge. But Foucault stresses the importance of local struggle. He advises us that power masks itself. Power fashions the mask of the autonomous individual, or the legal notion of the right to control the collecting, processing, storing, and dissemination of information about a person's attributes and activities. Myths are constructed that critical theory strives to deconstruct. The right to privacy does encompass the idea of ordering liberty, and freedom involves choices concerning the individual and his or her relationships with others. But the myths also must be confronted for what they serve: the automatic functioning of power through normalization.

The issues are broader than privacy and efficiency. The language of efficiency calls for challenge from the discourses of ethics and justice. In short, the situation is strategic. The long-term societal costs involving loss of individuals' sense of responsibility, distrust of government, and subjective feelings of impotency by significant numbers of people may prove much more costly to society than short-term efficiency interests.

Information Invades Privacy

Information is powerful, but in a manner we did not foresee. For many years, it has been technologically possible to construct electronic database files containing the equivalent of 20 pages of personal information on every man, woman, and child in the United States.[48] Moreover, the information on any individual could be accessed and retrieved in a matter of seconds. With the developments in information technology, there is no need for a monolithic national database system. Personal information can be correlated, integrated, and shared by participating governmental departments and business organizations. That such systems had not, in the past, been put on-line was due to the constraints and the policy choices made at the time concerning organizational goals and priorities. In 1972, the sociopolitical environment was not hospitable to such developments. Today, the environment has changed. The emphasis on management and efficiency practices has evolved at the expense of privacy interests. The Office of Technology Assessment reports that the growth of record-keeping at the federal, state, and local levels (interagency and intra-agency), as well as throughout the private sector, has resulted in steady encroachment on civil liberties.[49] Information policy is carried out with a view to enhancing efficiency, obscuring the broader ethical, social, political, and economic contexts. This focus on efficiency constitutes an invigorated and encompassing network of information and produces what we may term a mechanism of power. Electronic dissemination of personal information produces a knowledge of the recorded population.

Computerized data banks offer organizations information with which to exert considerable control over a person's health, welfare, and peace of mind. Life insurance, credit cards, employment opportunities, tax returns, government benefits, and rental agreements leave data trails of interest to organizations and agencies. Such womb-to-tomb surveillance has been called the "record-prison." The standards and procedures by which society makes judgments about people has and is undergoing tremendous change. David Kairys characterizes as ideological, endeavors that fall under the private rubric, but are not susceptible to the democratic ideal at work in the public realm.[50] Economic decisions affecting one's life are taken from the citizen's control, disguised by the discourse of private enterprise.

Today, landlords often decide to whom they will rent by enrolling in tenant screening services. The Unlawful Detainer Registry (UDR), one of the largest such services in the country, covers Southern California. It stores approximately 2 million records, that is, information on persons against whom apartment eviction court cases have been brought. In 1985, UDR received about 250,000 requests by landlords concerning potential tenants—900 requests a day for data searches. Legal actions for eviction in California are called unlawful detainers, and as such, they are a matter of public record. Once a landlord attempts to evict a tenant, a screening service can legally file the case, even if the suit is settled out of court or is dismissed. If a tenant enters into a dispute with a landlord and gives up possession of his or her apartment, that person could end up a cipher in a databank. In effect he or she is blacklisted. Legally, the way to remain off the computer list is to go to court, fight the case, and win. That, of course, is expensive. Gary Blasi, an attorney with the Legal Services Defense Center in Los Angeles, reports 40% of the 35,000 homeless in Los Angeles lost their homes because they were evicted.[51] Any person entered into the databank at UDR may not be able to find a place to live. "If you've been evicted from an apartment in Southern California since 1975, you're in the computer."

Frontline reported the story of one hapless tenant who lived under conditions so foul that the health department intervened. The landlord continued to refuse to fix the backed-up plumbing or to patch the caved-in ceiling. So, the tenant withheld her rent, a lawful tactic under such circumstances in California. The landlord then sought to evict her for not paying her rent. The tenant went to court, settled the case, and subsequently decided to move. Into the U.D. Registry she went. UDR Director Saltz:

> A lot of tenants feel like if they moved out that nothing happened. You know, if you stick your head in the sand, everything goes away. They may think there's nothing there. Until the shock comes to them that there really is. But I don't feel that that's something I should concern myself with, the fact that they choose not to recognize something that does exist.

Another tenant won a judgment over a rental dispute in court, yet one year later his name was still entered in the UDR computer file, in violation of California law.

The Unlawful Detainer Registry links-up with credit bureaus such as TRW, the largest credit reporting company in the country. TRW's California data center maintains credit records on over 120 million people, processing 300,000 credit reports a day, 30,000 reports an hour. Under current law an individual may not find out who is selling personal information about him or her until a derogatory report is released. Over 100 federal government agencies share data with the seven largest credit reporting companies.[52] The federal Fair Credit Reporting Act of 1970 guarantees a person the right of access to his or her credit file; it assures notice of adverse decisions made on the basis of a credit report, and the act provides restraints on investigative reporting. But it does not identify who has access to one's records, nor does it delimit the scope proper to information gathering.[53] The act specifies time limits on reporting and retention of harmful information, but allows for loopholes and disclaimers to the 7-year limit on maintaining information in a record.[54] The most common electronic searches involve computer profiling (screening) and computer matching. In a computer profile, records are searched for particular, selected factors with regard to a specific type of individual. A computer match compares two sets of files, record by record, to identify individuals (hits) who appear in both files. These techniques have been used to identify not only fraud, waste, and abuse, but also to identify men who should have registered for the Selective Service, or to screen prospective jurors. One section of the Deficit Reduction Act amends the Social Security Act, the Food Stamp Act, and the Internal Revenue Code, requiring public assistance and unemployment agencies to exchange information among one another and obtain unearned income data from the IRS, the Social Security Administration and state wage and unemployment insurance data files.[55] Further, DEFRA failed to mandate any oversight policies. In the future, individuals may even be "phased out" of the tax return process altogether and replaced by a process wherein the information will be disclosed directly to the IRS by employers, credit agencies, mortgage companies, and banks. In 1985, the federal government withheld approximately 750,000 tax refunds to people who, it was determined, defaulted on loans from the Department of Education, the Veterans Administration, the Department of Housing and Urban Development, and the Small Business Bureau.[56] Anyone delinquent on federal loans may have his or her name given to credit reporting agencies, and where applicable, have AFDC checks held.

Not surprisingly, civil rights advocates have raised concerns and fears on constitutional grounds. As currently practiced, computer searches and information exchanging may entail not only Fourth Amendment unreasonable search and seizure problems, but may violate due process as presented in the Fifth and Fourteenth Amendments and the equal protection clause of the Fourteenth Amendment. The presumption of innocence announced by the Fifth and Sixth Amendments may be endangered by searching the records of people who were not previously under suspicion of any wrong doing. Scrutinizing people without their knowledge and subjecting them to penalties without prior review disturbs due process. OTA argues that the equal protection clause of the Fourteenth Amendment prohibits the government, state or federal, from creating legal categories and carrying out policies that discriminate against persons in the created category. Nor has economic status been regarded as an acceptable category of classification for special treatment. "Computer matches are inherently mass or class investigations, as they are conducted on a category of people rather than on specific individuals," OTA reports.[57] Computer profiles categorize people according to selected criteria and, consequently, select a subgroup for special scrutiny or treatment, for example, persons suspected of underreporting their income, or persons believed more likely to commit violent crime or to abuse drugs. Formal computer profiles accentuate anticipated similarities while ignoring or downplaying significant differences. But the courts have not offered remedies for these problems.

While I consider the right to privacy to be implicit in common law, the public-private distinction emerged full-blown in American culture by way of Warren and Brandeis' 1890 article advocating a right to privacy.[58] Subsequently, public and private categories have been employed strategically to advance specific interests under the guise, historically, of a right to property and, currently, of the interest in management efficiency. Although agencies and organizations proclaim their intentions to minimize damages done to individuals by electronic recordkeeping, Marchand agrues that it is not in the nature, for example, of criminal justice recordkeeping systems to defray what he calls "social costs," for instance, the inadvertent injury to one's name or to one's sense of self.[59] Techniques of social control encumber everyone—the director and the subject interact within the system. Nor can we assume the pluralist notion that relevant interest groups will organize to undertake collective action to advance their interests. The size of the affected group does not guarantee it will act, neither does the social cost of recordkeeping transgressions imply that the system will necessarily adjust itself in the direction of liberty. The stigma attached to criminal records precludes many from taking any action they feel may call undo attention to the information. In fact, where criminal justice agencies have developed some privacy safeguards for information processing systems, "such a strategy has worked to preclude the expansion of conflict."[60]

The increased manipulation of personal information calls for new perspectives in our approach to power and privacy. Foucault's critical theory can be brought to bear on this problem. Foucault describes two approaches to the study of power and knowledge in society.[61] Mechanisms of power can be profitably analyzed from either of two schemas: legal or disciplinary/social. Foucault chooses to examine power relations, the production of truth, and the techniques of knowledge almost solely from the perspective of disciplinary strategies (at the micro or individual level) and normalizing techniques (at the macro or societal level). Normalization, the process by which individuals are made to conform, is furthered by the invasions of privacy suffered at the keyboards of information technologies. Disciplinary practices follow the discourse of maximum efficiency, sometimes at the expense of truth and fairness.

Public Versus Private

Warren and Brandeis write of the broad right to privacy and the need to protect that right by a narrower law of privacy. They distinguish a general, pervasive realm of personality, a societal right of privacy, and a legal claim for individuals to be let alone. They speak of these rights "against the world" as growing out of, but not limited to, the right of property—property in an extended sense, as one might own one's identity or liberty.[62] Property rights have broadened beyond any simple sense of ownership as something tangible. The right of privacy secures basic civil rights, among them "peace of mind,"[63] and "the right to one's personality."[64] Currently, the debate has expanded to encompass the need to protect information about oneself from exploitation and manipulation. Information is treated as property, and personal information is not necessarily controlled by the subject of the information but by the record holder. The generation of massive amounts of personal information, along with the technology to disseminate it, contributes to its marketability. This increasing dissemination of personal information has overrun into political as well as commercial surveillance tactics. The power tactics of surveillance have in part prospered as the very reversal of the American tradition of shielding the individual from the tyranny of social and political institutions. While Foucault claims that power relations are both intentional yet nonsubjective, their logic, aims, and directions are decipherable. Foucault contends that contemporary society has completed a reversal in perspective: We have passed from the ancient civilization featuring public spectacle to a culture of surveillance. The Greeks, for example, attempted to govern and control the population by exhibitions in temples and theaters—the strategy was to bring the question of politics, running the polis, to the public. Later, exhibitions and public spectacle were employed by Western monarchies to constrain their subjects, as Foucault so graphically depicts with the execution of Damiens.[65] But Western society gradually has downplayed the strategy of public spectacle in favor of its reverse: Instead of people attending to a public spectacle, data processors keep watch over us. Today, we discover the development of a virtual national database on citizens, a network for surveillance relations. Foucault writes:

> In a society in which the principal elements are no longer the community and public life, but, on the one hand private individuals and on the other, the state, relations can be regulated only in a form that is the exact opposite of the spectacle . . . .[66]

Through the use of property law, the public and private realms have again been reconstituted to constrain members of society through legitimizing current power relations. In fact, proclaiming the vitality of civil liberties deflects concern from the real situation of social control. If we decide that most of us really are free to pursue life, liberty, and property, then we may fail to see the critical problem. Those in control of the resources decide what policies will be pursued and which interests will prevail. For example, liberties may even be undermined by proclaiming the right to free speech. Individual rights, Kairys suggests, not only have been exaggerated in our society, but freedom of speech is strategically championed to mask real absences of freedom and democracy.[67] Choices affecting all are made by a few, and our free speech right to disagree deflects real opposition to fundamental inequalities. Free speech is used to legitimize social inequality. What one might term the hegemony of free speech, undergirding today's configuration of public/private, informs us we are free and society remains democratic.

One can locate here a deep disagreement between the liberal-pluralist school of thought and the critical approach. Does the public realm invade the private through the auspices of the bureaucratic "nobody?" Or does the individual right to do what one chooses with one's property really constitute a strategy of social control? Each view is valid from the perspective in which it is presented. Hannah Arendt correctly asserts that the public realm has usurped much of what used to lie within the private realm. Governmental collection and dissemination of personal information is carried out to advance, managers argue, public policy. But, at a different level, the formative power of the control over economic resources, including personal information, remains largely within the realm of private concerns. As Kairys notes, "Fundamental social issues, such as the use of our resources, investment, the energy problem, the work of our people, and the distribution of goods and services, are all left to `private'—mainly corporate—decision makers."[68] The legal configuration of the individual's right to property allows knowledgeable minorities to control the interests of the majority of us, while proclaiming democratic processes as the political rationale for so doing.

To speak of freedom, however, presupposes the guarantee to debate social issues; the civil rights of individuals uphold the dialogue at the public level. This conflicting nature of the public and private realms presents a fundamental problematic in liberal thought. Civil society is not simply the realm of free interaction, with each party equally able to maintain his or her own best interests. Liberal thought attempts to deal with social problems by relativizing issues, by balancing supposedly equal concerns, like the right to one's peace of mind with the right to property. Similar to Derrida's deconstructive turn, critical legal theorist Duncan Kennedy argues, "The point is that liberalism embraces contradictory reasoning techniques for resolving conflicts."[69] A plausible argument may be made for either privacy or property, depending on how one structures and frames the issues. The question, "what are rights?" may be answered, rights are results. What is to be accorded precedence—appeals to policy, social welfare, or personal well-being? We must grapple with the dilemma of the primacy of the public or the private. When the government collects personal information about us, it does so from the public realm. When a business collects personal information, it does so from the private realm. Examining the concept of power may help in attempting to understand the dynamic among the various realms and networks sustaining social relations.

Power Invests Discourse

Offering a positive, productive conception of power, Arendt structures her notion along lines of consent and undistorted communication. Power corresponds to the condition of unity built on plurality, that is, power rests on and works by consent. "Power corresponds to the human ability not just to act but to act in concert,"[70] she writes. Individuals and groups are empowered by coming together to decide what should be done, and this act ensures the ongoing dynamic of power. Any coercive notions, Arendt relegates to relations of force. Yet, power depends upon authority, but authority is characterized by recognition and respect by others. Power maintains the public realm, and public opinion in the public realm supports and continues power. This is why bureaucratic rule is nefarious: It weakens both the public and private realms, insofar as "nobody" is in control, no one accepts responsibility.

Alternatively, power may be viewed as command and coercion. Power is the production of intended effects, or the capacity to produce effects by controlling others' behavior. On this view, Meyrowitz writes, "Power refers to one's ability to coerce others (through physical, economic, or other means) to do one's bidding."[71] Dahl also describes power relations as related to the functions of control and coercion. Power is manifested in amounts; it is distributed within specifiable domains, and power is inscribed within a scope—one is not equally powerful in all circumstances.[72] Burnham defines power as "the ability to persuade others by overt or covert means to do one's will."[73]

Foucault's conception of power moves away from the emphasis on the power of someone to impel another to do what he or she would not otherwise do. It is not that Foucault would deny this happens; rather, it is beside the point for his analysis. At bottom, these definitions rest on a coercive or negative notion of power. Foucault stresses the productive aspects of power. Through discourses brought about over periods of time by experts, strategic micro mechanisms of power develop. Specialized knowledge, such as counseling single mothers, produces the mechanisms wherein individuals, as well as populations, are constrained, and these micro mechanisms dovetail into articulations furthering power tactics, such as aid to dependent families. Upon considering the uses of knowledge in the service of strategy, Foucault advises against reifying power. Power, he asserts, is not an institution, a structure, or even an ability. Power is merely the "name that one attributes to a complete strategical situation in a particular society."[74] As a form of social control, the practice of electronic record manipulation can be approached at various levels—individual effects, technological developments, public policy positions—while at the same time going beyond these strata to address other concerns, such as ethics and justice.

Foucault approaches truth as historical and political and power as relational. In terms of information and knowledge, one sees that information circulated within a network of interlinked databases, reported among information processors, most often without the knowledge of the subject, will effectively be treated as the truth about that individual. If and when the person discovers that information harmful to oneself is being circulated, he or she may have no practical way even to locate the source of the damaging information. The individual becomes subject to the control of the process and this, in turn, affects the way that person sees oneself and his or her role in our society. For example, a person who has been subjected to inclusion in the U. D. Registry and, consequently, is not able to find a home is likely to feel helpless. This sort of experience is spreading throughout society and illustrates what Foucault refers to when he describes disciplined individuals and normalized populations, made passive by strategies of control, observed by unseen recordkeepers, and inscribed within a regime of truth. This serves as an instance of the statement that truth is political, and, as will be seen, a recent transformation of information into knowledge. The law constitutes the other discourse of power by which we attempt to deal with what Gordon calls one of the more threatening aspects of life, "the danger posed by other people."[75]

The law depicts and regulates what society can and cannot do to and for the individual; the legal apparatus provides remedies for those whose right to control information about themselves is transgressed. Even so, the legal system works in accord with a disciplinary system, which argues that the individual must be allowed to function, not only around and upon oneself, but even within oneself, because one's self-image is fashioned intersubjectively. Legal analysis, however, traditionally concerns itself with how society sets limits to power. Truth, for example, is viewed as limiting power. One will not be falsely condemned. Repression can be vanquished by truth: The truth will set us free. The power of law limits legitimacy beyond which organizations cannot constitutionally go. But power invests discourse, producing truth. "We are subjected to the production of truth through power and we cannot exercise power except through production of truth,"[76] Foucault writes. The normalization process is made potent by means other than the law. Technique functions as a sort of shadowy area in contrast to the more clearly defined legal apparatus; it can undermine the social pact while restructuring laws. Techniques for control mold the polity. These social practices, while transitory, connect with other regulatory systems—for instance, credit or medical—to form strategies deployed through information processing tactics.

Foucault proposes a radical shift from traditional conceptions of power. First, he approaches power as relational, indeterminate, and immanent. Power is deployed through knowledge, spheres of specialization and expertise; conversely, knowledge directs power relations. Power and knowledge may be viewed as poles, punctuations, or emphases of a relation. This tactical productivity results in interpenetrating conjunctions of force relations and strategical integrations. Power and knowledge could be said to refract discourses that Foucault sees as resulting in a politics of the true, that is, social reality perceived as true and unquestioned. The federal government's emphasis on the crisis of management and efficiency as the key to solving the national deficit—downplaying civil rights costs—serves as an example of the politics of the true. Foucault writes of the relational aspects of power, and so he reminds us that the dominance of the government, the legal system, or any such conception of an encompassing organization of control should be taken itself as produced and not primarily as the agent.[77]

Second, power working in a network of relations is not exercised as a property, but advances as strategy in tension with other interests and along various trajectories.

> In short this power is exercised rather than possessed; it is not the `privilege' acquired or preserved, of the dominant class, but the overall effect of its strategic positions—an effect that is manifested and sometimes expanded by the position of those who are dominated.[78]

So, Foucault inverts the direction of the analysis of power often taken by critical theory; he asserts that the positive mechanisms of power, which generate knowledge, always generating more power, function in terms of a "will to power." Specifically, information technology, electronic recordkeeping as a technique, provides a discipline, knowledge that simultaneously surveys a population, while locating and inscribing individuals, circulating information distributing them within powerful networks.

Information Trumps Knowledge

Power traverses and produces discourses, resulting in knowledge. Conversely, knowledge structures and channels power. The resulting "regimes of truth" (in this case, recordkeeping), form institutionalized discourses. The various punctuations of the process make it vital. What counts as knowledge, and the status accorded to various sorts of knowledge, carries social and political import. Knowledge is used to legitimate power relations. Foucault contends that knowledge arises within social spheres of activity; never is it ideal or abstract, in the sense that it has no social foundation or function. Human interests and actions structure the field of possible further actions. Those persons in command of databases carry out activities that affect the future actions of individuals entered in the database. The actions of those who control and manipulate personal information structure the field of future possibilities for those included in, for example, a computer match. From the perspective of critical theory, the thrust of electronic database linking and processing with regard to personal information is not primarily to free people through increased access to information, but to control people by circulating information about them, which serves to categorize individuals along preconceived notions of relative worth. Individuals are categorized through information processing techniques that serve to characterize them in very specific ways: sick, poor, criminal, tax payer, credit risk, single mother, or litigant, to mention a few.

This interplay of unequal, immanent relations pulses throughout social fields, but, again, is refracted through structural and intentional considerations. In his report on knowledge, Jacques Lyotard emphasizes the need to rethink not only the power problematic, but to reconsider communication theory by focusing on "language games"—social discourses— incorporating an "agonistic" technique.[79] Foucault coins the term "agonism" to point up the same approach. Lyotard views the development and use of information technology for social control as a strategy, a discourse with rules, and as accepted practices and tactics, the "game" better understood by some players than others. "Agonistics," a theoretical approach based on contestation, clears a place, he argues, from which to consider combative strategies. This is a much needed advance over the instrumental or consensual conceptions of rationality. Insofar as information processing functions to expedite the practical functioning of society, the social body gets treated as some sort of leviathan. If we consider society from Lyotard's "provocative" perspective, we can escape the idea of society as a giant mechanism; we approach the social as diverse sets of social practices, techniques, and discourses. This allows for the entry of the principle of opposition. The oppositional principle advanced by Lyotard and Foucault runs counter to the information processing way of approaching problems; it runs counter to what has come to be known as systems thinking, which Machlup argues fosters a belief in "the rationality of the whole apart from its components and their interactive relations."[80] Lyotard accordingly supposes information processing will affect our learning processes and our lives, much as earlier advances in transportation systems or mass media.

Since the whole does not have a mind of its own, it is up to individuals to decide, somehow, what will pass for knowledge statements. According to Lyotard's analysis, knowledge today is taken to be information, information treated as a commodity indispensable to productive power. The traditional conception of knowledge is undergoing transformation. Upon considering power-knowledge relations, Lyotard distinguishes three "language games" (there could be others). These discourses concern various values: efficiency, truth, and justice. The discourse championing performance seems to have taken precedence in the information age. While social bonds are linguistic, they are not uniform or homogeneous. They are comprised of different strategic discourses, employing different rules, and drawing on various principles. The denotative discourse involves the distinction between what is true or false. To decide what will be viewed as just or unjust, one employs a prescriptive or legal discourse. Lyotard considers that technical discourse, involving the dialect of technology, allows one to decide what is efficient or inefficient.[81] Currently, the technological discourse appears to invoke the strategy wherein force relations are determined. While these discursive strategies interrelate, performance (efficiency) articulates knowledge. The goal of the contemporary configurations of language games is more power, not more truth or more justice. Power maximizes the input/output of information processing, resulting in compatible verifications (denotative discourse) and rationalizations (prescriptive discourse).

Lyotard writes:

> Now it is precisely this kind of context control that a generalized computerization of society may bring. The performity of an utterance, be it denotative or prescriptive, increases proportionally to the amount of information about the referent one has at one's disposal. Thus the growth of power, and its self-legitimation, are now taking the route of data storage and accessibility, and the operativity of information.[82]

Social relations are indeterminate relations, that is to say, the import of a situation is generated by social practices which are themselves not predictable. If this is so, then there may be no certainty in gauging the meaning or truth about something or someone, apart from socially generated schemes. This concern points to the importance of the construction of knowledge. Even admitting knowledge is socially constituted, that is, not based on any absolute or primal reality in itself, knowledge still forms the basis in accordance with which we interpret the world. Of course, one may construct various schemas or systems of categorization, but some schema or system will be employed to maintain and further whatever it is we decide to consider as "knowledge." The arrangements in the social sciences, for example, tend toward a system employing rules and norms. Foucault explains how, historically, norm and rule have displaced conflict and signification.[83] The structure of knowledge undergoes transformation through time. Such a transformation is occurring in the West presently. The "new order" collects data, articulating patterns of behavior, followed by bureaucratic classification, leading to regimes of truth about individuals. The person invoked likely will not be aware that information about him or her is articulated into a specific configuration or record. This "truth" loses its tentative character as information and gains the status of objectivity (neutrality and validity). The dynamics by which this process of "informing" the individual is effected might be termed a relation of power to knowledge.

Closely associated with the assault of efficiency on truth and justice is the technical appropriation of knowledge by information. Information has usurped what traditionally has been regarded as knowledge. As Foucault shows in his studies of madness, medicine, the prison, and sexuality, power relations are functions of what society accepts as knowledge. Following Foucault, Lyotard treats power and knowledge as aspects of social formation, that is, as areas of specialization. Lyotard asks; Who decides what is knowledge and what is to be decided? The technical discourse promoting efficiency places the dialogue in a context that naturalizes conflicts brought about strategically through essentially political decisions. Management efficiency, for example, is a strategy purposefully developed along a trajectory which can, however, be deflected. Linguistic clusters form meaning patterns; discursive formations and political strategies can be analyzed and redirected. Domestic policy tactics do not have to proscribe civil liberties, if individuals decide against the endless growth of social control mechanisms. Management efficiency is not necessarily the primary condition of social life. If power governs exchange, in this case the exchange of information, then those with interests in protecting privacy must promote tactics, productive mechanisms produced by discourse in which subjects see themselves as individuals *and* as objects of knowledge. But Foucault stresses the importance of local struggle. He advises us that power masks itself. Power fashions the mask of the autonomous individual, or the legal notion of the right to control the collecting, processing, storing, and dissemination of information about a person's attributes and activities. Myths are constructed which critical theory strives to deconstruct. The right to privacy does encompass the idea of ordering liberty. Freedom involves choices concerning the individual and his or her relationships with others. But the myths also must be confronted for what they serve: the automatic functioning of power through normalization.

In one area, Congress has made it a felony for isolated individuals to break-in on electronic record systems, and in another area, the federal advisory board of the NCIC has empowered and legalized the very kind of information surveillance the federal Privacy Act of 1974 was designed to prevent. Working at another level of social practice, Congress passed the Electronic Communications Privacy Act of 1986, making it illegal to intentionally intercept or disseminate electronic communications. The act, in part, protects persons against unauthorized access to electronic communications, including the storage of such messages. But it permits providers of communications systems services to intercept or access electronic records for the purposes of recordkeeping. It is unclear for what uses this loophole will be employed. On still another level, the federal Advisory Policy Board of the National Crime Information Center (NCIC) endorsed expanding the center's national computer file to exchange information on people *suspected* of a crime, not convicted of a crime, not charged with a crime, but suspected of a crime.[84] Finally, bowing to pressure from concerned civil rights groups, the FBI withdrew its $40-million plan to "modernize" their "electronic library" of information by including the names of suspects in the data base.[85] The FBI's de facto national data base, which comprises a network rising from local agencies up to the federal agency, receives about 540,000 inquiries daily from law enforcement officers. The advisory board also recommended that the NCIC should be linked to the Securities and Exchange Commission, the Internal Revenue Service, the Social Security Administration, and the State Department. Law enforcement officials would then have access to the personal records of persons suspected of a crime. As the vice chairman of the board said, "If the technology is available, why not use it?"

Currently, not only what is regarded as knowledge, but the processes by which society arrives at knowledge statements is undergoing a process of erosion, largely because of a permutation in what we take as our model of mind. Roszak is alarmed at the extent to which society at all levels, from government to business (public to private), from acclaimed institutions of higher learning even to grade schools, accepts what he calls the information processing model of the mind.[86] While Foucault's concern has been with how micro mechanisms of power are structured throughout a society over large periods of time, Roszak is concerned explicitly with the direction in which our fascination with computer technology is taking us, especially with regard to how we think and, consequently, what we think is important. Roszak documents the shift in Western societies from thinking as the attempt to evaluate ideas by forming meaningful, integrating patterns, to a data processing model of the mind, with its attendant emphasis on consistency and efficiency, to the exclusion of other aspects of thinking such as wisdom, ethics, truth, and aesthetics.

The sorts of intrusions resulting from electronic recordkeeping are occurring, in part, because society's priorities have shifted. Today, we are undergoing a cultural and epistemological shift, which justifies the constriction of civil liberties such as privacy. Historically, this change can be seen as the latest strategy of the empiricist tradition. Both Foucault and Roszak point to Bentham and the Utilitarians' demand for facts first;

observation resulting in the rise of the modern prison system for Foucault, and statistical recordkeeping to scuttle the British Poor Law resulting in "the draconian workhouse system" for Roszak. In both versions the emphasis on systematic observation and recordkeeping stengthened social strategies of discipline and normalization. Roszak remarks of the Utilitarians, "Lurking behind the investigation was a perfectly dismal vision of human nature and a grim obsession with cash values."[87]

Fundamentally, the information processing model of the mind is reductionist. It leads to a conception of knowledge as merely a collection of consistent facts. The mind does much more than process facts consistently; it formulates meaningful configurations from discrete events to decide among possible interpretations concerning what is worthwhile. This sort of process entails considerations of truth, justice, and wisdom. Collecting, processing, and distributing discrete packets of data does not constitute what Roszak calls thinking. The mind generalizes from relationships among ideas and information. In the attempt to reorganize vast amounts of facts, the mind searches out, indeed, creates patterns by enlarging on what is present to hand. The resulting patterns may or may not be adequate. Successfully discounting inadequate ideas traditionally has been another hallmark of thinking well. Ideas do not develop primarily from data or even from logic, but ideas come from experience, wisdom, and convictions. Information does not produce knowledge or ideas as the "cult of information" suggests.

Roszak highlights the antagonism between information as a sensible statement, communicating a "fact," and information as a quantity, an exchange along a channel, coded and then decoded by electronic impulses.[88] Seen quantitatively, as information processing, all information becomes equivalent. The criterion for qualifying accurate or private information is dissolved. How would information then be transformed into knowledge? Could knowledge be acquired without information being received? Machlup offers some distinctions between knowledge and information: Information is atomic and fragmented, whereas knowledge is structured and coherent; information is perishable and fleeting, while knowledge lasts; information carries a current of messages, while knowledge results in a pattern.[89] The prevalent technical discourse centers on efficiency, confusing information with knowledge. Consequently, information is regarded as powerful by those employing a technical discourse. Roszak reminds us:

> In our time, minds loyal to the empiricist love of fact have seized upon the computer as a model of the mind at work storing up data, shuffling them about, producing knowledge, and potentially doing it better than its human original.[90]

The quantification of information and the substitution of data for knowledge removes the problem further from reflection: Ideas make information; information does not constitute knowledge. The confusion of information and knowledge promotes the discursive strategy of efficiency over truth, and in turn glosses over issues of civil liberties, such as the right of privacy. I would like to suggest that the discontinuity Foucault examines between the law and the norm, the judge and the expert, is one that can be bridged. Foucault's choice of analyzing power strategies from social disciplines does not preclude critical analysis from the perspective of the law. The point is to develop analyses, descriptions, and explanations of power-knowledge strategies at work today. Foucault's critical theory initiates a different sort of critique of the "politics of truth" that constitute the forms of social hegemony in contemporary society.

Foucault does not presume to arrive at a program of change for others. Such "high altitude" theory places the theorist in an untenable position, a role in which he or she assumes some sort of knowledge above the particular that really only those directly involved could grasp. Nonetheless, resistance to power is a condition of its existence. Foucault writes, "It would not be possible for power relations to exist without points of insubordination which, by definition, are means of escape."[91] The task is to make forms of knowledge and networks of power problematic, to make, for example, electronic invasions of privacy subject to local criticism not dependent on a "regime of truth." Social theory ought to leave open the tactics for any specific contest to those involved in protesting constraint, but critical theory remains a perpetual provocation and a search for alternatives.

NOTES TO CHAPTER 6

1. S. Hall and T. Jefferson (eds.), *Resistance Through Rituals: Youth Subcultures in Post-War Britain* (London: Hutchinson, 1976), p. 12.
2. See S. Hall, "The Rediscovery of 'Ideology'; Return of the Repressed in Media Studies," in M. Gurevitch, T. Bennett, J. Curran, and S. Woollacott (eds.), *Culture, Society, and the Media* (London: Methuen, 1982), pp. 56-90.
3. Ibid., p. 86.
4. S. Hall, "The Problem of Ideology—Marxism Without Guarantees," *Journal of Communication Inquiry*, 10 (2): 1986, p. 42.
5. See S. Hall, "Encoding/Decoding," in S. Hall, D. Hobson, A. Lowe, and P. Willis (eds.), *Culture, Media, Language: Working Papers in Cultural Studies* (1972-1979) (London: Hutchinson, 1980), pp. 128-138.
6. See M. Foucault, in C. Gordon (ed.), *Power/Knowledge: Selected*

Interviews and Other Writings 1972/1977 (New York: Pantheon, 1980), pp. 194-228.

7. See S. Hall, "Cultural Studies and the Centre: Some Problematics and Problems," in S. Hall et al., *Culture, Media, Language*, pp. 15-47, and C. Weedon, A. Tolson, and F. Mort, "Theories of Language and Subjectivity," in *Culture, Media, Language*, pp. 195-216.

8. S. Hall, "Signification, Representation, Ideology: Althusser and the Post-Structuralist Debates," *Critical Studies in Mass Communication*, 2 (2), pp. 91-114.

9. Hall, "Signification, Representation, Ideology: ALthusser and the Post-Structuralist Debates," p. 93.

10. See L. Althusser, *Lenin and Philosophy and Other Essays*, trans. B. Brewster (London: New Left, 1971).

11. P. Anderson, "The Antinomies of Antonio Gramsci," *New Left Review*, 100, pp. 5-78.

12. S. Hall, "On Postmodernism and Articulation: An Interview with Stuart Hall," L. Grossberg (ed.), *Journal of Communication Inquiry*, 10(2): 1986, p. 60.

13. Foucault, in *Power/Knowledge*, p. 74.

14. See M. Foucault, in P. Rabinow (ed.), *The Foucault Reader* (New York: Pantheon, 1984) pp. 76-100.

15. M. Foucault, "The Subject and Power," in H. L. Dreyfus and P. Rabinow, *Michel Foucault: Beyond Structuralism and Hermeneutics*, 2nd ed. (Chicago: University of Chicago Press, 1983) p. 209.

16. M. Foucault, "Nietzsche, Genealogy, History," in Rabinow, pp. 76-100.

17. Foucault, *Power/Knowledge*, p. 10.

18. Ibid., p. 102.

19. See Foucault, *Power/Knowledge*, pp. 63-77, and A. R. Luria, *Cognitive Development: Its Cultural and Social Foundation*, trans. M. Lopez-Morillas & L. Solotaroff (Cambridge: Harvard University Press, 1976).

20 M. Foucault, *The History of Sexuality, Volume I: An Introduction*, trans. R. Hurley (New York: Vintage, 1980), p. 44.

21. M. Foucault, *Discipline and Punish: The Birth of the Prison*, trans. A. Sheridan (New York: Vintage, 1979), p. 23.

22. Foucault, "The Subject and Power," p. 217.

23. Foucault, *Power/Knowledge*, pp. 194-228.

24. Ibid., p. 55.

25. Foucault, *The History of Sexuality, Volume I*.

26. Foucault, *Discipline and Punish*.

27. Foucault, *The History of Sexuality, Volume I*, p. 143.

28. Foucault, *Discipline and Punish*, p. 207.

29. Ibid., p. 28.

30. N. Chomsky, "The Bounds of Thinkable Thought," *The Progressive*, October 1985, pp. 28-31.

31. B. H. Bagdikian, *The Media Monopoly*, 1st ed. (Boston: Beacon Press, 1983).

32. T. Gitlin, "The Greatest Story Never Told," *Mother Jones*, June/July 1987, pp. 27-31, 45-47.

33. H. Schiller, "Information: Important Issues for '88," *The Nation*, July 4/7, 1987, pp. 1,6.

34. N. Postman, *Amusing Ourselves to Death: Public Discourse in the Age of Show Business* (New York: Penguin, 1985), p. 80.

35. Ibid., p. 99.

36. G. Gerbner and L. Gross, "Living With Television: The Violence Profile," *Journal of Communication*, 26 (2): 1976, 172-199.

37. G. Gerbner, L. Gross, M. Morgan, and N. Signorielli, "Charting the Mainstream: Television's Contributions to Political Orientations," *Journal of Communication*, 32 (2): 1982, pp. 100-127.

38. G. Gerbner, L. Gross, M. Jackson-Beek, S. Jeffries-Fox, and N. Signorielli, "Cultural Indicators: Violence Profile no. 9," *Journal of Communication*, 28 (3): 1978, pp. 176-201.

39. Gerbner and Gross, "Living With Television," p. 177.

40. Gerbner *et al.*, "Charting the Mainstream."

41. Gerbner and Gross, "Living With Television," p. 193.

42. Gerbner *et al.*, "Charting the Mainstream," p. 106.

43. Ibid., p. 107.

44. R.A. Jones, "Computer War: Massachusetts Bucks the Trend," *Los Angeles Times*, August 17, 1973, p. 1.

45. D. Burnham, "FBI Says 12,000 Faulty Reports On Suspects Are Issued Each Day," *New York Times*, August 25, 1985, p. 1, 30.

46. Ibid., p. 30.

47 D. Burnham, "Wrongful Arrest Suit Cites Flaws In Computer Data," *New York Times*, January 19, 1986, p. 11.

48. See A.F. Westin and M.A. Baker, *Databanks in a Free Society*, (New York: Quadrangle, 1972).

49. U.S. Congress, Office of Technology Assessment, *Federal Government Information Technology: Electronic Record Systems and Individual Privacy* OTA-CIT-296 (Washington D.C.: U.S. Government Printing Office, June 1986).

50. D. Kairys, "Introduction," in D. Kairys (ed.), *The Politics of Law: A Progressive Critique* (New York: Pantheon, 1982) pp. 1-8.

51. "You are in the Computer," *Frontline*, #319, May 1985.

52. T. Roszak, *The Cult of Information: The Folklore of Computers and the True Art of Thinking* (New York: Pantheon, 1986), p. 183.

53. A. Miller, *The Assault on Privacy: Computers, Databanks, and*

Dossiers (Ann Arbor: The University of Michigan Press, 1971) p. 88.

54 J. Rule, D. McAdams, L. Stearns and D. Uglow, *The Politics of Privacy, Planning for Personal Data Systems as Powerful Technologies* (New York: The New American Library, 1980), p. 90.

55. U.S. Congress, "Federal Government Information Technology," p. 147.

56. D. Burnham, "IRS to Withhold Tax Refunds Owed Loan Defaulters," *New York Times*, January 10, 1986, pp. A1, A11.

57. U.S. Congress, "Federal Government Information Technology," p. 39.

58. S. Warren and L. Brandeis, "The Right to Privacy," 4 *Harvard Law Review* 193 (1890).

59. D. A. Marchand, *The Politics of Privacy, Computers and Criminal Justice Records*, (Arlington, VA: Information Resources Press, 1980).

60. Ibid., p. 308.

61. See Foucault, *Power/Knowledge*, pp. 78-108, and "How is Power Exercised?" in Dreyfus and Rabinow, *Michel Foucault*, pp. 216-226.

62. Warren and Brandeis, "The Right of Privacy," p. 213.

63. Ibid., p. 200.

64. Ibid., p. 207.

65. Foucault, *Discipline and Punish*.

66. Ibid., p. 217.

67. Kairys, "Freedom of Speech," in *The Politics of Law*.

68. Ibid., p. 164.

69. D. Kennedy, "The Structure of Blackstone's Commentaries," 28 *Buffalo Law Review* 205, 360.

70. H. Arendt, *The Human Condition* (Chicago: The University of Chicago Press, 1958), p. 44.

71. J. Meyrowitz, *No Sense of Place: The Impact of Electronic Media on Social Behavior* (New York: Oxford University Press, 1985), p. 62.

72. R. Dahl, "Power as the Control of Behavior," in S. Lukes, *Power* (New York: New York University Press, 1986) pp. 37-58.

73. D. Burnham, *The Rise of the Computer State* (New York: Random House, 1983) p. 88.

74. Foucault, *Discipline and Punish*, p. 93.

75. R. W. Gordon. "New Developments in Legal Theory," in Kairys, *The Politics of Law*, p. 228.

76. Foucault, *Power/Knowledge*, p. 93.

77. Ibid., p. 92.

78. Foucault, *Discipline and Punish*, p. 26.

79. J.F. Lyotard, *The Postmodern Condition: A Report on Knowledge*, trans. G. Bennington and B. Massumi (Minneapolis: University of Minnesota Press, 1984).

80. F. Machlup, "Semantic Quirks in Studies of Information," in *The Study of Information: Interdisciplinary Messages*, F. Machlup and U. Mansfield (eds.) (New York: John Wiley & Sons, 1983), p. 656.

81. Lyotard, *The Postmodern Condition*, p. 46.

82. Ibid., p. 47.

83. Foucault, "How is Power Exercised?"

84. R. Pear, "Crime Panel Backs Broad Expansion of Computer File," *New York Times*, June 11, 1987, pp. 1, 14.

85. M. Wines, "F.B.I. Rejects Plan to Widen Computer's Data on Suspects," *New York Times*, March 4, 1989, p. 6.

86. Roszak, *The Cult of Information*.

87. Ibid., p. 159.

88. Ibid., p. 11.

89. Machlup, "Semantic Quirks in Studies of Information."

90. Roszak, *The Cult of Information*, p. 103.

91. Foucault, " How is Power Exercised?" p. 225.

All
The News...

The first section of this study looks at aspects of a major newspaper's organizational practices from the perspective of a situationalist theory of leadership. This theory shares with phenomenology an appreciation for allowing an organizational situation to flesh out interpersonal and professional relationships from its administrative skeleton in the hopes of developing and nourishing an able-bodied, coordinated, well-adjusted team of professional people. Failing that, situational leadership theory claims a diagnostic function, offering intervention strategies. In contrast to Bill Moyers' cultural journalism or the radical anarchic approach at *Ramparts*, mainstream journalism stifles difference and weeds out dissenters, thereby maintaining the "integrity" of the bounds of thinkable thought. It seems an irony that those in the business of communicating on a massive scale so often miscommunicate on interpersonal levels. But that miscommunication masks a strategy of control, which in turn feeds into an informational system resounding with the univocal voice of the power elite. A deconstruction of the *New York Times'* coverage of El Salvador follows the organizational analysis.

The *New York Times* serves as our national newspaper of record. It is naturally accorded the respect and credibility which accompanies such accomplishment. Referred to more often by more people for serious news coverage of issues of import, the *Times* remains the most cited mass medium in the United States. The *Times* is an institution as influential and far reaching as many governmental agencies or departments. Its archives certainly reflect our culture's history. As our paper of record, it also shapes the present and indicates future lines of development. It is not merely a mirror of our society.

I contend that the daily foreign affairs practices of the paper rarely disturb Washington's foreign policy strategies and their communication to the American people. Of course, a paper such as the *New York Times* is made up of a vast array of professional goals, interrelationships, and functions. What concerns us here are the perspectives they do present. In fact, the best independent reporting often comes from freelancers or those who begin as freelance writers. Reporters who are brought along according to the usual socialization process display a definite pattern of compliance to the system of news gathering and, I argue, an acceptable, limited range of perspectives from which to present news that often involves life, death, and human dignity. As one young reporter puts it, "I've only had one or two stories spiked. But then I know what they want. How long do you think I would last here if I telexed them stories of how well the guerrillas are doing?"[1]

Which version of a situation emerges as the truth and in what manner it is constructed to a large extent depends upon the organizational structure of the newspaper. I attempt to examine the *Times* from a systems perspective. Of primary interest are the relationships between management/editors and workers/reporters. The sort of atmosphere one uncovers is, rather surprisingly, an institutional climate high in dogmatism with an unremitting reliance on authority, an environment that assumes reporters' conformity and subservience to management.

BEHIND THE FRONT PAGE

The manner in which individuals are treated at the *New York Times*, according to the reports by Chris Argyris and Gay Talese, serve as examples of behavioral, authoritarian attitudes, and stand in opposition to a phenomenological approach to the treatment of persons in the workplace. Conversely, leadership theory affords a method, or body of tenets, which is phenomenologically sound. The different proponents of leadership theory do not use the terminology of phenomenology, but the two methods are compatible.

One sees similarities between leadership theory's emphasis on appreciation of persons and Levinas' distinction between need and desire. The other is to be appreciated and learned from, rather than manipulated and categorized in the manner by which many of the editors of the *New York Times* do. From the editor's perspective, journalists are seen as objects, things to be channeled and controlled. This practice follows from the subject-object dichotomy phenomenology rejects as

illusory. Also, paralleling the distinction between competition and cooperation, the *Times* focuses on short-term competition hindering long-
term cooperation. Cooperation is a function of overall survival value.
Finally, the editors' rigid demands for conformity from those under
them leads to tunnel vision, ignoring critical insights to further specific
advancement. Argyris' study serves to highlight attitudes at work within a major mass communication medium.

Traditionally, investigations of mass communication have focused
on areas such as audience, the journalists themselves, and product: message receiver, message sender, and message. Less attention has been paid
to the organization of the process and the interrelationships of personnel.
My hypothesis is that internal relationships within the organization of any
newspaper affect the quality of that newspaper. This is a very complex
matter. The arrangement of internal relationships viewed as dynamic,
interacting influences on the quality of the product is rather novel in the
study of newspapers. My purpose is to examine a newspaper as a system.
System is a formal term that encompasses an array of subsets and departments which have specific functions with specific relationships to each
other and specific relationships to the whole itself. Specificity contributes
to the goal of the organization, and nothing is part of the organization
which does not contribute to the goal. A systems approach emphasizes
that "the interactions and interdependencies among the subsystems are at
least as important as the individual components."[2]

Chris Argyris' 3-year study of the *New York Times, Behind the Front
Page: Organizational Self-Renewal*,[3] is the vehicle through which we interpret
situational leadership theory. Argyris was not at liberty to divulge the
identity of the newspaper depicted in his analysis. This presents problems.
At times, it is not possible for Argyris to describe events in clear terms. A
sense of vagueness therefore pervades much of his study.

I further interpret Argyris' experience through the situational
leadership theories of Paul Hersey. Management is 90% communication.
Communication obviously is relational. Hersey's theories and observations are largely an amalgamation of his own and other motivation theorists. We focus on Hersey for the sake of clarity, but it must be stressed
that these views represent the work of a tradition in organizational
behavioral studies. Other theorists are mentioned as their theories
become clearly germane to the discussion. For Hersey, organizational
behavior and management practices are essentially situational. The situation presented here is *Behind the Front Page*. Both Argyris and Hersey
focus on the relational nature of management. Management is the
attempt to direct or modulate the behavior of others to accomplish a predetermined goal using available resources. This function is primary. The
ultimate goal of the manager in this sense is profit or selling newspapers

and advertising. But, if our hypothesis is valid, techniques employed toward this end will affect the internal structure of the newspaper, which in turn affects the product. Hersey and Blanchard write:

> [A]n organization is an 'open social system,' that is, all aspects of an organization are interrelated; a change in any part of an organization may have an impact on other parts or on the organization itself. Thus a proposed change in one part of an organization must be carefully assessed in terms of its likely impact on the rest of the organization.[4]

The process as well as the product require examination. The assumption is that a large metropolitan newspaper is subject to the same problems as a large corporation or government agency. Hersey contends: "Our greatest failure as human beings has been the inability to secure cooperation and understanding with others."[5] Argyris characterizes *The Daily Planet* (his pseudonym for the newspaper) as a "living system." A living system has distinctive qualities and attributes unique to itself as an entity, which enable or hinder it from functioning effectively. It is an abstraction designed to portray certain interdependencies and characteristics. In the case of *The Daily Planet*, Argyris writes:

> [T]his newspaper, even though an excellent one, was having credibility problems with many of its constituencies. Moreover, many members of the newspaper expressed a general sense of helplessness about changing these internal conditions, which included win-lose dynamics among reporters and between reporters and copywriters, management by crisis and with hypocrisy, and the conception of advocacy journalism held by many of the top young reporters.[6]

Argyris was concerned with analyzing the internal relationships within *The Daily Planet* as a system, to change parts of the system, and to induce capacity for self-examination within the system. His stated objectives were to understand the newspaper, to explain the given state of affairs at work within *The Daily Planet*, to be capable of predicting outcomes of events under specific conditions, and to aid executives in redesigning their living system. We will see that he had his hands full. Hersey concurs:

> In defining O.D. [Organizational Development] from our perspective, it is important to remember, . . . that the effectiveness of a particular organization depends on its goals and objectives. Thus, we do not accept a set of goals that are right for all organizations . . . .[7]

Obviously, one ought not approach the living system of *The Daily Planet* with the same assumptions with which one approaches, for example, an automobile factory. The employees are different kinds of people with vastly different functions, although both the persons and the systems share many characteristics. They work within a hierarchical situation, within the same economy, and, ultimately, for many of the same goals. Raising a family, securing housing, and planning for the future are but a few goals shared. Some of the common needs expressed by people at *The Daily Planet* are hard work, intellectual challenge, status, essentiality to the success of the organization, and competition. These needs tie in with the motivation theories of Maslow, Lewin, Herzberg, and McGregor, as presented through Hersey's situational leadership theory. One desires to fulfill needs; this creates motivation, the urge to act. Some of these needs when viewed from a dynamic of other needs and of others' coexistent needs, interact, collide, and result in frustration or the blockage of goal attainment. In general, there are two types of behavior displayed by individuals in a work setting: "task behavior," related to the job role, and "relationship behavior," between members of a group. According to Hersey's situational leadership theory: *"The more managers adapt their style of leader behavior to meet the particular situation and the needs of their followers, the more effective they will tend to be in reaching personal and organizational goals."*[8] If executives and editors are not meeting these situations through open and far-reaching dialogue, then Argyris states we can expect to find the management process within the newspaper to tend to be ineffective. It is incumbent on the manager, executive, or editor to diagnose the situation, to ascertain the relevant approach to a given environment. Further, it should be noted that the two types of behavior, task and relationship, are not discrete but should be coordinated by a manager in an integral manner. Task behavior features one-way communication from leader to subordinate; relationship behavior encourages two-way communication. Autonomy can be promoted through interdependent relationships.

Argyris selected the top 40 executives of *The Daily Planet* for study. He delineates as basic conditions for effective intervention three modes of commitment: valid information (self-maintaining), free choice (self-sufficiency), and internal commitment (self-learning). Argyris found that even at the top of the organization, the executives, while committed to valid information, were not committed to free choice or internal commitment. He reports: "When the top members of *The Daily Planet* had an opportunity to make their organization one that learns and examines itself, they retreated from the challenge."[9] Valid information refers to those factors and their interrelationships which cause the organizational problems. Free choice expresses the intention to modify the situation based on an accurate diagnosis of the situation from the individual's point of view, not simply from the point of view of those with control. Internal commitment means the individual internalizes the free choice to act, according to valid information, which will therefore fulfill his or her own needs as well as those of the system.

Abraham Maslow has articulated a hierarchy of needs which he believes represents the levels of interest an individual seeks to achieve as he or she matures throughout life.[10] The needs are: physical, food and shelter; safety, security and order; social, meaningful relationships with others; ego, sense of prestige and potency; and self-realization, transcendental understanding of self and environment. While I feel this hierarchy to be somewhat reductionist, it functions as a model from which others have synthesized more sophisticated articulations of motivation. The model is practical, that is, it is useful in interpreting why people behave in certain ways, and it posits references for the understanding of common needs. Particular individuals vary in their placements and degrees of achievement among various levels. These levels are not meant to be interpreted as exclusive, but are interconnected; people satisfy these needs to different extents at any given time or situation.

Douglas McGregor developed a theory of motivation derived from the assumptions of how managers regard human nature, especially the nature of those whom they manage.[11] The theory is dualistic. Theory X assumes the conventional, traditional view that motivation is best achieved through force, fear, power, monetary reward, and moral authority. This is a static conception which asserts that most people are by nature indolent, prefer to be externally directed, desire safety above all, and possess little capacity for problem solving. Contrary to theory X, theory Y assumes people may be properly motivated at all five of Maslow's need levels. Individuals may be self-directed, capable of creative problem solving, and able to enjoy productive labor. "Therefore, it should be an essential task of management to unleash this potential in individuals. The properly motivated people can achieve their own goals *best* by directing *their own* efforts toward accomplishing organizational goals,"[12] say Hersey and Blanchard.

Argyris' study reveals that the executives at *The Daily Planet* had more in common, in effect, with theory X than with theory Y, although they would express agreement with theory Y. Argyris' intervention theory primarily concerns itself with how persons behave, not how they say they behave. "The resistance that eventually stopped our progress was an example of individuals working the system to fulfill their own needs,"[13] he says. Argyris here refers to individuals at all levels of the organization, from the top down. Competition and fear overrode concerns for cooperation and self-acceptance. He describes the two types of leadership styles actualized within the organization as directive-controlling (employing harshness and anger as means) and passive-withdrawn (offering coldness and distance to subordinates and peers). "It is likely that the superior will not learn about a problem until it can no longer be contained, or becomes a crisis,"[14] he says. When an issue arose, it was predominantly dealt with in a competitive win-lose fashion; "71 percent of the administration and 88 percent of the news people reported the existence of win-lose interactions."[15] The individuals at *The Planet* imparted deep pessimism about the adaptability of human behavior; they felt it was the other person who was ineffective and competitive, and narrow interests leading to conflict were necessary conditions of the organization. This serves as a direct illustration of Hersey's theory X:

> Given the competitiveness, low trust avoidance of conflict, managerial secrecy, and centralization of decision making, it is not surprising that most of the *Planet* men I interviewed assumed that effective leadership is strong, directive, believes in competitiveness, and confronts impersonal conflicts covertly.[16]

Where are the commitments to valid information, free choice, internal commitment? Argyris admittedly is caught in a methodical paradox. He attempts to intervene in a system which applied information to individual needs for self-interest rather than organizational efficiency. The choices people often made reduced freedom; risk-taking was viewed as formally injurious; externalizing competitiveness was viewed as laudable. Egocentric behavior typified executive management practices. Once again, leadership personality is not only a matter of self-perception, but of how others perceive the leader. Leaders were seen as strong, authoritarian individuals who felt the effectiveness of the organization was dependent on directive, task-oriented behavior. The living system concentrated on high competition and low trust. Argyris states that when people did speak about what was on their minds, they did so in a manner which conformed to those values constitutive of the emotional atmosphere of *The Daily Planet*. People became incompetent when they discussed their true feelings, incompetent in the sense that they literally lost touch. "Conformity to ideas was the most frequently observed norm, concern for ideas was next,"[17] says Argyris. One finds this unsettling. A major institution whose function is to provide our culture with the truth before all else, which is protected by the Constitution, is itself mired in self-deceit and intellectual dishonesty.

Hypocrisy extended throughout the living system. Executive problem solving meshed within the system to avert situational crises in a contradictory manner.

> If organizational performance in one area becomes highly ineffec-
> tive, then they seek more aggressive executives, who are charged
> with 'cleaning up the mess' and get warned to 'go easy lest there
> be union difficulties or someone hurt.' This charge places the
> executive in a double bind. He is asked to make changes, which
> are intrinsically upsetting, in a system that magnifies the upset,
> without upsetting anyone! There is also the implied threat that if
> he does upset the system he will not be supported.[18]

Not only are the predispositions of management toward subordinates
authoritative and based on fear and control, but the attitude of management toward itself is of the same type, reification of theory X.
Management styles in themselves are not good or bad. The point is
whether a management style is effective. One questions the utility of theory X methods of motivation in properly addressing needs of highly
intelligent, competent, independent professionals. It would seem that
particularly in an area such as journalism, where the motivation ought to
be to produce the best communication vehicle one can, conditions of
authentic communication should be promoted, not regarded as renegade.

The dual factor theory of motivation is applicable to *The Daily
Planet*. Frederick Herzberg presents a conception which discriminates
between dis-satisfiers, hygiene factors, and motivating forces. Hersey
and Blanchard report "that when people felt dissatisfied with their jobs,
they were concerned about the environment in which they were working. On the other hand, when people felt good about their jobs, this had
to do with the work itself."[19] Both Herzberg and McGregor borrowed
heavily from Maslow's hierarchy of needs. Hersey combines their contributions along with others to formulate his theory of situational leadership. Hygiene factors can prevent people from becoming truly motivated. They reduce the effect of motivating factors. Hygiene factors are:
company policies, supervision, interpersonal relationships, working
conditions, and pay. All of the above, with the exception of pay, were
factors for concern within *The Daily Planet*.

Employees of the *Planet* felt group meetings were a waste of
time. Aggressive people did all the talking, while the more reserved simply weathered the verbal onslaught. No one dared state what was really
on his or her mind. People had predetermined roles in a script which
did not vary; it was viewed as errant behavior to step outside one's role
or to contradict a superior. Supervision was less than optimal on an
interpersonal scale. Hersey and Blanchard write:

> The present style of management *is* personality centered. The diffi-
> culty is that it is oriented toward the defenses and anxieties of
> people and that it tends to be covert about the orientation. All liv-

ing systems take into account aspects of personality of their members. Effectiveness depends on making this explicit so that the system can be oriented toward the growth and innovative aspects, and not the defenses and anxieties.[20]

Motivators, according to dual factor theory, center on achievement, recognition, challenge, responsibility, growth, and development. Many people at *The Daily Planet* appeared to be motivated in spite of the hygiene factors within the organization. Motivators are more potent as satisfiers than hygiene factors are as dis-satisfiers. Perhaps this partially explains why *The Daily Planet* managed to be one of the most respected journals. It employed only top-notch persons. Hygiene factors functioned as obstacles to need satisfaction. One receives the impression that many people at the *Planet* were personally unhappy because of the institutional atmosphere. Argyris predicted that, indeed, many of the younger reporters would go elsewhere. Motivators and hygiene factors are discrete and operate independently on different but intertwining planes. At the *Planet*, they combined in a pervasive atmosphere of anxiety. *The Daily Planet* also employed what is known disparagingly as a "star system." That is, a few high achievers were given singular status and privileges over the rest of the news staff. This situation caused much consternation, jealousy, competitiveness, withholding of information, distortion, and conformity. The situation led to compulsive, repetitive ineffectiveness within the interpersonal realm which contributes, according to Argyris and Hersey, to less effective goal attainment. Men and women contribute to the needs of the organization best when the meet their own personal needs at the same time in the job setting. Task behavior was not the primary problem; lack of growth and development on the personal level, however, influenced the rate of professional maturation, if motivation theory is accurate. "Organizations are only beginning to realize that their most important assets are human resources and that the management of these resources is one of their most crucial tasks."[21] It stands to reason that if the "human resources" of *The Daily Planet* were alienated, the organization itself would be adversely affected. The vital portion of the living system was diagnosed as ill. It may be a matter of conjecture whether the fever was caused by a common cold or cancer, but the hygiene factors worked abuse. Argyris contends, "A self-maintaining system, from an analytic view, is a system with built-in circularity. Built-in circularity means that every factor ultimately influences all the other factors."[22]

Situational leadership theory stresses inter-connection between task-behavior (directional), relationship behavior (socio-emotional support), and the job relevant maturity of subordinates. According to Guest, Hersey, and Blanchard:

> Maturity is defined in Situational Leadership Theory as the capacity to set high but attainable goals (achievement-motivation), willingness and ability to take responsibility, and education and/or experience of an individual or a group. These variables of maturity should be considered only in relation to a specific task to be performed.[23]

The relationships are curvilinear. I assume Hersey means a "built-in circularity," that is, they exert reciprocal influences upon one another. I assume the staff of *The Daily Planet* was at least of moderate to high follower maturity, else they would not be employed by a newspaper of such distinction and renown. Guest, Hersey and Blanchard point out:

> At this maturity level, people tend to have the ability to do a particular task but seem to lack the motivation. The initial leadership style that tends to be most effective in this situation would be high relationship/low task behavior . . . .[24]

Subordinates "should share in decision making through two-way communication, thus facilitating behavior releasing the blocked motivation."[25] After this has been accomplished and the group or individual attains high maturity, low relationship/low task behavior is prescribed. Argyris attempted through interviews, diagnosis, and, finally, through executive seminars to implement such a notion, but he failed utterly. He writes, "Many found the implications of practicing the new skills ranged from embarrassing to unbelievable."[26] One executive commented, "We need hypocrisy to survive and that is why we won't change."[27] This is an example of what Argyris refers to as a "self-sealing process," by which he means an individual interprets events in the world and reforms reality according to these interpretations. A self-sealing, self-perpetuating cycle is synthesized. Competition among everyone, from cub reporter to the president, led to insecurity, gave rise to incomplete, dishonest, narrow communication, which resulted in closed-minded inflexibility, which in turn produced a disequilibrium within the living system. The crisis, when resolved, activated the self-sealing, self-perpetuating cycle: a closed system. Since the system was closed with everyone affecting everybody else, the question of who manages whom took on a novel meaning. Levels of maturity may be assigned to executives. By standards of intervention theory or situational leadership, most of these men were immature. They did not function well at their essential task, managing effectively. Their motivation levels were poor. Argyris suggests:

> [I]ndividuals will not try to generate a new competence until they are relatively certain that they can learn it. But they will not discuss whether they can learn it unless they feel free to experiment with it. They will not feel free to do this unless they are acting within a culture, or a setting, in which experimentation is sanctioned and the fear of rejection by others is greatly reduced. But the fear will not tend to be reduced unless the others also want to learn about themselves.[28]

But no one at *The Daily Planet* was free. Further, the nature of operating a metropolitan newspaper restricted the organization; employees were bound by space-time constraints. These constraints remained inflexible. So, while the will was not there, to a significant degree, neither were the means. Coupled with this realization comes the revelation that, at first, old motivation techniques will be more effective than the new skills Argyris urges. Executives at The Daily Planet were busy, highly pressured men, and they reacted negatively to the training situation with sentiments much the same as Hersey predicts: "'How can we accept these things?' 'They are not usable.' 'They do not work in the real world.'"[29]

Perhaps the most frustrating aspect of the living system was its tenacity. The executives did not desire to change. They would admit to the inefficacy of isolated, closed system processes of communication on the one hand, while boasting of the effectiveness of hypocrisy and self-interest on the other. The argument can be made that high quality, accurate journalism is produced through competition. The better newspaper is the newspaper which is successful in the economic marketplace as well as the marketplace of ideas. Competition is a function of survival. Competition is attributable to the industry and the organization, as well as the individual. A circuit is fashioned. The industry competes for attention, the newspaper for circulation, the individual for job security and promotion.

Argyris does not deny this, but he argues that elevating competitiveness over cooperation is not really to the system's best interest. Competition may be expressed as a subset of systemic cooperation. Increased dexterity results when the left hand knows what the right hand is doing. Communication skills such as the ability to be open, accurate, direct, and considerate contribute to the competence of a communicator. The absence of such skills within the profession, organization, or individual increases the hygiene demands of all concerned. Tension will increase, overflow boundaries within the system, and eventually spread to the environment. There appears to be an ecology of communication similar to other types of natural resources. Pollution is by definition detrimental and affects the consumer. The closedness of communication practices within the boundaries of an organization will, in fact, spread to the environment. Argyris interviev ed a *Planet* reporter:

> Q: If I understand you, you dislike what your own competitiveness can do to others, yet you remain strongly competitive.
>
> A: Yes, I am always out for hurting people. I don't feel good about that as a human being, but I still seem to do it.[30]

This person is actively involved with people outside journalism as a major function of his job. Here, he refers to his peers, but clearly this is an instance of compulsive behavior. Compulsive behavior is an uncontrolled and repeated reaction to a stimulus, which triggers behavior without conscious intention. Argyris does not say to what extent this kind of behavior is bred into the living system, however. Clearly, the system did not discourage the reporter's behavior.

It was the practice of *The Daily Planet* to maintain more reporters on staff than they had stories assigned to cover. This example of structurally insuring competition is of questionable necessity.

All of the reporters Argyris interviewed:

> [R]eported that a highly developed sense of curiosity and distrust, or as one put it, 'functional paranoia,' was important; and all identified as important the needs of being recognized, of competitiveness, and of the need for immediate closure and feedback.[31]

Another reporter responds:

> I've always found it much easier to get a good easy-flowing conversation rather than be blunt with people. Take (a man whose views he has condemned in his articles). I established a good easy relationship with him and he talked and I got what I wanted out of him. I did it by sheer hypocrisy. It has always been my style. I'm not particularly proud of it. That's the way I am.[32]

That an intellectual/emotional split has been transmitted here is obvious. The dishonesty reached those within the *Planet*, the product itself (the newspaper article), and the individual interviewed. Argyris sees strong projections occurring within the minds of certain kinds of journalists; those he terms Reporter-Activists. This type of journalist-personality, according to Argyris, attacks institutions and individuals for practices, prejudices, and failings which he unconsciously ascribes to himself. The reporter cannot deal with these feelings psychologically; therefore, he or she projects the threat toward an object outside him-or herself. Feelings of hypocrisy, deceit, cowardice, ruse, anger, and the urge to dominate, the reporter cannot face within himself, so he or she lashes out at external instances of these self-same qualities in others. Argyris concludes that the reporter runs the risk of blowing up or breaking down. The reporter ignores the internal dilemma and does not confront either unpleasant eventuality.

Reporters at *The Daily Planet* needed intellectual challenges to overcome; 84% of Argyris' respondents found intellectual challenge to be a personal challenge, 94% sought it out. Evidently, such people are not essentially joiners or team players. They are independently oriented. Their predisposition is to work alone. Is this the kind of person who will make a good manager? Obviously not, at least not unless there are some intervening variables introduced into his or her attitudes. Yet, editors are gleaned from the ranks of the reporters. Recall that the function of a manager is to work through others to achieve a predetermined goal. Argyris says, "Seventy-four percent of my respondents said that groups were poor places to explore new ideas and think out loud; they felt that groups discussed only unimportant issues."[33] He further indicated that often reporters' opinions were based on valid observation. Aggressive individuals spoke the most at editorial meetings, but had little influence because of ineffective style, that is, they talked too much. Reserved people kept to themselves. The result was that a stalemate inclining toward indifference was produced as individual uniqueness did not surface. Moreover, highly competitive persons tend to over-respect authority. The respondents felt the meetings were most effective when well disciplined by a strong leader who had already arrived at his conclusions before convening the meeting. Ninety-four percent of the respondents registered this attitude. One person pointed out: "'Most of the executives really want participation until we disagree with them.'"[34] The situation is further complicated by factors Hersey labels "leadership personality" and "leadership style." Leadership personality refers to the leaders' perception of self, and how he or she comes across to others, as well as perceptions of those others. Leadership style is the leader's behavior as perceived by others; this does not involve self-perception. If there is a conflict or inconsistency between style and self-perception, behavioral incongruities may result. A leader may not be conscious of how he is perceived by subordinates. Hersey and Blanchard explain:

> It is unknown to the leader either because followers have been unwilling to share feedback with or communication ('level') to that leader on how he or she is coming across; or it may be that the data are there in terms of verbal and nonverbal behavior, but the leader is not able or does not care to 'see' them.[35]

At different times, all the above variations took place within the living system. The subordinates were thus placed in a double bind. They either were at fault with themselves if they withheld protest or faulted by the editor for speaking out against implied stricture. Argyris states that since "the living system contained a strong norm that one should not discuss such issues openly, the subordinates felt little freedom to discuss the dilemma."[36]

The situation was no better concerning horizontal communication. A reporter could not take a grievance directly across departmental lines. If a reporter was unhappy with the copy editor, he had to register his complaint with the editor who, in turn, informed the copy editor. This created tensions between a reporter and the copy editor, who felt he was victimized.

Perhaps a realistic approach to the problem would be to educate the editor to these kinds of problems through intervention theory, applying situational leadership insights. One might attempt to not only alter the leadership style to the situation, but the situation to the leadership personality. Argyris did not succeed in attaining a commitment to free choice to obtain valid information through any editor's internal commitment. He was stymied at a higher level: "As one executive put it, 'Good management and good organization begin with people who are tops, and in my opinion it practically ends there.'"[37] This executive, although extreme, affects an implied consensus among management at the *Planet*. They were fixated within theory X assumptions about static power, tradition, and authority. *The Daily Planet's* development was arrested at what Argyris concluded to be a dysfunctional level, which almost certainly would entail further cycles of crisis. Fixation occurs, according to Hersey, when a pattern of behavior is displayed repeatedly even though it's shown to be ineffective. Both Argyris and Hersey incorporate Kurt Lewin's tripartite change process. There is difference between them, however. Situational leadership assumes change as a goal: knowledge, attitudinal, behavioral, and organizational changes. Intervention theory assumes commitments to valid information, free choice, and internalization of valid information, and free choice. Change is auxiliary to these three commitments. According to Hersey, "Any change effect begins with the identification of problem(s)."[38] "*Change efforts involve attempting to reduce discrepancies between what is real (actual) and the ideal.*"[39] There is an ethical assumption explicit in Argyris which, while laudable, complicates the situation. If the organization does not agree to the three commitment tasks, by definition, change cannot be attempted, in principle or in practice. Part of the rationale for the commitments is to present the contradictions within the living system and individuals with undeniable clarity. Lewin's process of change calls for the unfreezing of attitudes, values, and practices; the effecting of change itself and the refreezing of the person's or system's value system to insure durability. Intervention theory rests on the dictum that the individuals must perceive discrepancies between professed beliefs and behavior to unfreeze behavior. Only through freely choosing to internalize valid information can intervention therapy work. "The process of confirming must be uncontaminated by the influences of others, so that the individual cannot find a way of assigning the responsibility for his incompetent behavior to someone else,"[40] Argyris says.

Argyris spent three years diagnosing *The Daily Planet*. Actually, the interviews and observations (diagnosis in the strict sense) were completed in two years. The third year was dedicated to actual intervention attempts. Situational leadership theory diagnosis entails, write Hersey and Blanchard:

> [T]echniques for asking the right questions, sensing the environment of the organization, establishing effective patterns of observation and data collection, and developing ways to process and interpret data. In diagnosing for change, managers should attempt to find out: (a) what is actually happening now in a particular situation; (b) what is *likely* to be happening in the future if no change effort is made; (c) what would people ideally like to be happening in this situation; and (d) what are the blocks or restraints stopping movement from the actual to the ideal.[41]

Inherent in this prescription for diagnosis is another variance between Argyris and Hersey. For Hersey, the role of diagnostician is performed by the manager himself. Situational leadership does not necessitate an outside consultant. Intervention theory formally requires an outside interventionist who, by requiring the three task commitments, safeguards his own independence from the living system. Curiously, another system is formed for treating the living system, which is itself unaffected by direct contact from the interventionist. Argyris' ethics appear to damage his logic. If, in fact, the interventionist does intervene, even if only to point out contradiction, he or she has induced a difference into the system which the members may act upon. If they do act upon information provided by the interventionist, has not the interventionist altered the system? Information is existential: It is real in that it can make a difference. I point out this inconsistency not to disparage Argyris, but to criticize an unnecessary complication within his practice. After all, his concern is that members of the system take responsibility for their actions and, hence, the consequences of self-actualization. Self-awareness is the concept which provides means for change; realization of the difference lies between what one says one does and how one actually behaves.

Argyris held a seminar for the top executives of the *Planet*. The executives' overriding concern for this meeting was that no one get hurt. By expressing this concern to the interventionist, executives were really saying that ultimate responsibility for the intervention process was to be the interventionist's. Argyris' fear was confirmed. The executives attempted to dodge self-awareness and, therefore, their share of the blame for failures in the living system. The living system referred to its internal structure as a justification for perpetuation. The open system strives for responsibility and increased confidence through widened communication capacities. However, there were three areas of discrepancy between client and interventionist: (a) the interventionist had to emphasize the importance of opening-up and risk-taking; (b) the client system tended to manifest unawareness of responsibility for systemic ineffectiveness; and (c) management attempted to define theory X leadership as effective. The seminar was an attempt to open up the top executives and concentrate on relationships this brought about. Reciprocal needs were brought to bear on the situation. Guest, Hersey, and Blanchard write:

> McGregor emphasizes that the power of a manager does not just come from position or from consent by subordinates... but by a *collaborative process of goal attainment.* Success may be achieved when the job requirements of leaders and followers are set by the *situation.*[42]

Influence must be generated vertically, up and down, as well as horizontally, interdepartmentally (e.g., news/editorial). By getting all levels involved in decision making and goal setting, one can convert restraining forces into driving forces. The interventionist or the manager must demand the leeway to act to reduce top-down pressure and restraining forces, that is, hygiene factors active in preventing accomplishment of need fulfillment. One can see the level of dogmatism at work from a few short exemplary dialogues from the seminar (X = Argyris):

A: I can't believe there isn't any risk-taking in our meetings.[43]

But even the most vociferous would not agree to playing back portions of the tape. I would not press them to do so.[44]

A: Everything you say is true. Do they realize the pressure we're under?

C: That's true—all of us are under pressure. Sometimes we get too preoccupied with a deadline that we don't look at the human problems.

A: Are we side tracking your presentation?...Well, do they want us to ask if the elevators should be painted blue, or do they want us to tell them to do it?

X: On unimportant issues, like the color of elevators tell them. On important, long-range policy issues, many want to be more involved.[45]

Later:

X: I gave an example where, in order to save face, management created two bosses for a particular group.

P: Yes, we did that and it was wrong.

X: But as far as I can see, you're still doing it.

P: Yes, you're right. It won't be easy to change.

E: But why is this wrong? Doesn't it show our organization has a heart?

F: Well, I can give you several examples of how this has harmed us, especially with our better young people. They believe we prefer to reward dead wood.

D: Frankly, I feel we also destroy people we think we're helping. They know that their jobs are meaningless.

E: I think a certain amount of subterfuge works because people like it.

X: If it does, I would say that could be a sign of sickness in the system.[46]

Later:

A: Let's suppose that we all now agree with the essentials of this report. I know I do. What do we do? One of the implications is that we should become more open. A lot of us have found that not being candid works well.

B: Yes, I have difficulty with the same question.

C: But we may think it works well, because a lot of information is kept from us.[47]

Dogmatism in a system is a qualitative measure by which one can gauge how open or closed a system or subset is at a given time. Dogmatism refers to one's capacity to deal with innovation; highly dogmatic individuals cannot deal well with innovation. Thus, Argyris strives to point out the relatively high level of dogmatism at work within the above dialogues. A sufficiently high level of dogmatism can lead to an entropic situation, a lack of energy, and calcification. One detects a sense of helplessness, a denial of difficulties, and a projection on to others of tacit duplicity.

Some time after the executive seminar, Argyris attempted to hold a seminar for the news department. He was informed kindly but in no uncertain terms that the choice made by those in the news department was not to internalize a commitment to valid information at that time. The head of the news department, R., had suggested the seminar; he approached Argyris full of enthusiasm. However, many in the news department told Argyris privately they did not believe that R. was actually in favor of the project. They felt the president of the *Planet* had pressured R. into suggesting it. No evidence pro or con was entered into the study. It was clear, though, that generally the president had ultimate control. One assumes that if he was in favor of the seminar it would probably have taken place. This is conjecture. This setback marked the termination of the intervention project.

Argyris predicted three consequences for the *Planet*: "They are: (1) its activities become compulsive and uncorrectable; (2) managerial innovation will come to be seen as deviant activity and will be inhibited; and (3) conflict and fear will be magnified."[48] He also believed the system provided oblique ways for reducing tensions. These means could only darken participants' needs to reexamine the living system.

I agree with Fred Fiedler's lack of optimism for basic structural altering of an organization, especially one as mired in tradition, ponderous reputation, size, complexity, time/space constraints, authoritarian direction and classic organizational structure as *The Daily Planet*. After all Fiedler writes:

A person's leadership style reflects the individual's basic motivational and need structure. At best it takes one, two, or three years of intensive psychotherapy to effect lasting changes in personality structure. It is difficult to see how we can change in more than a few cases an equally important set of core values in a few hours of lectures and role playing or even in the course of a more intensive training program of one or two weeks.[49]

Argyris did spend three years evaluating the *Planet*. But, he held only one seminar, although it ran for several days; he worked at the study during his free-time or at the convenience of the Planet. Argyris never played back any of the tapes for people to hear their contradictions or the psychological quagmires sucking in the vitality of the people at the *Planet*. It was a breeding ground for mistrust. "This organization is one of the most calculating living systems that I've ever been in,"[50] Argyris reports.

We have seen that high task/low relationship is about the worst situation in which highly intelligent, well-trained, aggressive professionals could find themselves. Management's assumptions about the nature of its subordinates are largely based on projections imbued with personality traits of persons not in control over their own hierarchy of needs. They tend to underestimate peers as well as subordinates because of interpretations made according to self-sealing meanings. The social needs and self-esteem needs of most remain unfulfilled. Self-actualization is not even spoken about. The president of the *Planet* was viewed by subordinates as concerned for profit over any other single consideration. People were intensely confused about their true loyalties. Fear, anxiety, hypocrisy, competitiveness, low trust, and high conformity were hygiene factors which disallowed satisfaction of the needs which motivate people.

Any changes that occurred at the *Planet* were short-lived. The executive group did not display the commitment necessary to generate new management skills or unfreeze established values in lieu of building a more vital communication organization through a new set of values. Argyris does feel that a newspaper that cannot generate valid information within its internal structure cannot realistically provide valid information about world events for our culture. This is the rub. *The Daily Planet* does an excellent job of presenting the news. To say it performs excellently, however, is not to assert it performs optimally.

Finally, I really question Argyris' methodology. If one is going to intervene, then I feel one should do just that and not hedge the bet. His motives and ethics are of the highest stripe; his effectiveness is not. He failed totally. This is not to say Hersey or anyone else could have succeeded where Argyris failed, but to constitutionally program frailty into one's system seems of questionable wisdom. Change should be a prime concern or else there is no reason for an interventionist's presence. A concern with change does not necessarily precipitate a leaning toward instability.

Argyris admits: "And perhaps more progress could have been made if I had worked at the organization full-time, attended more meetings, and continually exposed inconsistencies and organizational dilem-

mas."[51] Further, "Behavioral science intervention theory may be seriously limited in what it can do for client systems that cannot or do not want
to be helped."[52]

One must Agree.

MANAGEMENT OF THE KINGDOM AND THE POWER

It is now known with certainty that *The Daily Planet* is the *New York
Times*,[53] and that behind the helm stood Punch Sulzberger. Further, the
account of the *Times* throughout the 1960s and 1970s was one of turmoil,
upheaval, conflict, and drastic change. The hypothesis here is that internal relationships within the *New York Times* indeed affected the quality
of the newspaper. But clearly, external affairs with their extensive ramifications fused with and influenced the internal relations. The Ellsberg
affair and Watergate provide profound examples of this interchange.
One cannot dissect neatly activities of upheaval into cause and effect,
internal-external, or effort and goal. As Sulzberger comments, "It is
screamingly difficult to make any real change on this paper. It's equally
hard to make a mistake . . . I really think that I could take all the brass
away and the paper would still come out the next day and no one would
know how or why."[54]

While Sulzberger may be right, the brass has never been
removed nor the traditions eliminated. Gay Talese's account of the *New
York Times* provides vivid insight into the history and internal workings
of the great paper. *The Kingdom and the Power* carries the reader through
the *Times'* birth with Adolph Ochs through the 1960s and the schism
between two rival factions—New York and Washington.

One sees through *The Kingdom and the Power* that tradition and
formalism provide the bedrock upon which the *Times* stands. For
instance, a reporter's newsroom seating assignment identifies his comparative importance. Young, general-assignment reporters sit near the
back of the newsroom, near the sports department. As the reporter progresses from obscurity to better, more responsible beats, he or she moves
closer and closer to the front of the room. Thus, it appears glaringly
apparent that equality and cooperation do not form part of the seating
considerations. Talese recounts this story:

> There was one bright reporter who, after being told that he would
> help cover the labor beat, cleaned out his desk near the back of
> the room and moved up five rows into an empty deck vacated by
> one of the labor reporters who had quit. The recognition of the
> new occupant a few days later by an assistant editor resulted in a

reappraisal of the younger reporter's assets, and within a day he was back at his old desk, and within a year or so he was out of the newspaper business altogether.[55]

Motivation, according to theory X, is achieved through force, fear, power, and authority.

At the other end of the spectrum, editors at the *Times* were expected to wield their power covertly—modestly. The shape of power thus grew more amorphous at the higher levels of management. Talese points out that the price for promotion is individuality, the very uniqueness which, through theory Y, is fostered and nurtured. Reporters rarely know exactly who pulled what string. So with more power, responsibility, higher wages, and increased prestige went a concomitant modesty, caution, and loss of freedom. Talese refers to power at the *Times* as vaporous; indirection heralded major policy decisions so that at times it seemed "nobody really did anything."[56] Consequently, reporters relied solely on rumors, small significant alterations and, of course, effects. The managing editor, Turner Catledge, periodically scanned the vast newsroom through binoculars observing many reporters he had absolutely no familiarity with; he couldn't even see everyone at a single sweep. Stories were assigned according to the seating arrangement. Each morning, stories were assigned—the best to those occupying the front rows, the incidental to those at the back of the room.

Reporters whose style of writing became too noticeable, thereby insured their positions of stability near the rear. Talese writes:

> Younger reporters who wrote with style were never completely trusted by the city editor and his associates, the assumption being that 'writers' would compromise the facts in the interest of better literature. Such writers therefore were usually assigned to cover weather or parades or the Bronx Zoo and circus . . . .[57]

The young Timesman gained a clear perspective: he worked within a "fact factory," and he was instantaneously and completely replaceable. Talese describes the editors' communicating without contact; through a microphone and by memo the reporter often received instructions. Control and rigidity defeated the flow of information among the newsmen. A reporter from the Washington bureau sent Tom Wicker, bureau chief, this comment:

> We can make mistakes down here, and when we do, we should be hauled up short. But what takes the sap out of a reporter who is doing his level best to make the Washington report worthy of his idea of The Times is that all-too-apparent lack of confidence . . . .[58]

This comment was delivered before the reporter quit in response to treatment he received by the New York editors, to their insensitivity and routinely heavy-handed copy editing. It has been earlier noted that management is 90% communication. A win-lose strategy, and the high task-low relationship behavior of the *Times'* editors is evidenced by their practices. Such concerns as Maslow's hierarchy of needs is nowhere recognized by those supervising the reporters. Hygiene factors are in clear unabashed sight. Motivation must be drawn from the reporter's inner fortitude, while the opportunity for reinforcement appears unreal, disregarded at even the most basic levels.

Shortly after his appointment to assistant managing editor, Theodore Bernstein took it upon himself to produce an inner-house organ, *Winners and Sinners*, wherein one could find recorded for posterity any mistake he might wish to forget. Not content to include only the daily staff, Bernstein lent his efforts to Lester Markel's Sunday edition, also. Markel himself had the innate ability to transmit tension by walking into a room. "He had merely to enter, to stand in the aisle and look around for a few moments, and it was like a hot blazing sun curling caterpillars, legs tucking inward, bodies slowly bending . . .,"[59] says Talese. Markel engendered a love-hate relationship with his staff, capable of convincing those under him that they continually failed him. He didn't need Bernstein's aid. It was said the tension crept into the elevator as it passed Markel's department on the eighth floor. One of the maxims Bernstein announced stated that a single sentence should contain only a single idea. Markel commented in a memo.

"Mr. Bernstein: I have read with great interest your special edition on the short sentence—or rather—I have read your edition of Winners & Sinners. It is a special edition. It interests me. No end."[60] This exemplifies the atmosphere provided by the *Times* to foster confidence through "constructive criticism." In a battle with the chief foreign correspondent and indirectly with Catledge, Markel employed correspondent Greg MacGregor to check the game. Catledge proclaimed that foreign correspondents would channel their copy through the foreign-news editor. This was an innovation. MacGregor previously had sent his photos for the Sunday edition directly to Markel until he received a cable professing confusion from the foreign-news editor, Manny Freedman, about this practice. Confused, MacGregor found out through a reporter for the *Chicago Daily News* that the foreign-news editor was MacGregor's boss and had been for years. Whereupon MacGregor stopped sending photos to Markel. Markel questioned MacGregor about the disruption. MacGregor responded there was a reason but that he did not want to discuss it. Markel pressed him asking, "'Do you think you're working for Manny Freedman or for the *New York Times*?'"[61] Markel told

MacGregor not to worry, that he would speak with Freedman personally. But first, Markel went to Sulzberger. Freedman never forgave MacGregor for Markel's behavior. As events eroded the relationship, MacGregor resigned from the *Times*, caught inextricably in a web of management's device.

In January 1956, an editorial appeared in the *Times*:

> And our faith is strong that long after Senator Eastland and his present subcommittee are forgotten . . . long after all that was known as McCarthyism is a dim, unwelcome memory, long after the last Congressional committee has learned that it cannot tamper successfully with a free press, *The New York Times* will be speaking for the men who make it . . .[62]

However, not wanting a single communist on the payroll, Sulzberger told his employees to cooperate with the subcommittee and advised them not to take the Fifth Amendment! One copyreader refused to cooperate and invoked the Fifth. Sulzberger fired him. Talese recalls that the publisher made many speeches about freedom of the press, but, when a strike was called, the *New York Times* banned the press from its business meetings. If questioned on the strike, they would not comment.

When a news editor proposed the budget for the new Western edition, Catledge proclaimed his support. Catledge, "Look, if this is what you absolutely think we'll need, then let's go and get it."[63] At the meeting the general manager told them to cut the budget by $25,000. Catledge advised the general manager that he himself had checked the figures, and they were correct. The general manager lost his temper.

> 'I'm very busy,' he snapped, and would not discuss the matter further. Catledge turned and left Bradford's [the G.M.] office. 'Well,' the editor said in the corridor, walking with Catledge toward the elevator, 'What do I do now?' Catledge's face was red with anger and humiliation, and he glared at the editor, saying, 'Do what he says!'[64]

When Punch Sulzberger took over the paper from his predecessor, the first thing he did was to shut down the Western edition. This was the beginning of his massive effort to consolidate power in the New York office. Catledge was named executive editor, subsuming all editorial departments under his authority. The attempt aimed at placing within a monolithic structure that which had previously allowed plurality and diverse attitudes and philosophies. Now, went Sulzberger's plan, the *Times* would speak with one voice: the voice of authority. The Sunday editor, the Washington bureau, the New York newsroom, as well as all foreign bureaus would answer to Catledge. With the coming of the computer age and the advances in electronic communications, there was no longer a need for strong bureau chiefs. New York could instantly beam its orders to Timesmen and women all over the world. Editors could be turned into clerks. Talese indicates that the *Times'* own coverage of its internal shifts and machinations was reported in the paper in such vague terms, so lacking interpretation, that a reader would have no clues as to the significance of this managerial *coup d'état*.

"It was said that Sulzberger liked the chain-of-command management style of the Marine Corps, a single line of authority from top to bottom."[65] This approach, while ideally suited for an organization designed to seek and destroy, is not optimal for the management of an organization whose expressed purpose is to give news impartially without fear or favor. According to leadership theory, dialogue forms a necessary component of effective management. Obviously, Sulzberger's attempt was to swing the decision-making process toward one directional flow, to simplify what was structurally complex.

Salisbury argues [66] that Argyris' mistake lay in the consideration that profits were the most important—more important than editorial integrity. Salisbury's reading of *Behind the Front Page* is incorrect. He writes, "But few in the newspaper profession shared Argyris' conclusion that 'affirmative feedback' was more important than the First Amendment to the U.S. Constitution which guarantees the freedom of the press."[67] That is not Argyris' conclusion. His argument is that within the attempt to manage highly intelligent, aggressive men and women, one must take into account their needs as human beings as well as journalists, noting their maturity levels. To treat everyone from a distance is a mistake. Further, if one's management is faulty, the quality of the product will suffer. The argument has nothing to do with freedom of the press recognized within the First Amendment, or First Amendment considerations as to whether the quality of the product is so far below acceptable standards that the people's right to know is impaired. Argyris argues that while this could happen, the *New York Times* is an excellent newspaper.

Moreover, one must conclude that, according to the bottom line—profits—of which Salisbury speaks, the *New York Times* was managed excellently. The paper by 1966 had become more cost effective. In 1966, there was a net profit of more than $9 million, up more than $5 million from 1965. Ad rates climbed 8%.[68] Advertising, circulation, and production departments were consolidated.

The massive consolidations necessitated many changes in personnel which in turn lowered morale. Aware of this decline, Sulzberger brought in an inter-office public relations adviser, Granger Blair, to facilitate changes and improve morale. But the problems ran deeper than instituting higher wages and profit-sharing for the editors.

Events hit the fan when the New York office attempted to bring the Washington bureau under its control. They coexisted, Washington as its own entity, subordinate to, yet independent of, New York. Although a certain amount of hostility flared time and again; the flames were fed from constant battle between reporters, copy-editors, and editors, not among editors themselves. For example, if a Washington reporter had a problem with his copy and New York's handling of it, the reporter formally channeled his after-the-fact complaints to the Washington bureau chief who sent it to the managing editor in New York; he in turn sent it down the many levels in New York from national news editor to copy-desk, virtually a dead issue.

Sulzberger intended to appoint a New York man as head of the Washington bureau. This had never been done. Always, the Washington bureau chose its own chief. James Reston, for example, appointed Tom Wicker. Catledge and Rosenthal decided to replace Wicker with James Greenfield, a man not only from the New York office but with only seven months on the *Times*. Sulzberger approved the choice and traveled to Washington to explain—after the fact—his decision to Reston and Wicker. Upon his arrival, Sulzberger invited both Reston and Wicker to dinner. Reston declined the invitation. Wicker appeared tense and nervous throughout the dinner. He was so upset he stayed up all night, too agitated to retire. When the next morning arrived, Wicker told Sulzberger that he wanted to announce his resignation. Sulzberger told him not to. At this point, a total breakdown in management had occurred, the degree undetected by the New York office.

Greenfield had already presumed the job was his. He had accepted congratulations informally yet surely. He even told a *Newsweek* reporter he had the position. Reston at this time flew to New York. Talese is not clear as to the exact transpiring of events, but assumes the three top Washington editors threatened resignation over Greenfield's appointment because shortly after their arrival at the *Times*, Sulzberger reversed his decision. The results: Greenfield, betrayed, quit; the executive editor, Catledge, crushed, was eventually replaced by Reston. The New York leadership, through employing theory X, self-destructed. "The executive leadership in the News department had been shattered by the recent Washington-New York confrontation, and Sulzberger felt compelled to replace his old friend and advisor, Turner Catledge."[69]

Reston, in his new position as executive editor, was expected to reconcile the differences brought about through covert management practice. Salisbury writes of the situation, "There was no way, I felt, in which Reston could regain command of the situation."[70] He did not.

Rosenthal took over in 1969. This was the situation Argyris encountered. People walking on eggs. Nor was Argyris aware that Ellsberg was making his transactions with the *Times* during this most difficult period. Win-lose dynamics were taking place for the *Times* externally as well as internally, but Argyris was not privy to this information.

FRAMING EL SALVADOR

The *New York Times* has not constructed a monolithic framework by which it reports events in El Salvador, publishing *only* that which meets editorial standards set by authorities, but it does adhere to political parameters established in Washington, and those policies influence the nature of news coverage. Elite interests in Washington and San Salvador make available to the press news they think is fit for consumption. Yet, the *Times* occasionally will publish stories causing consternation at the State Department. But most often, the *Times* relies on government made maps and seeks out official sources and officially sanctioned leads. Some areas are restricted and some closed during certain seasons.

Among news workers, some disagreement exists over what news is fit to print. But be forewarned that if any reporter violates State Department policy boundaries in a significant manner, there are journalists eager to blow the whistle on the miscreant. This sort of self-inflicted media bashing does not happen often, largely because reporters are trained to be responsible and can be trusted not to go into restricted areas or to interview questionable sources. In spite of all precautions, disasters do occur. Things happen.

The reporting of a disaster, like the murder of six Jesuit priests, their cook and her daughter by members of the Salvadoran military, will reflect the story in the light of the U.S. foreign policy disaster it is. Such news will be reported as a catastrophe; much will be made about how, despite the efforts of the democratic regime, tragedy strikes. I contend that in covering El Salvador, reporting follows shifts in U.S. foreign policy. Salvadoran elites promote the idea that their government is a reform minded, humane institution, which, while plagued by isolated, errant sociopaths and saddled with a ponderous, inefficient bureaucracy, is nonetheless a healthy, stable democracy that champions the interests of the Salvadoran people and remains a safe place for continued stable investment. Also U.S. elites present the image of a struggling, tentative democracy ravaged, torn, and bleeding, pressured from the fascist fringe on the right and threatened by the Marxist guerrillas from the left. Overall, I contend, the *New York Times* legitimates these views by the way it frames events in El Salvador.[71]

As with any industry, the news industry employs managers, and they come equipped to direct policy according to certain strategies. The installation of Abe Rosenthal as managing editor marked a conservative change in the editorial course for the *New York Times*. The self-proclaimed "bleeding heart conservative" fit in especially nicely with both Carter and Reagan administration policies in El Salvador, shaping, nurturing, socializing reporters on their way to upper echelon positions, while cutting back, weaning, alienating reporters who regularly questioned the wisdom or veracity of American policies. Even proven journalists had to watch out not to cross too far over the line. For instance, Rosenthal referred to Pulitzer-prize winner Sydney Schanberg (killing fields of Cambodia) as "St. Francis"[72] for his liberal, critical views concerning the *Times'* prodevelopment positions. Falling into disfavor, his column was canceled.

Another journalist, Raymond Bonner, suffered a similar fate for his reporting in El Salvador. Bonner is a Stanford educated lawyer turned freelance journalist who landed a job with the *Times* in 1981. Rosenthal pulled Bonner out of El Salvador in August 1982 and achieved his resignation by July 4, 1984. "It's hard to write against the prevailing wisdom in Washington, no matter who is in power,"[73] says Bonner. "The real problem was that my reporting didn't fit the tenor of the times, or the *Times* under Abe Rosenthal."[74] As managing editor, Rosenthal believed his job entailed keeping the paper politically "non-discernable." At the *Times* that meant, "I had to watch out for drifts left of center, very rarely right."[75] Rosenthal claims that he recalled Bonner because he did not know how to be a correspondent, which in this case implies that he did not understand the danger, professionally, of bucking the State Department policy line. In 1982, Jose Napoleon Duarte was elected president of El Salvador; Bonner questioned the integrity of the U.S.-backed election process. This, in effect, struck at the heart of American policy in El Salvador because the Carter, Reagan, and Bush administrations' justification of aid to the country rested on selling it as a democracy to the American public. Rosenthal declared, "I don't want to see any more of Bonner's pieces on electoral fraud."[76] Bonner took a leave of absence from the paper to write a book on American policy in El Salvador titled *Weakness and Deceit*. It was published by The Times Book Company, which ran a promotional ad campaign for the book. In the context of the powerful criticisms of Bonner's reporting by the mighty in government as well as in the conservative press, combined with Bonner's investigative writing on the nature of Salvadoran society, one ad read in part, "now we know Ray Bonner is telling the truth," that his was the "true story." Max Frankel, currently executive editor of the *Times*, wrote a memo to Times Books, complaining that the ad implied that the *Times'* (essentially the official government) view of the events in El Salvador, then, was not the truth.[77] Frankel was correct, it was not, and the ad was changed.

Since 1979, the Carter, Reagan, and Bush administrations shared two propositions: The violence in El Salvador is due to rabid extremists of both the right and left, with everyone else consequently suffering, and that only U.S.-sanctioned elections will guarantee the maintenance of democracy as exercised by a decent, honest, honorable government, a government which has, since it is freely elected, the people's interests at heart. These two propositions, I argue, have been faithfully reflected in the reporting of the *New York Times*.

Elections are not the issue. Three out of four Salvadoran peasant children suffer malnutrition, and diarrhea is the leading cause of death. Ninety percent of the Salvadoran population does not have safe drinking water. One in five of the over 5 million people has fled the country altogether.[78] Seventy-five thousand people had been killed as of March 1991.[79] As expressed in a *Times* editorial, "What is a conscientious American to think?"[80] I would like to suggest that ethical coverage of El Salvador might come to recognize that elections are not the issue. Values are the issue.

A foreign service officer working in El Salvador during both the Carter and Reagan presidencies tells Bonner that it is his opinion that the government, at least since Vietnam, has been persistently attempting to sell the American public on some issue or other. "Why not just tell the American people the truth?" he asks a reporter for the most often cited news medium in the U.S. "We're not used car salesmen for chrissake. Tell them what's happening and let them decide."[81] Bonner acknowledges that at first he accepted the government sponsored official version depicting a freely elected, moderate Salvadoran government trapped between the extreme right and left. Not only did he support it, but most editorial writers and reporters believed the Carter and Reagan officials. Even recognizing that the military has been in control of the government since 1931, when it massacred 32,000 peasants, journalists in general, and from the *Times* in particular, have accepted this position. Why? There are many factors, ranging from the socialization process and management practices discussed earlier to relying almost exclusively on those who create the policies as sources. Whatever the particular tactics employed (toward the media structurally, on the consciousness of individual journalists, or by the organization of facts in a story used to sculpt information), one can detect a patterned agenda by which certain officially sanctioned versions of reality are offered to the public, sometimes in the face of glaringly contradictory evidence. We see that the practice of objective reporting easily leads to the dangerous pitfall of accepting whatever officials and experts design, and, with Edward Herman and Noam Chomsky,[82] I conclude that often times the discourse effected by the media is developed within the executive branch of the federal government.

However, it is my opinion that we must urge the recognition, often underplayed by both Chomsky and critical theory in general, that voices of difference do matter. It is of course true that systems are pervasive, but they are not impermeable, which Bonner's work illustrates. Even though Bonner's dedication to independent thinking, honesty, and accuracy cost him a career at the *Times*, he did get his version out. The New York Times Company did, after all, publish his book—even if it reviewed it negatively. His work has spurred on others, albeit a minority, in the mainstream press.

Essential for our description and analysis of the *Times'* coverage of El Salvador is, what sort of government *really* runs the country? Is it at all consonant with its American mainstream media portrayal? The 1989 presidential campaign chant for the Nationalist Republican Alliance (Arena) went, "Christiani to the presidency, d'Aubuisson to power." Roberto d'Aubuisson was president for life of the Arena party. Lindsay Gruson, while acknowledging that Arena had been linked to some of the "country's worst human rights abuses and assassinations," claims in a preelection piece that it is unclear who has control over Arena. Gruson writes, "Mr. Cristiani says that he and Mr. d'Aubuisson have 'had our differences of opinion in the past' but that they remain 'good friends'." Gruson continues on saying that Cristiani declines to criticize d'Aubuisson for his ties to death squads, and that he defends d'Aubuisson whenever the latter is linked to "growing violence."[83]

Two days before the March 19 election, Gruson's story emphasizes an army officer's opinion that the liberal Convergence party candidate has a right to run. "The major's tolerance of his enemy's political allies is a sign of the tentative progress in the American-backed effort to remove the army, *probably* the most powerful single institution in El Salvador, from *direct* involvement in politics."[84] Slowly, Gruson says, the country is beginning to tolerate dissent. Gruson's lead for this story merits attention. In order to frame the relative, newly won "tolerance," Gruson begins by reporting that in 1981, before the 1982 elections, the army put out a death list and bounty for 138 "leftists." That no such death list circulated in March 1989, one supposes illustrates progress. Why else would Gruson lead a news story with an 8-year-old incident? Gruson further down reports a "thinly veiled death threat against poll takers," broadcast by the rebels. He does not offer any more specifics. Prior to this 1989 story, the *Times* failed to report the issuance of the army death list. It was not reported at the time it occurred because, as Herman suggests, this would have raised doubts about the earlier elections, but it could be used to highlight the comparable openness of the 1989 election.[85]

While pointing out that Arena had in the past been tied to death squads and human rights abuses, and had been formed as a paramilitary organization by d'Aubuisson, Gruson writes after the Arena victory, "Mr. Christiani took pains . . . to project an image of moderation and conciliation for himself and his party. . . ." Christiani went on, Gruson reports, to compare Arena to the U.S. Republican party with its conservatives, moderates, and liberals, that the party's poor image was a product of "misleading news reports."[86] That June, Gruson's report reflects the image of Christiani as a moderate, calling for negotiations with the guerrillas, to work for human rights, and to improve education. "'The only privileged people in our society will be the very poor,' he said. . . ." Gruson writes that at this point Arena and the government seem to be separate entities, with most cabinet members being "American trained technocrats," however, allies of d'Aubuisson had been appointed "to key ministries overseeing security matters. . . ."[87]

One sees a similarity between the classic good cop-bad cop and the structure of this news story. But it is more complicated than that. American policy suggests an attempt to legitimize the pragmatic Christiani by contrasting him with extremists.[88] Let's look at a security matter, since that is d'Aubuisson's province. On June 13, Vice President Quayle met with d'Aubuisson, and let him know in no uncertain terms, Robert Pear reports, not to "embarrass" Cristiani. Pear says, "the Vice President wanted to give him a 'lecture' about the need to respect human rights and to end political violence." In the fourth and fifth paragraphs, Pear affords two sentences to the "arrest" of a prominent labor leader whom the government accused of being involved in an attack on an army barracks. He was arrested, Pear notes, "just a few hours after he received a visa to visit the United States, where he was to meet with several members of Congress."[89] At roughly the same time Quayle is lecturing d'Aubuisson, government security forces are torturing labor leader Jose Mazariego.

Dennis Bernstein writes that there was no indication that Pear attempted to find out any further information concerning Mazariego's fate beyond his arrest. He made no attempt to contact his family, the union or any rights groups.

> Three days later, says Mazariego, his kidnapers finally identified themselves as Treasury police and brought him before a judge who ordered his release. Mazariego, a leader of Salvador's telephone workers union, came to the U.S. a week later bearing the bruises and scars of several days of torture.[90]

Upon arriving in Washington, Mazariego told a *Newsday* reporter that the security forces put his head in a bag of lime and tied it around his head until he passed out. He regained consciousness as the police were pouring acid on his knees. They repeated this torture—capucha—four times. The *New York Times* failed to cover Mazariego's visit to Capitol Hill. Adding insult to severe injury, the *Times*, Bernstein relates, published a piece by Quayle on its op-ed page minimizing Mazariego's torture, dismissing the experience as "'the brief detention and alleged mistreatment of a pro-FMLN (Guerrilla) union leader.'"

Former Ambassador Robert White told Congressmen in 1984, "Arena is a fascist party modeled after the NAZIs and certain revolutionary communist groups." Bonner says in his book that d'Aubuisson himself is one of those American-trained technocrats, attending the U.S. Army school in Panama and the International Police Academy outside Washington, D.C. D'Aubuisson actually told European journalists, "You Germans were very intelligent. You realized that the Jews were responsible for the spread of communism, and you began to kill them." Yet, most reporters write as if the death squads are separate from the government and the government is distinct from the military. Salvadoran Army Captain Ricardo Alejandro Fiallos testified to a Congressional Committee in 1981:

> It is a grievous error to believe that the forces of the extreme right, or the so-called "Death Squads," operate independent of the security forces. The simple truth of the matter is that "Los Escuadrones de la Muerte" are made up of members of the security forces and acts of terrorism credited to these squads such as political assassinations, kidnapings, and indiscriminate murder are, in fact, planned by high-ranking military officers and carried out by members of the security forces. I do not make this statement lightly, but with the full knowledge of the role which the military high command and the directors of the security forces have played in the murders of countless numbers of innocent people in my country.[91]

With all the intelligence and resources of the *New York Times*, isn't this sort of information known to the *Times'* readers? Upon being interviewed for a PBS *Frontline* program, a death-squad member recounted that, in his estimate, the vast majority of death squad members are educated in the U.S. Largely, they are not uneducated illiterates, but members of Salvadoran middle and upper-middle class families, often trained in the United States. Toward the close of 1989, Salvadoran Army intelligence unit case worker Cesar Vielman Joya Martinez came to Capitol Hill after deserting the army. He applied for political asylum in the U.S., after first testifying to the Mexican Academy of Human

Rights and telling his story to members of Congress and the press. He says that as a former death squad member he participated in eight murders and saw the orders for 72 murders altogether. The victims were tortured, beaten, and had their throats cut. Joya Martinez was assigned to a special forces unit of the Salvadoran Army First Infantry Brigade, which receives assistance from the United States.

"The U.S advisers paid the unit's operating expenses, with thousands of dollars in cash and checks, but were careful not to receive any details of the special operations carried out by clandestine death squads,"[92] Joya Martinez says. Not only does he allege U.S. financing and knowledge with a nod and a wink, but he also charges that President Cristiani is familiar with death squad activities, that the Salvadoran military is involved at the highest levels, and that death squad victims are targeted by a military committee whose members include the intelligence unit's section commander as well as the commander of the First Brigade, Colonel Juan Francisco Elena Fuentes.

"There are no death squads here (in the army),"[93] claims Elena Fuentes. But he does charge Joya Martinez with murder and theft, along with desertion. The *New York Times* does not report these events. The pattern that emerges from this discussion, I believe, is damning and substantial. Joya Martinez says, "I see all the people I've killed in my sleep. I just wanted people to know that U.S. money paid for these murders."[94] The effect of the *Times'* ignorance of such atrocities is to exclude them from public perception, to place them outside the horizons of our awareness. The formal, official version of events channeled through the elite media create the agenda for discussion and by so doing shape societal perspectives. The power-knowledge grid energized by channeling only some sorts of information, according to officials, experts, and allies, produces a false reality. Is it an ethical defense to claim, "We just didn't know"? Or that while Joya Martinez's testimony was of legitimate concern to Congress and others, it somehow did not meet the standard of proof for notice by the *New York Times*? Isn't it the most profound obligation of our paper of record to investigate and report so we do know?

The *Times* shows its readers what it considers important to do in both its reporting and editorial positions on El Salvador. A November 16, 1989 editorial reads, "The battlers in this unending war continue to stagger against each other, neither strong enough to deliver a knockout blow, each unwilling to end the contest." It continues, "Salvadorans appear to need no outside prompting for violence." Although the Salvadoran government receives almost $1.5 million per day in aid from the U.S.,[95] and had received over $1 billion as of 1989 in military materials,[96] the *Times* does not recognize this as prompting violence. Analysts agree that without massive military aid the Salvadoran government could not hold, especially in light of the massive guerrilla offensive of November. This implies that the government lacks popular support. But the *Times* does not promote this view. In fact, the *Times'* editorial on the situation on November 30, 1989 leads off, quite consistently with the tenor of its news stories, "An ultra-right Government in El Salvador seems indifferent when its soldiers are accused of murdering priests. Cuba and Nicaragua are believed to arm guerrillas who kill civilians in the name of peace." No existing documentation suggests that the guerrillas murder innocent civilians, but such documentation does exist in connection with the military murder of innocent civilians. The official position of the paper included the number of Salvadoran dead at 61,000. The editorial writers used this incorrect figure on several occasions, so it was not unintentional. Whenever a figure is mentioned in the news stories during this period, 1989-90, it was consistently 70,000. One assumes that the official voice of the paper knows what its reporters write, yet the editorials contradict their own news stories. On December 14, the editorial writers are again busily framing the situation in terms of "President Alfredo Christiani, whose elected regime is besieged by Sandanista-aided insurgents."

The *Times* supported the fiction that Arena, and Cristiani, were reformed democrats struggling to rein in renegade fascists, while defending their freely elected government against Nicaraguan backed, Marxist terrorist revolutionaries. But it seems that the evidence points to the position taken up by another elite paper. The *Los Angeles Times* editorial of March 2, 1989 asks its readers to question whether the White House and State Department are financing a fascist government. Admitting this to be a harsh charge, the editorial points out that the party was founded by violent rightists, backed financially "by a small oligarchy whose selfish rule created the conditions for the rebellion in the first place."[97] The term "fascism" carries strong emotional overtones and ought to be used sparingly and carefully. Fascism refers to a hierarchically organized reactionary movement, one which espouses extreme nationalism personified by a charismatic leader, championing money and property over people and their labor. Fascism appeals strongly to the irrational. The lifetime president of the Arena party, Roberto d'Aubuisson, embodies these characteristics. D'Aubuisson, the *Los Angeles Times* editorial asserts, planned the murder of Archbishop Oscar Arnulfo Romero and plotted to assassinate a U.S. ambassador. The White House and State Department claim they must honor democratic elections, yet we did not give foreign aid to Hitler. The *L.A. Times* recalls, "But when the Nazis first came to power in Germany, it was through elections."

REPORTING ON HUMAN RIGHTS VIOLATIONS

A November 18, 1989 *New York Times* editorial uses much the same information, but structures it quite differently. Admitting that the "dirty, decadelong war" has made outsiders suspicious of the right, the *Times* lists some of the more well-known atrocities, including the Romero murder during mass, the murder and rape of three nuns and a lay missionary, and the assassination of two American labor advisers. This editorial represents the *Times'* official reaction to the execution of six Jesuit priests, a cook and her daughter. But it is different this time, we are told. America is horrified and impatient. And now comes the majestic warning, "Unless President Alfredo Cristiani of El Salvador presses a fast, full and credible search for the killers, *he risks loss of U.S. aid.*"[98] Assumed in this is that those in charge of prosecuting the outrage are innocent of that outrage. In the face of common sense and an eye witness, the *Times* supports the idea that it was not the military behind the murders, or that perhaps it was some renegades under d'Aubuisson. Never mind that Cristiani might also have been under d'Aubuisson.

Considering the situation in El Salvador, it is of interest to look to the reaction of Ambassador William Walker, who maintains that "whoever did this was doing the work of the FMLN."[99]

> I have stood at this platform and said what I think about the presence in this country of mad, pathological killers at both ends of the political spectrum, and we will do everything in our power to bring those elements at the two extremes of the spectrum under control.[100]

Speaking of the rebel offensive, "There's trouble here, just like there's a drug war in Miami. That doesn't mean the basic democratic institutions aren't sound."[101] Besides the murders of the priests and their cook and her 15-year-old daughter, there remain 20,000 other unsolved homicides in a country where the security forces had expanded from 12,000 to over 55,000.[102]

While I argue that there is a pattern to the *Times'* coverage of foreign affairs in El Salvador, it is not a White House publication, and its reporting is sometimes critical, although it closely monitors developments in Washington and relies on sources in the Capital to articulate the field of discussion. Further, we need to remember reportorial and editorial differences. Lindsay Gruson's piece on the killing of the priests reflects thoughtful, incisive, and fair reporting. His lead for the story comes from the eyewitness who described how the victims were dragged from their beds and shot in the head with army issue high powered rifles. The third paragraph quotes Rev. Jose Maria Tojeira, "They were assassinated with lavish barbarity," he says, "they took out their brains."[103] One cleric described this act as a warning to those who think and to those who enable others to think. Gruson cites Bush administration officials, the priests' colleagues, Salvadoran official denial of responsibility, and Americas Watch observation of soldier's surveillance of the university and prior search of the rectory. He offers context and a sensitive narrative, writing that a sign close to the bodies claiming rebel responsibility amounted to "amateurish dissimulation," and pointing out that the day before the killings d'Aubuisson publicly threatened "rebel sympathizers." The casual newspaper reader, however, might get a different take on Gruson's piece. On scanning the page one headlines, he or she would read at the top, "SIX PRIESTS KILLED IN A CAMPUS RAID IN EL SALVADOR," under which, "ASSAILANTS IN UNIFORMS," and beneath that, "Government Denies a Role and Hints at Rebel Plot—Inquiry Is Promised." The message constructed by the copy editor, who writes the headlines, is quite different than what Gruson wrote.

Chris Norton reports at least two witnesses said they saw the murderers enter and drag out the priests. His report is more critical of the government per se than Gruson's, who implicitly makes a distinction between the Cristiani government and d'Aubuisson. Treasury officers, Norton writes, searched the Jesuits' quarters the night before, attempting to determine exactly where the priests slept. "Apparently the rooms were covered with fingerprints and it shouldn't be hard to match prints, especially with FBI help."[104] Moreover, Norton expresses a widely held skepticism as to whether the government has the will or the power to pursue evidence leading to the military. On the day after the murders, a First Brigade army sound truck blared, "Ignacio Ellacuria and Martin Baro [two of the priests] have fallen. We will continue killing communists."

As the murder investigation continues, we can see the official Washington version of events resurface in the *Times'* coverage. Gruson's lead on December 11 reads, "President Alfredo Cristiani and officials close to the investigation into the slaying of the six Jesuit priests last month say a woman who linked the army to the killings failed six lie-detector tests."[105] Who are these "officials close to the investigation?" The lie-detector tests were administered by the FBI at their headquarters in Miami where the witness, Lucia Barrera de Cerna, and her family were transferred from the Spanish Embassy in San Salvador for "their own safety," and where she changed "vital elements of her account at least three times."

This is a classic example of objective reporting. Relying on official sources (thus absolving the *Times* and Gruson of ethical or professional responsibility), the *Times* clearly conveys the impression desired by Cristiani and, I believe, the American Embassy that her description of the events "seemed coached." Looking at the lead in the *San Francisco Chronicle* story for the same day, concerning the same issue, written from the same city, "Archbishop Arturo Rivera y Damas accused the U.S. government yesterday of brainwashing Lucia Barrera de Cerna, believed to be the only eyewitness to the killing of six Jesuit priests, their house-keeper and her daughter."[106] It is significant that for the *Times* the incident happened only to the six priests and not to the housekeeper and her daughter. The *Chronicle's* second paragraph quotes Rivera y Damas, "Instead of being protected, as people of the United States Embassy in El Salvador had promised, she was submitted in that country to an authentic brainwashing."

Neither newspaper indulges in inaccurate reporting; both selected phenomena from a horizon by which to present the field of events, by structuring those events according to what we will call an institutional intentionality, a *way of making sense* that is consonant with the pattern of events the institution intends. If one reads the *Times'* piece further, one will find in the middle of the story the quote cited by the *Chronicle* following and reflecting its lead. Conversely, the *Chronicle* story reports the charges of the "sources involved in the investigation" further down in its account. Many of the facts expressed in each story are simply framed differently by one than the other. But the message conveyed by each story is quite different. Whose version do we accept? It depends largely to which story one has access.

The San Francisco Bay Guardian is a weekly with a much smaller circulation than the *San Francisco Chronicle*. Writing in the *Bay Guardian* Chris Norton takes the trouble to describe the background to the situation. He says that the Jesuits claim that an arrangement was arrived at with the U.S. Embassy by which Cerna would be transferred to them, but upon arriving in Miami, the FBI grabbed her to undertake a "risk assessment." Cerna remained in FBI custody for eight days. She underwent "intense and inappropriate" interrogation, according to the president of the U.S. Jesuit Conference. Norton quotes the statement issued by the Jesuit Conference:

> The witness, exhausted, a stranger in a strange land, with very unpleasant experiences of Salvadoran legal and military officials back home, and dreadfully afraid for her four-year-old daughter, finally yielded to the pressure exerted on her and said that an official of the archdiocese of San Salvador suggested she give the testimony she gave.[107]

A director of the Lawyer's Committee for Human Rights interviewed Cerna to determine who was right, the Jesuits or the FBI. Attorney Scott

Greathead, assistant district attorney in New York, found that Cerna's interrogation was "coercive." "It is clear to me that this was an effort to get her to recant what she had said in El Salvador," Greathead says.

Norton provides us with a fascinating example of media manipulation aimed at furthering the perceived interests of the U.S. by the Embassy. Earlier, on December 9, the American and El Salvadoran governments undertook what Norton says was an apparently coordinated attack on the witness' credibility. Cristiani kicked off the strategy by holding a press conference in which he declared Cerna's testimony false. Next, Ambassador Walker called in and briefed "selected journalists off the record;" this is known as background briefing. In other words, Walker became one of those "sources close to the investigation." Here is the conception of the *New York Times* version of the story. Walker declared that Cerna had failed lie detector tests six times and had changed her story three times. The American Ambassador also implied to the reporters that the head of the Catholic Church's human rights office had coached and invented Cerna's testimony.[108]

Father Jose Maria Tojera, provincial for the Society of Jesus in Central America, reports in the *Los Angeles Times*, "Thirteen Green Berets were training those charged with the murders up until 48 hours before the crime."[109] Maj. Eric Buckland told the FBI that then army commander Col. Rene Emilio Ponce (who later became defense minister) had known of the plan to murder the Jesuits two weeks prior to the murders. Buckland later recanted his testimony and was considered "emotionally unstable" and "unreliable."[110]

Coincidentally, on November 17, 1989 the United Nations released two reports on human rights violations. One report accusing Iran of massive human rights abuses was reported in depth by the *Times*; the other criticizing the Salvadoran government for a increased resurgence of torture, rape, and execution of prisoners was not even mentioned by the *Times*.[111] Both reports were carried by the wire services. Chomsky argues that victims of repression at the hands of U.S. allies or "client states" are reported by the *Times* very differently than abuses suffered at the hands of America's enemies, an argument he and Herman document pervasively.[112] Although the *Times* treatment of client states suffers from an institutional bias, it is not without exception. The 1989 General Accounting Office report critical of U.S. Central American policy was duly reported. The authors of the study declared that the U.S. should lower its profile and concentrate more on "supporting Central American peace efforts rather than military solutions." Robert Pear writes, "United states policy had had 'unintended negative consequences,' increasing the power of local military forces at the expense of civilian rulers."[113] Mark Uhlig reports that Americas Watch charged in November 1989 that the Bush administration had covered up abuses by the Salvadoran Army, saying that the armed forces had committed "unspeakable abuses." If Bush

> is in fact powerless to exert any meaningful control over them, the report says, referring to the armed forces, 'then the Bush administration's fiction that the U.S. supports a legitimate government is really no more than a thin veil to cover up its support of a murderous military.[114]

But when Salvadoran Jesuits charge the U.S. with withholding information that could provide insight into the murder of the Jesuits, their housekeeper and her teenage daughter,[115] the *Times* is silent about this, reporting instead that the Salvadoran Army seemed to be carrying out a planned operation and that the Salvadoran justice system was not doing its job in bringing a strong case against the four privates, three lieutenants, and a colonel.[116] Amnesty International found killings by death squads and the military had increased sharply during 1990, more than double than for the same period one year before. "Bodies of victims have been found mutilated, some with their faces completely destroyed and others with signs of having been brutally tortured."[117] The *Times* did not publish anything on the quite graphic report. Representative Joe Moakley issued a report, endorsed by State Department officials and covered by the *Times*, pointing out that the investigation into the killing of the Jesuit priests had come to a "virtual standstill."[118] But on the anniversary of the massacre the Lawyers Committee for Human Rights issued a report pointing "to an explicit coverup by the Salvadoran government and military, the U.S. government and the U.S. Federal Bureau of Investigation."[119] The *Times* failed to run anything on this. It seems an imperfect pattern, but a tendency nonetheless, that when wrongdoing is alleged on the part of the U.S. government, the *Times* fails to report the story. If the malfeasance is placed on the shoulders of the Salvadorans, then the *Times* covers it. But not always. Moakley issued another report, ignored by the *Times*, on January 7, 1991, quoting a Salvadoran government official: "The armed forces wrote the first act of the Jesuits' case by murdering the priests; now, they are writing the final act by controlling the investigation."[120]

What about human rights and the peasant population? Little about the outlying peasant regions of El Salvador is reported by the *Times* and what is often takes the tenor of Uhlig's piece on March 3, 1989. Uhlig begins waxing poetic about the descending darkness over the rugged mountain highlands, allowing the Salvadoran refugees an opportunity to observe "through the cool, thin air, the percussions of aerial bombing just a few miles away in the rocky slopes of Morazon Province in El Salvador."[121] He explains that 13,000 Salvadorans have at last found a refuge from the fighting, but it is a refuge of fear and controversy. Uhlig describes a situation in which the refugees are imprisoned by harsh terrain and the Honduran Army, ruled by "pro-guerrilla Salvadorans who wield almost absolute authority over their fellow refugees." He notes that one sees few young people, as they are conscripted by rebel armies. Paradoxically, Uhlig writes, the repressive atmosphere of these camps can be traced to the successful protection of the refugees from outside harm, particularly the Honduran Army. The piece is organized into five sections. The well-written, poetically crafted lead is followed by a section on the pro-guerrilla leadership, which sets up two briefer sections describing refugee suspicions of outsiders and concluding with more surprise at the lack of young people and the rigid nature of the camp. A characteristic passage reads,

> Aid officials say that, understaffed, they encouraged the growth of refugee leadership committees to help organize the basic distribution of food, clothing and shelter to camp residents. From that seed of authority has grown a structure of campwide regimentation and orthodoxy that appears as inflexible as it is efficient.

Uhlig quotes an unnamed diplomat, "It is an inward-looking, suspicious society that has organized itself to survive, but it has lost its sanity." The inhabitants work long hours without, Uhlig is taken aback, vacations.

This sort of reporting without context, historical perspective, or evidence of the most fundamental understanding of what these people have suffered is the heir to the reporting of the refugee plight by Raymond Bonner. Uhlig notes in passing, midway in his story, that the first refugees came to Honduras in 1980, when they accused the Honduran and Salvadoran armies of abuse, prompting the United Nations to intervene from 1982 until the present to protect the refugees from "intimidation." Such haughty understatement goes beyond ignorance to fashion misrepresentation by omission. Uhlig makes only the most fragmented comments on the need for absolute authority and who created this atmosphere of fear, or why the refugees require United Nations protection. The UN is not there to protect them from their own leaders.

The guerrillas, it is true, are led in part by Marxist revolutionaries. Yet former Ambassador Robert White told a Congressional subcommittee, "The guerrilla groups, the revolutionary groups, almost without exception began as associations of teachers, associations of labor unions, compesino unions, or parish organizations which were organized for the definite purpose of getting a schoolhouse up on the market road."[122]

And "the guerrillas have accepted elections as the legitimate path to power.[123] In 1982, Bonner met, traveled, and followed into battle (Bonner was an officer in the Marines with Vietnam combat experience) the guerrillas in Morazon Province where Uhlig reports he could see, "warplanes fire lines of glowing tracer bullets into the black Salvadoran countryside." Bonner reported on those who met the other end of those tracer bullets. Based on scores of interviews with the peasants that made up the rank and file of the guerrilla units, Bonner painted a composite:

> born and raised in the department [province] and quite likely never travelled beyond it; only two years of formal education; at least one parent, child, or sibling murdered by the government soldiers, frequently after having been hacked with a machete; living family members part of the revolution.[124]

In Morazon Province during a 10-day period during December 1981, the elite Atlacatl Battalion,[125] trained by U.S. advisers, carried out a military operation in which about 1,000 people were killed. Soldiers wrote on the wall of one village where they had killed many, "The Atlacatl Battalion will return to kill the rest." Bonner came upon the scene of indescribable slaughter while traveling with the guerrillas. From his account, he figures that the first column arrived in the town of Mozote at around 6 a.m. The villagers were ordered out of their homes and into the town square by the army. Systematically, "The men were blindfolded, taken away in small groups of four and five, and shot. Women were raped. Of the 482 Mozote victims, 280 were children under fourteen years old."[126]

Bonner, referring to himself in his story as a visitor traveling through the area with those fighting the government, interviewed a 38-year-old survivor who had managed to escape into some nearby bushes during the confusion. The woman reported hearing her son scream: "Mama, they're killing me. They've killed my sister. They're going to kill me."[127] Rufina Amaya's blind husband, her son aged nine, and her three daughters aged five, three, and eight months were butchered. Amaya told Bonner she overheard soldiers' talking from her hiding place. "'Lieutenant, somebody here says he won't kill children,' said one soldier. 'Who's the son of a bitch who said that? the Lieutenant answered. 'I am going to kill him.'"[128]

The very next day after Bonner's story ran on page one of the *Times*, Ronald Reagan said that the Salvadoran government "is making a concentrated and significant effort to comply with internationally recognized human rights." Assistant Secretary of State Thomas Enders told Congress, "There is no evidence to confirm that government forces systematically massacred civilians in the operations zone, or that the number of civilians even remotely approached the 733 or 926 victims cited in the press. . . ."[129] The *Wall Street Journal* ran an editorial claiming systematic bias by Bonner and others. The *Journal* referred to Bonner's reporting of the massacre as a "propaganda exercise." "Realistically, neither the press nor the State Department has the power to establish conclusively what happened at Mozote in December, and we're sure the sophisticated editors of the Times recognize as much."[130] Bonner was there. So was a reporter for the *Washington Post*. George Melloan, who wrote the *Journal* editorial, went on national television denouncing Bonner. He said on the *MacNeil-Lehrer Report*, "I think some reporters tend to identify with guerrilla and revolutionary movements to some degree. . . .Obviously Ray Bonner has such an orientation." This sort of attack on the truth had the desired effect. "The foreign editor of one major newspaper sent copies of the editorial to his correspondents in Central America. 'Let's not let this happen to us,' was the message, according to one of the paper's reporters."[131] The weakness and deceit Bonner writes about within the government is practiced as well by the press. This appears to be the incident which caused Bonner's fall from grace with Managing Editor Rosenthal. Rosenthal traveled to Central America and spoke with Bonner in 1982, by 1983 Bonner was no longer in Latin America.

More than 10 years after the *Wall Street Journal* accused Bonner of propagandizing, the *Times* ran a front-page story underneath a photograph depicting the excavation of 38 children. The caption under the photo says, "In the village of El Mozote, El Salvador, forensic experts have uncovered a site holding the skeletons of 38 children who were among the 792 local villagers reported massacred in 1981 by American-trained soldiers." Reporter Tim Golden writes that "the bones have emerged as stark evidence that the claims of peasant survivors and the reports of a couple of American journalists were true."[132] The government authorized forensic team concluded that the evidence buried in the mass grave corroborates Amaya's account.

CONCLUSION

The Bush administration shifted foreign policy emphasis away from Central America.[133] As the U.S. downplays the significance of developments in El Salvador, the *Times'* coverage reflects this marginalization. Congress voted to halve military aid to El Salvador in the wake of the murder of the Jesuit priests, their housekeeper and her daughter.[134] Bush threatened to veto the 1991 foreign aid bill if it contained the reduction in aid to El Salvador. On January 2, 1991, FMLN guerrillas executed two American soldiers whose helicopter had been shot down. The FMLN subsequently offered to cooperate in the investigation of the deaths of the U.S. servicemen.[135] The executions led Bush on January 15 to free the $42.5 million in military aid frozen by Congress.[136]

Within a week of the resumption of military aid (suspended to pressure El Salvador to prosecute those guilty of murdering innocent civilians), 15 peasants were massacred just outside San Salvador, in El Zapote, by hooded men in uniform.[137] This was the worst human rights abuse since the murders of the six priests, their housekeeper and her daughter. Archbishop Arturo Rivera y Damas has charged the Salvadoran military with the deaths.[138] The *Times* carried a brief Reuters news release leading, "Leftist rebels today accused the Salvadoran armed forces of killing 15 peasants this week in a village north of San Salvador."[139] This is followed by a FMLN denunciation of the armed forces' attempt to intimidate the population, which then is "balanced" with a quote from Salvadoran Justice Minister Oscar Santamaria categorically rejecting the charge. "I don't think it is a serious position. It is pure speculation," he says. The last paragraph of this 6-paragraph story concludes, "The rebel group presented no proof to back its accusation. . . ." Again, while there are no factual misstatements, the structure of the objective report, its length, and placement inside the newspaper indicate the relative unimportance attributed to the massacre.

Would a similar occurrence in another country have been treated so lightly? "27 Die in Attack by Zulu Raiders in South Africa" is a page-one story given a 30-paragraph treatment, complete with a photo of a man covering the body of a dead resident.[140] Some of the subheads are "Police Complicity Charged," "'We Didn't Have a Chance'", "Bodies Lie in Street" and "Police Escort Reported."

A free press is indispensable for a true democracy. El Salvador's opposition press was destroyed by those in power. Less than one month after the reinstatement of military aid, the only remaining Salvadoran newspaper that reported both sides of the civil war was burned down. Associated Press put out a dispatch carried by the *New York Times*, "Salvadoran Paper Damaged by Fire."[141] The same report appeared in the *San Jose Mercury News* under the head, "Arson destroys Salvador paper; director accuses government."[142] Perhaps layout concerns explain the different interpretations. "Arsonists on Saturday destroyed the only Salvadoran newspaper that covered the rebel side of the civil war, and the director of the paper blamed the military and the right-wing government," says the lead in the *Mercury News*. "The director of an independent newspaper whose presses were destroyed in a fire that officials described as arson said today that the paper would continue to publish," goes the lead in the *Times*. No mention is made of the editorial nature of the paper or that the director blames those very people the *Times* attributes as a source for their account of the fire.

Much of the same information is presented in each paper, but the framework ordering each story provides for a different interpretation of the same event from an Associated Press dispatch. The *Times* places the director's accusation of government guilt down in the third paragraph. The fifth paragraph of the *Mercury News* account reads, "Workers gathered outside the smoldering plant Saturday said it seemed the paper's files had been searched before the fire and documents and photographs taken." There is no similar expression in the *Times*. The *Mercury News* quotes the director, Francisco Valencia, in the twelfth paragraph, "We know who it was. It was the people who commit massacres with impunity, the same people who assassinate priests, who attack unions, who attack anyone who doesn't agree with ideology of the government and this country's power groups." The *Times* does not use this and instead quotes editor Jorge Armando Contreras, who says the fire was started by "the dark forces that have always tried to impede the exercise of free press in El Salvador. The country is now sufficiently mature to know who these forces are and we are not going to waste time in pointing fingers at those who appear to be irresponsible" (sic). It may be that Salvadorans are sufficiently mature to recognize who is responsible, but it seems better journalism to report Valencia's plain, precise, and specific charges, rather than innuendo. This is an editorial decision.

As Abe Rosenthal says, "For a paper with the resources and intelligence of the *New York Times*, there are no excuses. The only things there are, are values—what we think it is important to do."[143] So values are embodied in what the *Times* does. This is a sophisticated statement on the interrelation between fact and value in journalism. If one says that values are all there is, and that there are no excuses for what one does because one realizes that, at a fundamental level, journalism is the promotion of values, then it is a damning statement as well. A truly free press must feel at liberty, even obligated, to criticize the powers that be, especially in matters that concern the character and makeup of a whole society and which involve matters of life or death for many in the society. Yet, I believe that at least insofar as foreign policy and El Salvador are concerned, the *New York Times* displays a profound pattern of accepting, promoting, and disseminating the official government line.

NOTES TO CHAPTER 7

1. Reporter is not identified as a *Times* correspondent, quoted in R. Erlich, "EL SALVADOR: PRINTING THE NEWS TO FIT," *The San Francisco Bay Guardian*, September 14, 1983, p. 12.

2. E. Huse and J. Bowditch, quoted in Robert H. Guest, Paul Hersey, and Kenneth H. Blanchard, *Organizational Change through Effective Leadership* (Englewood Cliffs, NJ: Prentice Hall, Inc., 1977), p. 12.

3. C. Argyris, *Behind the Front Page: Organizational Self-Renewal in a Metropolitan Newspaper* (San Francisco: Jossey-Bass, Inc., 1974).

4. P. Hersey and K.H. Blanchard, *Management of Organizational Behavior: Utilizing Human Resources* (Engelwood Cliffs, NJ: Prentice Hall, Inc., 1977), p. 305.

5. Ibid., p. 1.

6. Argyris, *Behind the Front Page*, p. x1.

7. Hersey and Blanchard, *Management of Organizational Behavior*, p. 302.

8. Ibid., p. 101.

9. Argyris, *Behind the Front Page*, p. 275.

10. A.H. Maslow, *Motivation and Personality* (New York: Harper and Row, Publishers, 1954).

11. D. McGregor, *The Human Side of Enterprise* (New York: McGraw-Hill Book Co., 1960).

12. Hersey and Blanchard, *Management of Organizational Behavior*, p. 55.

13. Argyris, *Behind the Front Page*, p. 253.

14. Ibid., p. 30.

15. Ibid., p. 11.

16. Ibid., p. 28.

17. Ibid., p. 9.

18. Ibid., p. 40.

19. Hersey and Blanchard, *Management of Organizational Behavior*, p. 65.

20. Ibid., pp. 95-96.

21. Ibid., p. 72.

22. Argyris, *Behind the Front Page*, p. 4.

23. Guest, Hersey, and Blanchard, *Organizational Change*, p. 18.

24. Ibid., p. 20.

25. Ibid., p. 20.

26. Argyris, *Behind the Front Page*, p. 141.

27. Ibid., p. 142.

28. Ibid., p. 140.

29. Hersey and Blanchard, *Mangement of Organizational Behavior*, p. 12.

30. Argyris, *Behind the Front Page*, p. 50.

31. Ibid., p. 50.

32. Ibid., p. 58.

33. Ibid., p. 12.

34. Ibid., p. 12.

35. Hersey and Blanchard, *Management of Organizational Behavior*, p. 237.

36. Argyris, *Behind the Front Page*, p. 31.

37. Ibid., p. 61.

38. Herse ˙ and Blanchard, *Management of Organizational Behavior*, p. 256.

39. Ibid.,] 256.

40. Argyr. . *Behind the Front Page*, p. 139.

41. Hersey and Blanchard, *Management of Organizational Behavior*, p. 274.

42. Guest, Hersey, and Blanchard, *Organizational Change*, p. 80.

43. Argyris, *Behind the Front Page*, p. 77.

44. Ibid., p 78.

45. Ibid., p. 77.

46. Ibid., p. 80.

47. Ibid., p. 81.

48. Ibid., p. 64.

49. F. Fiedler, quoted in Hersey and Blanchard, *Management of Organizational Behavior*, p. 148.

50. Argyris, *Behind the Front Page*, p. 225.

51. Ibid., p. 280.

52. C. Argyris, *Intervention Theory and Method: A Behavioral Science View* (Reading, MA: Addison-Wesley Publishing Co., 1970), p. 25.

53. H. Salisbury, *Without Fear or Favor, The New York Times* (New York: The New York Times Book Co., Inc., 1980).

54. Ibid., pp. 66-67.

55. G. Talese, *The Kingdom and the Power* (New York: The World Publishing Company, 1969), p. 108.

56. Ibid., p. 120.

57. Ibid., p. 214.

58. Ibid., p. 428.

59. Ibid., p. 259.

60. Ibid., p. 256.

61. Ibid., p. 227.

62. Ibid., pp. 243-44.

63. Ibid., p. 286.

64. Ibid., p. 287.

65. Ibid., p. 340.

66. Salisbury, *Without Fear or Favor*, p. 68.

67. Ibid., p. 68.

68. Talese, *The Kingdom and the Power*, p. 457.

69. Ibid., p. 517.

70. Salisbury, *Without Fear or Favor*, p. 413.

71. "Brave Stand for Justice in El Salvador, " *New York Times*, January 1, 1990, p. A14.

72. A. Rosenthal, quoted in J.C. Goulden, *Fit to Print: A.M. Rosenthal and His Times* (Secaucus: Lyle Stuart, 1988), p. 243, and cited in M. Hertsgaard, *On Bended Knee: The Press and the Reagan Presidency* (New York: Farrar, Straus, Giroux, 1988) p. 201.

73. R. Bonner, quoted in Hertsgaard, *On Bended Knee*, p. 191.

74. Ibid., p. 202.

75. A. Rosenthal, quoted in Hertsgaard, *On Bended Knee*, p. 198.

76. A. Rosenthal, quoted in Goulden, *Fit to Print*, p. 341.

77. Ibid., p. 343.

78. D. Helvrag, "Whodunit?" *The San Francisco Bay Guardian*, November 29, 1989, p. 19.

79. R. Boudreaux, "Both Sides See Talks Next Week as Best Chance for Peace in El Salvador," *Los Angeles Times*, March 30, 1991, p. A19.

80. *New York Times*, November 23, 1989, p. A26.

81. R. Bonner, *Weakness and Deceit: U.S. Policy and El Salvador* (New York: Times Books, 1984), p. 9.

82. E.S. Herman and N. Chomsky, *Manufacturing Consent: The Political Economy of the Mass Media* (New York: Pantheon Books, 1988).

83. L. Gruson, "As Salvador Vote Nears, Which Way for the Right?" *New York Times*, March 12, 1989, p. 6.

84. L. Gruson, "As Salvador Vote Nears, Dissent Gains a Toehold," *New York Times*, March 17, 1989, p. A4 (emphasis added).

85. E.S. Herman, "Suppression, Then Disclosure," *Lies of Our Times*, 1 (1), January 1989, p. 6.

86. L. Gruson, "New Latin Leader Urges Peace Talks," *New York Times*, March 23, 1989, p. A7.

87. L. Gruson, "Newcomer Sworn as Salvador's Leader," *New York Times*, June 6, 1989, p. A3.

88. L. Gruson, "Salvadoran Foes Open Venezuela Negotiations," *New York Times*, May 17, 1990, p. A8.

89. R. Pear, "Quayle Meets Salvador Party Leader and Urges Respect for Rights," *New York Times*, June 14, 1989, p. A3.

90. D. Bernstein, "The New Improved, Moderate Arena Party," *Extra!*, Summer 1989, p. 26.

91. R. Alejandro Fiallos, quoted in Bonner, *Weakness and Deceit*, p. 327.

92. J. Crogan, "Tales from the death squads," *The San Francisco Bay Guardian*, December 20, 1989, p. 19.

93. Ibid., p. 21.

94. Ibid., p. 21. Joya Martinez also charges that his unit infiltrated the

University of El Salvador, shooting at Salvadoran soldiers in the area, and that this was then reported in the local newspaper as evidence of FMLN activity at the university.

95. "Salvador suspects arrested," *San Francisco Examiner*, January 14, 1990, pp. A1, A22. The daily amount averages $1.1 million, L. Gruson, "As Salvador Vote Nears, Which Way for the Right?" *New York Times*, March 12, 1989, pp. 1, 16.

96. C. Norton, "Witness to murder," *The San Francisco Bay Guardian*, December 20, 1989, pp. 19, 21.

97. "Salvadoran Shake-Up," *Los Angeles Times*, March 2, 1989, p. 6.

98. "The Suspects in El Salvador," *New York Times*, November 18, 1989, p. 26 (emphasis added).

99. Walker, quoted in Halvarg, "Whodunit?" p. 19.

100. M.A. Uhlig, "Salvadoran Security Forces Raid Episcopal Church, Arresting 17," *New York Times*, November 21, 1989, p. A9.

101. D. Helvrag, "Whodunit?" p. 19.

102. Ibid., p. 19.

103. L. Gruson, "6 PRIESTS KILLED IN A CAMPUS RAID IN SAN SALVADOR," *New York Times*, November 17, 1989, p. A1. In fact, the force of the gun blast shattered their skulls.

104. C. Norton, "El Salvador's Tet," *The San Francisco Bay Guardian*, November 29, 1989, p. 19.

105. L. Gruson, "Witness in Slaying of Six Jesuits is Said to Fail Lie-Detector Tests," *New York Times*, December 11, 1989, p. A1.

106. "Archbishop says U.S. Brainwashed Witness," *San Francisco Chronicle*, December 11, 1989, p. A1.

107. Norton, "Witness to murder," p. 19.

108. Ibid., p. 21.

109. J. Maria Tojeira, "Tipping the Scales of Justice," *Los Angeles Times*, April 26, 1991, p. B5.

110. Ibid., p. B5.

111. N. Chomsky, "WHOSE HUMAN RIGHTS?" *Lies of Our Times*, 1 (1), January 1990, p. 11.

112. Herman and Chomsky, *Manufacturing Consent*.

113. R. Pear, "Report is Urging Major Overhaul of U.S. Central American Policy," *New York Times*, March 3, 1989, p. A7, emphasis added. Tellingly, on the same day the *Times* carried eight stories on page one, three of which dealt with the Soviet bloc's need for policy reform. The GAO report appears on page seven.

114. M. Uhlig, "Rights Group Accuses U.S. Over El Salvador," *New York Times*, November 27, 1989, p. A4.

115. "Salvadoran Jesuits say U.S. holds evidence," *San Francisco Examiner*, August 12, 1990, p. A7.

116. L. Gruson, "NEW ALLEGATIONS IN JESUIT KILLINGS," *New York Times*, August 12, 1990, p. A9.

117. "Salvador Slayings Reportedly on the Rise," *San Francisco Chronicle*, October 24, 1990, p. A4.

118. R. Pear, "SALVADOR ACCUSED ON JESUIT INQUIRY," *New York Times*, May 1, 1990, pp. A1, A4.

119. J. Kavanagh, "El Salvador, U.S. rebuked for role in investigations," Toronto, *The Globe and Mail*, November 17, 1990, p. A13.

120. A. Cockburn, "Fight Some Butchers, Pay Others," *Los Angeles Times*, February 18, 1991, p. B5.

121. M. Uhlig, "Fear Controls Salvadoran Refugees in Honduras," *New York Times*, March 3, 1989, p. A4.

122. R. White, quoted in R. Bonner, *Weakness and Deceit*, p. 88.

123. L. Gruson, "Salvadoran Foes Open Venezuela Negotiations," *New York Times*, May 17, 1990, p. A8.

124. Bonner, *Weakness and Deceit*, p. 111.

125. The members of the army arrested in connection with the murder of the six priests, their housekeeper and her daughter are or were members of the Atlacatl Battalion. Colonel Guillermo Alfredo Benavides Moreno, charged with ordering the murders, was the commander of the battalion on November 16, 1989 when the eight people were slain.

126. Bonner, *Weakness and Deceit*, p. 338.

127. R. Bonner, "Massacre of Hundreds Reported in Salvador Village," *New York Times*, January 27, 1982, p. A1.

128. Bonner, *Weakness and Deceit*, p. 339.

129. Reagan and Enders, quoted in Bonner, *Weakness and Deceit*, p. 340.

130. *Wall Street Journal*, February 10, 1982, p. 26.

131. Bonner, *Weakness and Deceit*, fn. p. 340.

132. T. Golden, "Salvador Skeletons Confirm Reports of Massacre in 1981," *New York Times*, October 22, 1992, p. A1.

133. W. Friedenberg, "Central America consigned to oblivion," *San Francisco Examiner*, October 21, 1990, p. A16.

134. J. Hackel, "Aid cut seen as turning point for Salvador," *San Francisco Examiner*, October 21, 1990, p. A14.

135. L. Gruson, "Salvadoran Rebels Offer to Help Investigation of Helicopter Deaths," *New York Times*, January 7, 1991, p. A2. The FMLN subsequently decided to prosecute those involved in the murders and to allow the participation of independent observers, Cockburn, "Fight Some Butchers, Pay Others," p. B5.

136. R. Boudreaux, "Both Sides See Talks Next Week as Best Chance for Peace in El Salvador," *Los Angeles Times*, March 30, 1991, p. A19.

137. R. McKerrow, "Atrocities and Elections: Grim Cycle in El Salvador," *Lies of Our Times*, April 1991, pp. 14-15.

138. Cockburn, "Fight Some Butchers, Pay Others," p. B5.

139. "Rebels in El Salvador Say Military Killed 15," *New York Times*, January 25, 1991, p. A7.

140. C. Wren, "27 Die in Attack by Zulu Raiders in South Africa," *New York Times*, May 13, 1991, pp. A1, A6.

141. "Salvadoran Paper Damaged by Fire," *New York Times*, February 11, 1991, p. A3.

142. "Arson destroys Salvador paper; director accuses government," *San Jose Mercury News*, February 10, 1991, p. 14A.

143. A. Rosenthal, quoted in Hertsgaard, *On Bended Knee*, p. 342.

8

Jurisprudence and Access to the Media

Media theory is inseparbably bound up with media rules and norms. The First Amendment informs possibilities and structures the dialogue on free speech and press. I begin the discussion of the critical phenomenology of legal theory with two questions: What do the principles of positive law and the development of legal rules have to do with our understanding of the way we live among one another, and how should such relations enter into our thinking concerning the problem of access to the cultural conversation? Does the law have a materialistic base or is it above and apart from the churning grind of daily life? It is my position that, contrary to the pure theory of law, the law is impure, it is essentially part of cultural life. Legal thinking, or theory that involves legal relations, must be based within the intersubjective life world of experience. Law is misrepresented to the extent that it is described as pure, and jurisprudence is idealistic and often unresponsive to the degree it refuses the social world.

Law mediates our relations with one another; that is where it works and makes meaning. In its essence, then, law cannot be objective, transparent, or adequate to itself. The law involves value and fact, not facts alone or facts to determine value. Law is value-based examination and ordering of the phenomena. Rules are historically determined by experience. Recognition of this process does not weaken legal studies, but works as a much needed corrective to the purist ideal. For, to mention one of Derrida's favorite Americanisms, if things were simple, word would have gotten around. We look at an instance of pure theory and move on to critically based impure notions in order to address the problem of who should be allowed to speak and write in the media. Who counts and who is counted upon are considerations implicit in the question of access to the media.

Democracy relies on the marketplace of ideas, so who should be admitted? Really, in fact, who should be allowed space and time? Access is viewed as either an affirmative opportunity or a prohibitive limitation on government interference. This framing of the issue allows for two separate lines of questioning the future of society. For an idea to gain currency, it, of course, must be heard. The tradition has put forth a series of concepts, ordered according to which are the most powerful over those that are judged to be less so. Facts deserve our attention, if for no other reason than their mere accessibility. Values do not carry nearly the same weight, if for no other reason than their subjective nature. Facts are by definition objective and values subjective. This is a view with which I wish to take issue. A critical phenomenological approach recognizes the essential nature of value as a fundamental strand of social life. In *fact*, value opens up the very determination of facts. Value structures facts. We value some facts and not others. Doesn't the Declaration of Independence attest that we hold some truths to be self-evident? Those truths are the intersubjective values of life, liberty, and the pursuit of happiness. The Bill of Rights is a series of assertions of value, not empirically verified facts.

JURISPRUDENCE

Pure Theory of Law

Any effort to describe communication, with its multifarious manifestations, stemming from dialogue through mass communication, does well to consider the legal and societal underpinnings of the communication process. Considering the First Amendment guarantees of freedom of speech and the press, Hans Kelsen's philosophy of law offers a perspective for grounding the basic structure of those rights. Kelsen presents a pure theory of law. His philosophy is pure; it contains no ideological preferences, no sociological observations. He provides only a logical schema as the prerequisite of a legal system. Kelsen operates, then, at a level of logical abstraction, similar to the epistemology of Immanuel Kant. Acts are separated from rules. Rules occupy the realm of consideration. Authority founds a legal realm in which Kelsen considers only cognitive justifications for constitutional applications. The science of law becomes an object of cognition; it has a constitutive character.

Kelsen's position is known as legal positivism. Legal positivism forms a school of thought often contrasted with natural law theory. This latter school holds that human laws are in some sense derivable from nature or God. Natural law contrasts with laws that spring from the mind of man. This distinction is presented to place Kelsen's theory in historical context, not to champion either theory. Kelsen's positivism must be further distinguished from logical positivism. Clearly, if Kelsen holds that a theory of law is an object of cognition, much of its truth can be said to be virtual as opposed to actual. Logical positivism claims that only empirical, observable actions or states-of-affairs can be said to be meaningful. But a norm does not exist, for Kelsen, in the same ways as a judge or a policeman; a norm is virtual.

Kelsen asserts that a person, in the legal sense, emanates from an interconnection of willed meanings Kelsen calls norms.

> A legal person is the unity of a complex of legal obligations and legal rights. Since these obligations and rights are constituted by legal norms (more correctly: *are* these legal norms), the problem of the 'person' is in the last analysis the analysis the problem of the unity of a complex of norms.[1]

Only if the law forms a reciprocal order of behavior can it be distinct from nature; only then does jurisprudence become a social science. One commits an inaccuracy upon asserting a necessary connection between a norm and a future event. Laws, norms, and sanctions refer to future events, but they do not assert that specific actions will take place. One needs the distinction, "ought" and "will."

But "ought" makes legal as well as ethical sense. Like Kant, Kelsen upholds a moral realm; one is obliged to behave in certain ways because it is one's ethical duty. A moral imperative, Kelsen argues, attaches no reward or punishment for behavior. As this is the case, ethics must consist in a more rarefied realm than the legal order. Considering ethical judgments, Kelsen maintains one cannot separate motive from motivated behavior. To posit impartiality and add objective validity, the law must draw a distinction between ethics and law.

> The fundamental difference between law and morals is: law is a coercive order, that is, a normative order that attempts to bring about a certain behavior by attaching to the opposite behavior a socially organized coercive act; whereas morals is a social order without such sanctions.[2]

Moral orders are socially compelling in themselves, for Kelsen, whereas legal norms imply sanctions. Thus, the judgment that an action is legal or illegal results from a specific, normative interpretation. A norm confers meaning through a judgment, an act, which in turn receives its legal status or determination from yet another norm.

A perplexity is found in the differential, "ought" and "is." Upon asserting a norm, one means an event ought to occur in a specified manner. A norm is the meaning of an act by which behavior is permitted, commanded, allowed, or admonished. Kelsen clarifies:

> From the circumstance that something *is* cannot follow that something *ought* to be; and that something *ought* to be, cannot be the reason that something *is*. The reason for the validity of a norm can only be the validity of another norm.[3]

By valid, Kelsen means binding. One norm guarantees another norm in a hierarchical fashion. The progression continues, each judgment that an action is or is not as it ought to be, until the ultimate norm—the norm based only on its own presupposition—is reached. This norm is the act of creating a constitution. The constitution, for Kelsen, is ultimately objectively valid, that is, an agreement that forms the principle of justification for the rest of the system. The system contains itself, but it has boundaries. The constitution functions as the positive value judgment, the basic norm. The basic norm supplies reason for the validity and content of all the other norms deduced from it. However, the body that constitutes the authority to assert a constitution presupposes its own validity through what, if successful, becomes a coercive, legal order.

The act of constitution supplies validity for the system, but remains logically distinct from the system and the constitution. Kelsen writes:

> The basic norm is the presupposed starting point of a procedure: the procedure of positive law creation. It is itself not a norm created by custom or by the act of a legal organ; it is not a positive but a presupposed norm so far as the constitution establishing authority is looked upon as the highest authority and can therefore not be regarded as authorized.[4]

The basic norm stipulates laws are to be enforced in conformity with the constitution. Therefore, the rules of a legal order are not arranged horizontally, but form a hierarchy beginning with the constitution. The basic norm forms the transcendental-logical condition for the validity of the rest of the system.

From this follows the validity of all coercive acts, laws, and their obligations. Efficacy is not the determining quality. However, a legal system functions effectively when behavior conforms with norms. If behavior conforms with the norm, it is valid, utilitarian or not. The norm is differentiated from the obligation. A norm stipulates an obligation. A sanction will be attached to opposite behavior. The sanction forms the coercive act that constitutes the legal obligation. The penalty for not obeying the law confers an obligation to conform with the norm. Consequently, any given law fits as a part in a whole legal system or normative structure. The law draws its legality only from this situation, according to Kelsen. Behavior either is or is not prohibited. Kelsen's system, on the logical plane at least, allows for no ambiguity. If a certain behavior is not prohibited, it must be allowed by the legal order. Any behavior thus regarded, by necessity, is regulated by the normative order. Legal freedom exists only in a negative sense. Some behavior permits the person to work within the system. On the other side, any behavior not prohibited qualifies as positively guaranteed behavior.

Again, all norms fan out from one basic, presupposed norm. This norm, at least for a "democratic" system, is born by writing a constitution. For any system, the basic norm is not established by a positive legal act, something put forth with justification from an antecedent state-of-affairs. Rather, the presupposed legitimizing act, Kelsen writes:

> [I]s interpreted as establishing a constitution and the acts based on the constitution are interpreted as legal acts. To make manifest this presupposition is an essential function of legal science. This presupposition is the ultimate (but in its character conditional and therefore hypothetical) reason for the validity of the legal order.[5]

One infers that somewhat arbitrary, contingent forces bring about rational societies. Kelsen admits that democracy, indeed any form of government, does not depend upon laws of nature, a decree from God, or even binding links with history for legitimization, but rather, a fortuitous assembly of assertive individuals taking matters into their own hands.

Once the structure is in place, the continued existence of any normative order must rely on an effectively functioning state. The legal order forms the state. Nonetheless, effectiveness conditions and sustains validity; it is not validity itself. Expanding the purely rational structure of his positivism, Kelsen argues that the rule of law is not essentially imperative. The rule of law asserts a judgment, a statement about an object of cognition, a virtual ideality. As a result, the science of law, jurisprudence, must fulfill a descriptive, not a prescriptive, function. While the law consists of "ought" statements, and the different branches of government comprise legislation, interpretation, and execution of norms and sanctions, jurisprudence functions to describe legal phenomena. With his description of legal phenomena, Kelsen's positivism resembles Husserl's earlier phenomenology of intentionality with its constitutional emphasis.

Since, within the normative order, the fact that one is held accountable for his or her actions forges responsibility. If a person's acts conflict with a norm, another connection is fashioned—a delict. A sanction is imputed to the delict. Kelsen takes care to point out that the sanction is not "caused" by the delict. The delict does not bring about the sanction through necessity. The norm, "ought," comes into play between the condition and the consequence. The responsible individual *may* be punished. To say one is responsible for one's actions means behavior is imputed to the person in question. The sanction is imputed to the delict, but the sanction is not caused by the delict. The connection between sanction and delict is not, as traditional legal theory ascribes, causal. The connection is one of imputation, the state of being charged with a delict.

Kelsen writes, "It is significant that the Greek word for cause, *aitia*, originally meant guilt: the cause is 'guilty' of the effect . . . "[6] But it cannot be the case that the delict is guilty of the sanction. The person may be charged with the delict for which he or she may be sanctioned. The individual is the final term of an interpretive process based on a normative order. Kelsen asserts that man as legal agent, as moral actor, is free. Deliberation represented by the concept of imputation must be taken into account within the description of the phenomena. Inevitability and causality find no place in the legal reasoning of human responsibility. The principle of imputation connects discrete acts of human behavior. The contingent character of imputation allows for freedom of deliberation and choice. Kelsen's science of law directs its act toward legal norms, not facts or instances; the legal norms form the meaning for the facts.

Kelsen intends jurisprudence to cover only a limited, well-defined field. His concepts are systematic, yet qualified and relative, tentative and delicate. "Imputation, like causality is a principle of order in human thinking, and therefore just as much or just as little an illusion or ideology as causality, or category of thinking," says Kelsen, "which—to use Hume's or Kant's words—is only a thinking habit or category of thinking."[7] Normative statements about legal affairs cannot be reduced to temporal facts of acts of the will. Pure theory makes judgments about characteristics that facts display. But normative judgments do not dig into the mire of individual, corporeal life; they remain aloft in the unspoiled atmosphere of reason.

Constitutional rights do not in themselves confer the right to act in a certain manner. They serve as prohibitions. But the prohibition, for example, against abridging freedom of speech or the press, does not function as a restriction against enactment of laws that do violence to this right. The constitutional guarantees merely allow the courts to strike down such legislation as unconstitutional. A statute enacted by the legislation functions according to a principle of legitimacy; that is, it is valid until another norm terminates its validity in accordance with a higher norm. As long as the presupposed norm holds, then the positive legal lattice-work is valid, too. One ought to behave in accordance with the U.S. Constitution because it is established and effective. Consequently, one ought to behave according to the normative order because its validity is assured. This applies, however, only so long as the legal order is effective.

Positive law, then, differs essentially from natural law. The basic justifications are not the same. Natural law theory places the validity of any positive legal order upon its consistency with its derivation from nature or God. Positive theory, Kelsen's pure theory, makes no such claim. A valid legal system could exist in contradiction to God or nature as long as the presupposed norm remains functional, and the tiers of the structure conform in such a way that an effective, coherent system exists. Natural law theory is obligated to reject any positive law that contradicts natural law. The positive law would necessarily be invalid. Clearly, this is not the case for Kelsen's positive law.

The pure theory of law differs from critical phenomenology in style and scope. The field of concern gives rise to dissimilar horizons. Critical phenomenology concerns itself with the content and form of actual laws coupled with their actual effects on people. Kelsen limits his pure theory to the validity of norms to avoid committing what he considers a fundamental error, that is, attribution of causality. A critical phenomenological approach attempts to link laws, interests, and circumstances together, producing an interactional grid. Not only the law itself but other phenomena must be included in the field of study. Kelsen rejects this as the proper field of study for jurisprudence; he maintains that one thereby loses the distinction between "ought" and "is." Ought would be demoted to the causal dimension of "if . . . then state-of-being justification." When imputation is ignored, error results. The resultant confusion of legal authority with other authority conceals justification of legitimacy. Kelsen argues that society is validly upheld only if the presupposition of the basic norm functions as justification for that society. The presupposition of the normative quality of obeying the constitution of a state ensures its validity, if not its truth. Critical phenomenology provides no such justification.

Kelsen's pure theory is epistemologically similar to Kant's critique, "'by presupposing the basic norm that one ought to behave in accordance with the subjective meaning of the constitution—creating act of will—according to the prescriptions of the authority creating the constitution,'"[8] Kelsen quotes Kant. With his concern for safeguarding sanctity and validity of this presupposed norm, Kelsen has effectively separated form from content. Content becomes irrelevant. Pure theory insures only the internal consistency of the system. Merleau-Ponty holds that context—the difference between form and content—generates sense. Kelsen tells us that content and, consequently, context, muddy the legal waters.

Perhaps the way off the horns of the dilemma is to posit varying levels of constitution. At the epistemological level, Kelsen may be correct. But epistemology, separated from psychology, sociology, and carnal life, is illusory and escapist. Morals, justice, and fundamental well-being constitute aspects of life that a legal system is designed to protect.

Kelsen writes:

> Since the basic norm, as shown, as a norm presupposed in the foundation of the validity of positive law, is only the transcendental-logical condition of this normative interpretation, it does not perform an ethical-political but only an epistemological function.[9]

Kelsen's pure theory is aptly named. But the law functions nowhere discorporately. The net effect, if one brackets Kelsen's pure theory of law, amounts to performing a "mind-body" split on legal theory. The history of philosophy is replete with this triumph of the separation of fact from value, reason from passion. Self-enclosed and sanctified, pure theory lacks the flesh of life.

Impure Theory of Law

For a critical phenomenology, interpretation does not merely follow understanding; rather, understanding already interprets its object in a process of mediation between identity and difference, representation and alteration. So, interpretation constitutes a manifest mode of understanding. From a situated point of view, then, judgments of fact and value are intertwined and hence problematic. Legal matters transpire within an interpersonal realm. The text calls for an integration different from, yet part of, a pressing and historical context. As Husserl points out, upon considering an object, mental or physical, one mentally constitutes the side not seen, thereby mediating one's prior perspective. Any standpoint affirms incompletion. Moral and political considerations insist on legal deliberations. Legal structure inheres in moral, political issues. In stark contrast to Kelsen, Justice William Brennan warns, "We cannot delude ourselves that the Constitution takes the form of a theorem whose axioms need mere logical deduction."[10] Because, as both Levinas and Derrida declare, reason is most versatile and incisive when reason questions itself. Law, in its positive moment, conserves our cultural conversation by aiding in the promulgation of ethics as openness and exposure of one person to another. Here we locate the normative basis for differences of interpretation. Without an ethical, intersubjectively oriented foundation, law is only the police.

Derrida's central question is, I think, essentially Kantian. If, as Kant thought, we are to obey the dictates of reason in matters of ethics, if we are to act as if the rule of our action is to become the rule of a universal, natural law, then we ought to ask what this "as if" signifies.[11] Throughout Derrida's writings, one encounters the question, put in many ways, so to provoke discussion, "Is the reason for reason rational?"[12] This is a responsible question—a question questioning our social responsibility—and an ethical question (contrary to many of his critics): "But is the answering *to* the principle of reason the same act as answering *for* the principle of reason?"[13] It is not. Reason—law as the embodiment of reason—entails authority, to be sure, but does it not also have to do with a standard to be met? Reason must itself meet a critical standard. And Derrida's style, deconstruction, presupposes this affirmation of civility, fairness, decency, and dialogue with the other as the basis for reason and law. But reason does not always come up to its own standards in the law, or the tradition more generally. Pure theory answers for the principle of reason, while deconstruction, critical legal studies, and critical phenomenology respond to the tradition. As Derrida repeatedly has pointed out, his is an internal critique of, not a frontal assault on, the tradition.

Kelsen asserts that the difference between law and morals is that law is a coercive order and morals is a social order without the power of force. Morals are compelling in themselves; they are voluntary, while laws must rely on sanctions. Certainly, morality is a social realm, but the point of contention lies with the idea that the essence of law is coercion. While coercion forms a part of the law, assent and openness toward the other constitute the recognition of obligation, which in turn presupposes the possibility of transgression and coercion. Does law cross morality, or does morality, value, remain distinct from law and force? Or do ethics provide the possibility of law? While it is clear that because one has the legal right to do something, for example, to refuse access to an opposing point of view, it may not thereby be ethical. What becomes of the relation of doing something that may be ethical, but not legal? What about the civil disobedience that prefigured the American Revolution and the subsequent formation of the United States? Was it right or legal of the American colonists to disavow the Crown, to sever ties with a valid, sound, constitutional legal system? Under what conditions does breaking the contract become moral or legal according to pure theory? Is the moral moment distinct from the legal one? Once the constitution is breached, by right or might, then the act of founding a new legal order becomes the assumed condition for another constitution. Such considerations pollute pure theory with the logic of events. How does one assume responsibility for society? Did the signers of the Constitution found the United States? Or was the nation born with the Declaration of Independence? Does life begin with conception? Or is there a period when an insurrection is not yet viable, has not realized an essence? Does England, in its estranged relationship, and later as divorced progenitor, have any "rights?" It remains problematic from a "reasonable" viewpoint. The founding fathers violated a binding, preexisting social contract with England. The constitution, Kelsen says, functions as the positive value judgment, the basic norm. How would pure theory view the Declaration of Independence? So, in the American experience, that basic norm was itself based on an illegal act, a revolutionary act, sounding the death knell for a perfectly legal state of affairs. The basic norm, the constitution, supplies reason with the validity and formulation of all subsequent norms. Pure theory is not up to explaining this.

Kelsen argues that if a certain behavior is not prohibited, it is allowed. But certainly the Declaration of Independence was prohibited by King George, the Parliament, and the rule of law. Kelsen seems to argue that founding, positive acts of constitution are compelling. Yet the Civil War argues against this interpretation. So, was the presupposed legitimizing act of forming the constitution itself illegal? Then all subsequent sanctions for delicts themselves are based upon an illegality. We cannot account for this pollution by a pure theory. Such a conclusion, that the laws governing American citizens today are not genetically legitimate, not being a realistic or reasonable conclusion, implies that pure theory is not consistent with its own standards. Not only Kelsen's positive value judgment, the basic norm, the constitution, should be regarded as a phenomenon that one brackets, but pure theory itself becomes integrated into the field it investigates. The phenomenological, critical point here is, then, that the theory cannot claim to be truly impartial, and it must come under a similar analysis to the one it undertakes of more restricted horizons. It is in a mediate position with not only what it purports to analyze, but with history and events that come before it and make its understanding possible.

This contaminates the purity of the theory. Theory must go past this tradition, and turn this "infelicity into delight," to cite Derrida's light-footed phrase. The tradition has much to gain by transgressing self-imposed, internal limits. "Logic, the logical, the *logos* of logic cannot be the decisive factor here: rather, it constitutes the object of the debate, the phenomenon that must first be explained before it can be accepted as the deciding instance,"[14] says Derrida. The possibility of misunderstanding the positive value of the Constitution or of free speech rights needs to be accounted for. By that I mean values must leave room for the play of interpretation; the positive moment of the tradition's basic norm is itself predicated on situations that affected it and overdetermine the possible uses and values said to spring from its realization. Interpretation of the meaning of the rights set forth in and by the Constitution of the United States is a continuation (and discontinuation) of a process embedded in a history of conflicted interests, contested facts, and multiple values.

The surplus, and thereby the discord of the law, its scene and its right constitute the phenomenon of law, which is both transcendental, as Kelsen would have it, and imminent. Rights transcend the individual, but inhabit the relations among people. This is why we attempt to adjust traditional theory, phenomenological and positivist, to take account not only of rights and freedom *from* restraint, but further to adjust rights and freedom for renewed opportunity. I think that is what it means to conserve and explain the values fundamental to our system of law. Once again, we look past the legal or social system as solely a grid of prohibition and repression to the productive nexus, the freedom and space provided by mediation of constitution and constraint.

The Declaration of Independence furnishes us with an essential instance of *"différance,"* a declaration which differs from, in this case the Crown, and defers, is the U.S. declared or constituted by this declaration? Is the Declaration performative or declarative? Derrida thinks that this is not strictly decidable. It performs and describes in the name of a people that cannot preexist the statement as performative, yet gives power to the people as a declaration. This issue reaches down into the very structure of determination. The ambiguity, the undecidability sets forth the conditions for determinability; it provides the opening by which something, not preexistent, may occur. The Declaration evidences a "fabulous retroactivity."

The structure of this instituting language has to work to institute a new political, cultural entity as well as represent those who in some sense preexist the actual performance of the document. The "good People of these Colonies" perform through their signatories an act which transforms them into the United States of America. Again, one cannot strictly speaking decide whether a state springs into being or a state formally announces itself. The description/production of independence is structurally necessary for it to produce the effect it does. The positing of a right is prefigured between the birth and the declaration. Derrida writes,

> In signing, the people say—and do what they say they do, but in differing or deferring themselves through (*différant par*) the intervention of their representatives whose representivity is fully legiti-

mated only by the signature, thus after the fact or the coup (*aprés coup*) . . . "[15]

Implicit in Derrida's statement is a critique of our theories of truth. A truth is not original or adequate to itself. Truth relies on context because the context forms the horizon, which phenomenologically structures events or texts in time. The Declaration carries the structure of a "fabulous event" as do all texts. But the fabulous structure of this particular text emerges in the wrenching away and simultaneous affirmation of history to which the Declaration attests. The process traces out a series resulting in the Constitution and the Bill of Rights. The signing of the Declaration of Independence does not correspond to a state of affairs, nor does it discover the truth of an event: It creates the truth of the event; it produces the meaning not yet fully realized by the people or their representatives. The event itself is porous and ambiguous, even though the unalienable rights of life, liberty, and the pursuit of happiness may be self-evident. This means that the truth of these values are displaced while being reaffirmed by the actions of the people; they are revitalized in their inscription in the Declaration and made other than what the Crown said they were.

The professed strategy of this sort of analysis is to indicate phenomena beyond the norms and considerations of the tradition of, for example, pure theory. Derrida sets out to confront the tradition with its other, contesting the hierarchy of values favored by our tradition, not to destroy them, but to challenge specific constellations of values and their right to dominance and sovereignty. The tradition's championing of fact over value, reason over feeling, logic over rhetoric, technique over substance, and uniformity over plurality calls for a critical, phenomenologically based questioning. To strip legal reasoning of its presumption of neutrality aids in rethinking the reality, the "presence," of our situation. Critical theory means to subvert the tradition, that is to say, to question the divisions between oppositional terms and to begin to reorganize these inherited hierarchies. Our effort is not to do away with hierarchy (that is not possible), but to undermine the fixation with form, and to sensitize ourselves to the desire that constitutes us as humans. To recognize the face of the other, we do well to rethink the problem of rights consciousness. In fact, it may be that a large measure of society's formalization and malaise is produced by promoting the fiction of the rights-constituted person marking out the existence for the person of flesh and blood. This obsessional dependence on legal rights blocks other modes of intersubjectivity, causing, not relieving, alienation.[16] Our experience becomes "legalized." The right to experience accordingly creates much of our experience, and we see each other in court and administrative hearings, instead of paying attention to the other person's appeal in the ongoing life world.

While the grid of rights created by the American legal system symbolizes progress over past systems, we pay a price for the current centrality of form over experience. We should recognize the historically developed nature of the system, in order to move beyond the present predicament. Justice Brennan points out that the judicial branch of government was not produced on the peaks of pure theory; it was hammered out in power struggles over partisan politics.[17] The American experience does represent democratic progress over antecedent legal systems. Our break with the conception of parliamentary sovereignty, and the idea that the legislative body and its actions embody the constitution heralded an advance in the progress of due process. The Madisonian theory that the people, not the government, are sovereign, initiates a radical theory of law: The authors of the Constitution viewed government as an agreement constituted by persons with one another, rather than a concord between the governors and the governed.

"The framers bequeathed to us a vision. . . .In this vision, the *essence* of the relationship between the state and citizen is the relationship between one human being and another,"[18] Brennan says. Of course, this advance was marked by a forcible cut from a government that precipitated events by its arbitrary use of power, denying freedom to the individual. In the on-going attempt to realize the new radical theory of law, a fight centered over what limitations should be placed on the judiciary's proper right to express political views versus the control which Congress would apply by, if necessary, impeaching judges who fell out of line with the official interests of the party in power. An impeachment process was brought by the Republican president and Congress against an outspoken Federalist supreme court justice. The independence of the judiciary won out as the Senate recognized the danger of subordinating the bench to the other branches.[19] The Senate followed form over substance, passion followed reason in this case, and the integrity of the system was won. "The origins of the formalist conception of law and the judicial process lie in the reaction, at first entirely healthy, to the spectre of politicization that hung over the Court in its early years,"[20] Brennan concludes.

What has been lost is the awareness that the context has changed. Form has usurped from passion the kind of control the framers feared; today, society suffers from the triumph of form over experience. Phenomenology recalls the primacy of intersubjective experience. Reason should be guided by wisdom, but insight is a product of experience and compassion, not a function of protecting the rightness of one's actions by blindly following the rules. Each ruling or policy holding takes place within a context, and contexts shift, alter, merge, and develop over time. Deconstruction would remind us that law does not ultimately take place above contextual situations (strictly speaking, that is not conceivable, yet formalism acts *as if* decisions could be taken outside of the arena of experience). New social and political contexts call for a reconsideration of the rules, I do not mean that new contexts completely break with preexisting traditions, but that the notion of context displaces the absolute center pure reason presupposes. There are no unshifting anchors outside of human experience. "In our own time," Brennan warns, "attention to experience may signal that the greatest threat to due process principles is formal reason severed from the insights of passion."[21]

Access as a Matter of Interpretation

Recognizing that a person has the right to carry on in a specific fashion, according to a constitutional guarantee, means also that this person may be entitled to bring legal proceedings against another for violation of a right occasioned by the other pursuing his or her legal actions. The problem of access to the press provides a paradigm for illustrating a basic conflict within the normative structure of the legal order. Is the First Amendment guarantee of freedom of speech and press a freedom from government regulation or a freedom for individual expression? Does the First Amendment protect and encourage maximum diversity of expression, or, was the original conception a protection from outside interference? To whom does the right belong? Is access a positive affirmation or a negative prohibition?

The access issue presents a dilemma. Perplexity arises from a divergence of perspectives. The individual's interests crash against the bulwark of institutional autonomy. A tug from another direction situates a legislative entanglement—the Federal Communication Commissions's stipulations concerning radio and television. Pure theory is made problematic by the apparent contradiction within the normative structure.

The issue of access has its roots in British common law. The history of licensing publishers, coupled with censorship of expression, crossed the Atlantic, and its cultivation was begun in the colonies. But the cultivation was unsuccessful. Eventually, the First Amendment germinated. However, as Benno Schmidt points out, "Access may be neither justified as an extension of that which history has opposed nor attacked as tantamount to something history has rejected."[22] The Bill of Rights, generally, has been construed negatively as the prohibition against governmental interference in the marketplace of ideas. Schmidt refers to this as the "prophylactic conception" of the First Amendment. The current conception of the First Amendment is founded primarily on social utility over freedom of conscience.

Notwithstanding the difference of perspectives and interests, the contradiction explicit within the access issue lies in the opposing conceptions of freedom of speech and the press with regard to print and broadcast media. The *Red Lion*[23] and *Miami Herald*[24] cases present portraits of just how differently various instruments of freedom of expression have been treated. These two cases were decided roughly six years apart. *Red Lion:* "It is the purpose of the First Amendment to preserve an uninhibited marketplace of ideas in which truth will ultimately prevail, rather than to countenance monopolization of that market . . ."[25] *Miami Herald:* "A responsive press is an undoubtedly desirable goal, but press responsibility is not mandated by the Constitution and like many other virtues it cannot be legislated."[26] Clearly, these decisions are not compatible, unless some distinction between print and electronic media is drawn. Both form part of the "press," to which the First Amendment ascribes freedom. From where does the Supreme Court draw justification for such a schism?

Of course, a distinction has been drawn. The legal status of electronic media is different from that of print. While the functions are quite similar, their structures vary, calling for divergent treatment. In *Red Lion*, Justice Byron White delivered the 8-0 opinion of the Supreme Court; Justice William Douglas did not participate. Predictably, Douglas' view differed from his colleagues, "T.V. and radio stand in the same protected position under the First Amendment as do newspapers and magazines."[27]

Red Lion Broadcasting Co. owned WGCB radio station in Pennsylvania which had aired a 15-minute broadcast by Rev. Billy James Hargis. During his show, Hargis criticized a book, *Goldwater—Extremist on the Right* by Fred Cook. Rev. Hargis charged that Cook had been fired from a newspaper for making false charges against city officials; he had worked for a publication with communist ties; and he had defended Alger Hiss, attacked J. Edgar Hoover, and the CIA. The charges were unfounded. The FCC decided that Rev. Hargis' broadcast constituted a personal attack on Cook.

The Supreme Court held that Red Lion must grant free reply time to Cook. The right to reply to an attack serves "to enhance rather than abridge the freedoms of speech and press protected by the First Amendment . . ."[28] The Court's concern was not to protect Cook from personal attack; the law against defamation of character covers that. Under the fairness doctrine of the Communications Act, the other side of a public issue must be presented. A broadcaster must provide adequate coverage of public issues; it must be fair, that is, accurately reflect opposing views.[29]

Obviously, the FCC and its enforcement of the fairness doctrine effects government control over the press. Justice White, referring to radio, writes, "Without government control, the medium would be a cacophony of competing voices, none of which could be clearly and predictably heard."[30] The broadcasters argued that the rules of the fairness doctrine violated their First Amendment freedoms of speech and press. They contended that they ought to be able to employ their frequencies to broadcast what they choose and to exclude from it whom they choose. At this point, the court pointed out the different standards between print and broadcast media. "Where there are substantially more individuals who want to broadcast than there are frequencies to allocate, it is idle to posit an unbridgeable First Amendment right to broadcast comparable to the right of every individual to speak, write,or publish."[31] The Court continued, saying that a broadcaster had no constitutional right to monopolize a frequency, excluding all others. Referring to Meiklejohn's theory of freedom of expression as allowing for a knowledgeable and therefore functional citizenry, the court invoked the government's right to legislate the airwaves.

> Nor can we say that it is inconsistent with the First Amendment goal of producing an informed public capable of conducting its own affairs to require a broadcaster to permit answers to personal attacks occurring in the course of discussing controversial issues, or to require that the political opponents of those endorsed by the station be given a chance to communicate with the public.[32]

The court cited *Associated Press v. U.S.*, which involved a monopoly by the wire service in a blatant attack on freedom of the press.[33] The point being made by the court in the earlier case had a totally different application than the modified use to which it was applied in concluding *Red Lion:* "Freedom of the press from governmental interference under the First Amendment does not sanction repression of that freedom by private interests."[34]

From *Red Lion*, the court clearly sees broadcasters as public trustees, rather than fiats of free speech. Broadcast autonomy simply vanished after *Red Lion*. The division champions public access and thus necessarily curtails freedom of the medium. Does such a decision affect what in the *Miami Herald* case is described as an editorial function of the press? The court argues this function is protected by the First Amendment. Is *Red Lion* a broadcast case or a press case? The emphasis imparts significance. One sees that the right of free speech can conflict with the right of freedom of the press; both are protected by the same constitutional guarantee.

Within Kelsen's theory, the consistency of a particular norm in *Miami Herald* is seen not to be valid, according to the Supreme Court's interpretation. Therefore, it was within the *Herald's* legal authority to demand annulment of the statute. The Florida statute requiring any newspaper attacking the character of a political candidate to afford free space to the attacked candidate for reply was judged to be unconstitutional. The case concerned the *Miami Herald's* refusal to accept a political candidate's reply to editorial comments made by the newspaper. The editorials attacked Pat Tornillo's character. He was running for the Florida legislature. A Florida right-to-reply statute demanded the *Herald* accept Tornillo's rebuttal. The circuit court found the statute unconstitutional, but the Florida Supreme Court reversed the lower court. Justice Warren Burger announced the 9-0 decision of the Supreme Court, holding that the statute requiring a newspaper that attacks the character of a political candidate to afford free space to the attacked candidate to reply is an abridgment of freedom of the press. One assumes that the court feels quite strongly for men of conflicting opinion such as Marshall, Brennan, and Douglas on the one side and Burger and Rehnquist on the other to concur. For instance:

> Burger carefully made sure that important cases in criminal law, racial discrimination and free speech were kept away from Douglas, Brennan and Marshall, his ideological "enemies," as he called them. If necessary, the chief would switch his own vote to retain the assignment power, thus preventing them from writing ground-breaking decisions . . . ."[35]

On the other side, Marshall, Stewart, Brennan, and Douglas considered the chief justice inadequate, if not downright deceitful.[36]

Tornillo's defense argued that the government is obliged to make sure a wide spectrum of views reaches the public.

> It is urged that at the time the First Amendment to the Constitution was ratified in 1791 as part of our Bill of Rights the press was broadly representative of the people it was serving. A true marketplace of ideas existed in which there was relatively easy access to the channels of communication.[37]

It appears, though, that government-guaranteed access to private media has almost no historical support or precedent. It is not mentioned in the Constitution.

The Florida Supreme Court, upholding a right of reply for political candidates attacked by the press, ruled in favor of access for reply, not for protection from intrusion. "The First Amendment did not create a privileged class which through a monopoly of instruments of the newspaper industry would be able to deny to the people the freedom of expression,"[38] said the court. This is an echo from *Red Lion*. Yet, nowhere does the Supreme Court mention *Red Lion* in its *Miami Herald* decision. Schmidt writes that while such broad access right-of-reply rules exist in France, Germany, Norway, Hungary, and Austria, the United States is not inclined to admit such a guarantee. Citing *A.P. v. U.S.*, Burger included in the decision that freedom to publish includes everyone and not just some, and the freedom is guaranteed by the Constitution. But, Burger argued, citing *CBS v. DNC:*

> The power of a privately owned newspaper to advance its own political, social, and economic views is bounded by only two factors: first, the acceptance of a sufficient number of readers—and hence advertisers—to assure financial success; and, second, the journalistic integrity of its editors and publishers.[39]

Finally, Burger concluded that the choice of material and amount of information included in a newspaper, and the treatment of public issues and officials, fair or not, is the function of editorial judgment. It has yet to be demonstrated how government regulation of this primary function can be consistent with the First Amendment guarantee of freedom of the press.

Miami Herald is not among the Supreme Court's more elegantly reasoned decisions. Precedents cited in *Miami Herald* do not consider access to newspapers and magazines, nor, as previously mentioned, did the Court ever refer to *Red Lion*. Both Justice White in *Red Lion* and Burger in *Miami Herald* quote *A.P. v. U.S.* to buttress their respective decisions, but *A.P.* dealt with the monopolization of news sources, not access to news outlets. *Red Lion* implies that the First Amendment allows access rules if they will aid in preservation of the free marketplace of ideas. *Miami Herald* asserts that a responsible press is not mandated by the First Amendment. The first case heralds an enhancement of public debate, the latter argues against a right of reply. Implicit in *Miami Herald* is the distinction between print and broadcast media. Obviously, the First Amendment makes no such distinction. Schmidt suggests excuses for the weakness of the Supreme Court's decision in *Miami Herald*. The opinion was rushed through at the end of the term; the specter of Watergate reared its visage and usurped the concentration of the Court. But, Schmidt concludes, "The Court's opinion is almost devoid of reasoned support, its use of precedent is disingenuous, and the constitutional principle announced is not consistent with other rules grounded in the First Amendment."[40]

The texts of *Red Lion* and *Miami Herald* offer discordant interpretations of access. No one dissented in either case, although Douglas did not participate in *Red Lion*. The area of access remains ambiguous. The decision reached by the Burger Court is inadequate when viewed from

voices which are representative of his community and which would otherwise, by necessity, be barred from the airwaves."[66] Further, it is consistent with the First Amendment to make the granting and renewing of licenses conditional upon a demonstrated willingness to present controversial issues of public importance within the community.[67]

Just as the *1949 Report on Editorializing* relied largely on the *Associated Press* decision, so the *1974 Fairness Report* based much of its discussion on *Red Lion*. The Commission's report, largely based on the scarcity of spectrum space justification, noted that the "purpose and foundation" of the fairness doctrine is to be found in the First Amendment itself.[68] The Commission did not consider the doctrine to go too far in the direction of crabbing the free speech and press rights of broadcasters, insofar as the Commission's role was to regulate and not to censor. For instance, if a given broadcaster presented one side of a controversial issue, he was not required to present opposing views on the same program or series. "He is simply expected to make a provision for the opposing views in his *overall programming*."[69] The licensee was subject, finally, to standards of reasonableness and good faith. No sanction was to be brought to bear against any offending broadcaster for isolated fairness violations during the term of the license. The FCC would ask him or her to provide for an opposing point of view.[70] Since the broadcaster is the expert in his or her community on what constitutes a controversial issue of public importance, he or she would be in a position to recognize one. The basic test was whether the issue involved a social or political choice, measured against his or her judgment concerning the impact that such an issue might have on the community. The Cullman rule did remain a thorny issue.[71]

The Commission admitted the system was "far from perfect." Even so, it thought the doctrine represented the best solution to a thorny problem by providing a mechanism by which to assure public enlightenment on significant issues, yet burdening broadcast journalists with a minimum of governmental intrusion. The Commission included a provision warning that should things not work out, should the doctrine prove inadequate to its design, the Commission would have a future opportunity to reassess its actions, according to the First Amendment and the public convenience. In 1985, it did.

One sees the extent of disagreement presented in the clash of opinions of two of the Supreme Court's most stalwart champions of freedom of expression in *Columbia Broadcast System, Inc. v. Democratic National Committee*.[72] Justice Brennan reminded the Court that "'the ultimate good is better reached by free trade in ideas.'"[73] That being the case, the fairness doctrine was not only necessary, but as it stood in 1973, the doctrine was not strong enough to provide for the free trade in ideas. Because:

> [B]roadcasters retain almost exclusive control over the selection of issues and viewpoints to be covered, the manner of presentation, and, perhaps most important, who shall speak. Given this doctrinal framework, I can only conclude that the Fairness Doctrine, standing alone, is insufficient . . .[74]

Yet Justice Douglas, no less resolute, wrote, "The Fairness Doctrine has no place in our First Amendment regime."[75] He disagreed with the unanimous decision in *Red Lion*, and he implied that the fairness doctrine was compatible with societies in which there exists no commitment to freedom of expression.

The Revocation

The FCC, since 1949, had consistently and persistently justified the adventitious nature of the fairness doctrine on grounds that it served the public interest and enhanced the freedom of expression of diverse points of view, which would by necessity be excluded from the airwaves were it not for the doctrine. Then, in 1985, it turned on its own progeny.

The Commission reassessed its previously professed allegiance to the traditional policy, declaring that the mere longevity of the doctrine ought not get in the way. Longevity provides no protection against constitutional scrutiny and challenge.[76] Notwithstanding the Supreme Court's decision upholding its constitutionality in *Red Lion*, times and marketplaces change. The factual predicates upon which the Supreme Court had relied had shifted. After all, the framers intended, the Commission claimed, to promote free speech by prohibiting the government from intruding into the marketplace of ideas, and the agency doctrine intrudes into the broadcaster's marketplace.

The Court's decision in 1969 was, the FCC pointed out, "narrowly circumscribed." The Court had relied upon the Commission's judgment that the doctrine did not lessen the presentation of controversial issues over the airwaves. But the hearings conducted by the FCC in 1985 showed conclusively that the doctrine did in fact constrict the amount and nature of programming of controversial issues. Justice White wrote for the Court:

> If the experience with the administration of these doctrines indicates that they have the net affect of reducing rather than enhancing the volume and quality of coverage, there will be time enough to reconsider the constitutional implications.[77]

The premise upon which the Court had relied in *Red Lion*, that there was a scarcity of spectrum space, was no longer a viable assertion. The marketplace had grown, developed, and diversified in ways unforeseen in 1969. Now there is plenty of space.

The FCC reported that there had been a 48% increase in the number of radio stations since 1969 and a 30% increase since the *1974 Fairness Report*.[78] Television stations had grown 44.3% since *Red Lion* and increased 28% since 1974.[79] Additionally, new technology allowed for even further diversification of the market. Cable systems had increased by 195% since 1969[80] and projections showed that 69% of American homes would include VCRs by 1990.[81]

The *1985 Fairness Report* claimed that the expansion of the marketplace rendered the fairness doctrine obtrusive. The public had adequate access to the marketplace of ideas without intrusive government regulation. The Commission asserted that its reappraisal of the fairness doctrine rested on three prongs: the doctrine restricts, rather than expands, its constitutional objective, that is, to guarantee access and debate over controversial issues of public importance; the costs to the Commission and broadcasters in terms of money and time are prohibitive; and the transformation of the marketplace no longer warrants the intrusion the doctrine placed upon First Amendment rights of broadcasters. According to testimony, the FCC found a "significant danger that broadcasters will minimize their presentation of controversial issue programming in order to avoid the substantial dangers associated with the fairness doctrine."[82]

The FCC decided that the doctrine operated to promote mainstream, orthodox views and thereby to exclude the expression of marginal, innovative positions. Of even more concern, the doctrine provided a weapon by which the government could intimidate and coerce broadcasters not to cover some issues. Suggestions to manipulate the networks this way were made by some in the Nixon White House.[83]

The Supreme Court has so far refused to reconsider the soundness of *Red Lion*, "'without some signal from Congress or the FCC that technological developments have advanced so far that some revision of the system of broadcasting regulation may be required.'"[84] The Court of Appeals noted that the *1985 Fairness Report* constituted such a signal. Noting that the enforcement of a policy, generated by the Commission itself, which it no longer believes to be constitutional, could violate the Commissioners' oath of office to obey, support, and defend the Constitution, it ordered the Commission to consider Meredith's claim that enforcing the doctrine against it violated Meredith's constitutional rights (unless the Commission were to decide not to enforce the doctrine at all "because it is contrary to the public interest").[85]

Based upon its experiences administering the doctrine, constitutional considerations, the *1985 Fairness Report*, and occasioned by the situation and series of events which led to its reconsideration of *Syracuse Peace Council*, the FCC concluded, "the fairness doctrine, on its face, violates the First Amendment and contravenes the public interest."[86] Intending no irony, relying on *Red Lion*, the Commission reasoned that the constitutionality of the fairness doctrine becomes suspect on showing that it serves to chill press expression, consequently thwarting its intended purpose.

> Therefore in response to the question raised by the Supreme Court in *League of Women Voters*, we believe that the standard applied in *Red Lion* should be reconsidered and that the constitutional principles applicable to the printed press should be equally applicable to the electronic press.[87]

Seen in this light, the fairness doctrine obstructs the constitutional landscape, obscuring the focus of broadcasters and, by so doing, blinding those license holders to the interests of the rest of us—a blindness that resulted from extremely blurred vision brought on by regulatory cataracts, whose surgical removal, the FCC assures us, will restore the social vision of the broadcaster.

The Logic of Exclusion

There has been a rupture. The FCC of the 1980s has torn the doctrinal fabric of its regulatory heritage. A social practice has been disrupted by the discontinuation of a long-standing safeguard. The Commission of the 1970s saw the fairness doctrine as an instrument for maintaining a healthful balance between the power of broadcasters and public access to the airwaves. The Commission of the 1980s has come to see the doctrine as an obstruction to freedom of expression. Deconstruction and textual criticism provide conceptual tools with which to elucidate the implicit differences between rhetoric and logic. The sense of public policy, law, and written or spoken communication is not always tantamount to the stated intentions of the communicators. Deciphering the intentions of authors or authorities forms at most only a part of the task of the interpretation of meaning. That is to say, the stated intentions of the 1980s FCC provided only a fraction of the sense of what they did, and what they accomplished must be placed in relief against the tensions of various interests.

We can see that a policy has been reversed. This doctrinal reversal has taken a text, the fairness doctrine, and shifted it to the margins of practice. An authoritative message has emerged. From the Supreme

Court communicating in *League of Women Voters of California* its hesitation over altering the precedent set in *Red Lion*, through the FCC's *1985 Fairness Report* differing with that affirmation, to the Court of Appeals admonishing the Commission to reconsider the constitutionality of its ruling concerning Meredith (according to current technological developments in the marketplace), to the abolition of the doctrine itself, a pattern is in evidence. The disruption and discontinuation has been embedded in a wider legal process of repetition and continuation. The revocation was woven into the legal and governmental power process by which the decision was legitimated by a consensus of authorities, both governmental and professional.

Within the constellation of protected interests, the broadcaster's was not supreme. The public's interest was the primary term. "It is the right of the viewers and listeners, not the right of broadcasters, which is paramount."[88] By shifting the appeal from the primacy of the public interest to the indirect achievement of that end by linking the broadcaster's First Amendment rights, a slippage occurred. The formal rights of the broadcaster became the primary term, thereby subtly, yet decisively, restructuring the entire set of policy assumptions. License holders came to be seen as those who speak, and therefore those who must be protected, rather than those holding conflicting views on matters of public importance. This reversal of protection was promoted under the guise of efficiency. It was maintained by expert testimony in the 1985 hearings and was bound to a policy by broadcast experts, authorities, and professionals whose strategy was a realignment of power relations labeled deregulation. This amounts to increased liberty for the few in the name of public interest.[89]

In a very real sense, the FCC is in the process of deconstructing itself in a way unforeseen by practitioners of critical interpretation. The Commission appears to be solidifying the hierarchy of privileged voices and positions by renouncing its own power and policy. The year of the contra was at hand. By inscribing their "liberatory" discourse on the course of events they fostered radical conservatism. In transposing the interests intended by the courts and Congress, of providing access to those who would otherwise have no access, the Commission has relied on a new application of the term reasonable. In 1972, the Court of Appeals stressed the wide degree of broadcaster discretion permitted under the fairness doctrine:

> Thus, in opinion after opinion the Commission and the courts have stressed the wide degree of discretion available under the fairness doctrine and we have clearly stated time after time, *ad infinitum ad nauseum*, that the key to the doctrine is no mystical

formula but rather the exercise of reasonable standards by the licensee.[90]

Reasonable access since the abolition of the doctrine still will be interpreted by the broadcaster, but not in accordance with the affirmative duty to seek out and present views. Instead, the marketplace will determine which views will be presented. This instance of instrumental, technological reason has taken over for the more principled reasonableness standard advocated by the Court of Appeals in 1972. The state of being reasonable differs from acting in such a way as to maximize participation in a marketplace of goods and services. The dissemination of views according to market shares is not at all equivalent to seeking out contrasting points of view over controversial issues of public importance in order to insure robust, wide-open debate. The instrumental rationality of the contras has transgressed the regulatory role that Congress foresaw and still demands from the FCC. In 1987 President Reagan overrode the Congressional bill which would have codified the fairness doctrine into law. This technological rationality, or instrumental technique, can be seen as a tactic for increasing the social control of those owning media, who are often allied with those in control of the major corporations that the media report on.

The Discourse of Deregulation

Deconstruction coalesces with the critical legal studies movement in the mutual recognition that formal analysis will yield individually valid, yet comparatively contradictory outcomes to legal and social issues. If the struggle is over responsibilities and rights, the strategy concerns knowledge and power. If one accepts the premises of the 1974 *Fairness Report*, the conclusion that the doctrine serves the public interest follows inescapably. Equally compelling, from a formal point of view, are the deliberations leading to the conclusion of the 1985 *Fairness Report*.

Broadcast regulation reflects, on a particular scale, the essential dilemma that resonates throughout American society. We live in a society that espouses democratic, pluralist values, yet is driven by a market economy. Broadcasters are placed in the unenviable position of embodying both. They are expected to champion the stockholder's economic interests as well as the community's social well being, to trade conceptually in the economic marketplace and to deal profitably in the marketplace of ideas. Alternatively, the licensee claims First Amendment free speech and press rights, while advocating his or her autonomy as a private citizen with the right to maximize profits by contracting with whom he or she sees fit, even if the raw material of the medium is a public resource. The freedom of the broadcaster as an autonomous individual conflicts with the privilege of a trustee communicating in the public interest, convenience, and necessity. Individualism confronts social responsibility. The critical legal studies scholars frame this dilemma as central within the legal system.

Professed ideals sometimes collide with actual social practices. A semblance of consensus presents a visage masking a contentious, contradictory system of power-knowledge strategies. The social and economic systems often are not compatible. The irreconcilable assumptions of the market and political systems of activity founder when joined with the values put forward by competing views of culture and society. Duncan Kennedy has identified the divergence between appeals to socially responsible policy and individually based rights as the original contradiction at work in society.[91] These inclinations toward individualism and social responsibility are deeply based predilections around which are organized ethical, economic, and social issues within the legal system.

Discussions about the ends or ultimate values of the social order find no place within the liberal, individualist regime, and that is because, while in everyday life individuals may act and depend on one another, the individualist tradition recognizes no intersubjectivity within the moral order. Ethics is considered a subjective project. Facts constitute the objective realm, while values are seen to be subjective and arbitrary. Values do not give themselves up to rational analysis because it is not possible, ultimately, within the liberal tradition, to determine the actual experience of another. So facts inhabit a separate domain from values. Since one is not able to evaluate the subjectivity of another person, and each individual is free to maximize his own ends, then it follows that individualists will place great value on a structural or formal approach to policy and legal decision making. Individuals form alliances to further private goals. The government, then, is an arena for struggle, not a means for progress. Reason guarantees a means by which to further individual autonomy and self-interest. Justice must rely on the formal neutrality of process inherent in the structure of decision making.

The competing and contradictory tendency within society, according to Kennedy, is the regulation of justice seen as an order of shared ends. From this perspective, values are seen as purposive and discoverable through discussion. Ethical discussion is prized as a higher form of rationality than that espoused by the individualist tradition. Intersubjectivity undergirds individuality and identity. From the social responsibility perspective, reason is not primarily instrumental, but consensual and principled. The grammar of this system emphasizes the social sphere. Values make sense and literally aid in the construction of society. Law and social policy can function in a positive sense. The social responsibility advocate will rely more on substance over form; he or she will emphasize the substantive part of the process over the formal structural guarantees of neutrality.

> The essence of individualist certainty-through rules is that because it identifies for the bad man the precise limits of toleration for his badness, it authorizes him to hew as close as he can to those limits. To the altruist this is a kind of collective insanity by which we traduce our values while pretending to define them.[92]

Kennedy contends both traditions, individualist and altruist, get stuck. The explanation for the muddle is that both sorts of persons in modern society believe both sets of assertions, even though they contradict one another. Recognition of this can of worms does not take us out of it, but it does point to the futility of attempting to justify either tendency according to concepts like precedent, fact, or principle. Kennedy's seminal description of the nature of our conflicted heritage at least opens the way to the recognition that, contradictory though they may be, there is a discernible reliance of individualism on form, and a social responsibility connection to substance. These paradigms are not based on other justifications, logical or factual, but are historically developed, rhetorically motivated appeals.

I have attempted to examine manifest appeals to better understand the terms of the discussion, the rhetoric of the debate between the substantive issue of access to the airwaves of citizens and the formal appeal to First Amendment rights of the powerful. The Supreme Court's conviction, as voiced in 1945, does not persuade the contras of today:

> Surely a command that the government itself shall not impede the free flow of ideas does not afford nongovernmental combinations a refuge if they impose restraints upon that constitutionally guaranteed freedom.[93]

What is not said is often as important as what is. No mention of this sentiment is made in either the *1985 Fairness Report* or the decision to abolish the fairness doctrine as unconstitutional and a contravention of the public interest.

If being persuaded by an argument really does influence the kind of person one is and becomes, then being dissuaded is equally a function of style and interpretation. Deconstructing the rhetoric of those representing powerful institutions may aid the rest of us in comprehending those institutions that influence our individual and social lives. Rhetorical appeals attempt to identify with our common experiences concerning the ways in which we dwell with one another in society and how we cultivate values.

The contras champion the dual principles of an open, free marketplace and protection from burdensome government regulation, which leads to a chilling of broadcast media.

> As we have observed in other proceedings, marketplace forces are the primary determinants of information oriented programming. Moreover, given our previous analysis regarding the chilling effect of the fairness doctrine, we believe it reasonable to expect an increase in the coverage of these types of issues.[94]

The Commission determined that one factor contributing to this chilling effect was the cost. The Commission asked broadcasters for their expert testimony. This is parallel to asking employers if affirmative action hiring practices dampen their willingness to employ workers. Or, because libel law may restrict the presentation of some reporting, we do away with libel. The 1974 *Fairness Report* concluded the fairness doctrine did not inhibit coverage of controversial issues. The 1985 Report admitted that while fear of fairness obligations did not lead to a systematic avoidance by broadcasters, it did serve to deter them. "For example, fearing the imposition of onerous regulatory burdens, Meredith Corporation states that one of its stations elected not to air a paid program on the nuclear arms race."[95] Meredith also testified that one of its stations simply chose not to editorialize on issues of public importance as a matter of policy. From such testimony, are we to conclude with the FCC that absent the doctrine Meredith would do an about face and broadcast contrasting viewpoints on issues such as the nuclear arms race? This is the same corporation that argued that building a nuclear power plant is not a controversial issue of public importance. In response to the charge that testimony evidencing a chilling effect might be self serving, the FCC admitted that might be true. Nonetheless, it continued, the same could be said of all parties presenting any point of view.

Precisely the point. Appeals to the motivations of actors must take into account the various vested interests and the intentions and goals of any parties. Knowledge structures power, and power is the exercise of knowledge. There are not neutral parties. The question is how best to give voice to competing interests in furtherance of the marketplace of ideas. It's not so much that the truth will thus win out. But left in the hands of license holders to exclude voices, truth may well not present itself for cultivation. Truth is not discovered but produced. The appeal to an open marketplace is invariably the economic market, not the market of ideas. Open market is an oxymoron. Free market is a contradiction. All markets are structured by controlling, hierarchical forces competing not only to maximize their own interests but ultimately to exclude competing forces. Competitive marketplace is a euphemism for preserving a discriminatory structure.

Over 25 years ago, Marshall McLuhan proclaimed the medium is the message. The message of any technology is the changing scale, pace, and pattern that it introduces into our lives. Television is on over seven hours a day in the average home. The FCC tells us that there is a strong marketplace incentive to provide coverage of newsworthy issues. On what basis do we see that evidenced? Corporate investment tycoons such as Laurence Tisch control CBS, ABC was bought by Capital Cities for $3.5 billion, and General Electric paid $6.28 billion for NBC.[96] Rupert Murdoch's aptly named organization, the News Corporation, owns 20th Century-Fox Film, Fox Broadcasting (now considered to be a fourth network), and television stations in Boston, Chicago, Dallas, Houston, Los Angeles, New York, and Washington. He negotiated the purchase of Triangle Publications, Inc., publisher of TV Guide, for $3 billion.

While the number of corporations controlling the majority of American media in 1988 teetered precipitately at 26, some Wall Street analysts predict that the number could fall to about six corporations. Our conception of the public interest is better served by protecting public access to the airwaves than emphasizing the priority of broadcasters' First Amendment rights. This is so not because broadcasters ought not to enjoy free speech, but because the rest of us ought to be given the opportunity as well. For instance, General Electric (NBC) owns nuclear power plants. If they were to advance the wisdom of further investment in nuclear power plants in New York, should we assume that they would behave differently than Meredith Corporation did in Syracuse?

The argument that deregulation dismantles a restrictive fairness doctrine masks the real issue. Revocation of the fairness doctrine defuses the structural potency of governmental regulation by replacing it with the authority of corporate structure. One system of control takes over for another. But at whose expense? The fairness doctrine was put in place to control corporate selfishness and power. Corporate power and control over the media is consolidating at an alarming rate. The subsequent constriction of diversity can only limit debate on issues of public importance. Clearly, those on the boards of corporations champion similar values, and they guard the status quo. The production of culture is an industry, and the health of vigorous minority views can fall prey to monopoly control just as readily as control of broadcasting stations falls into the hands of interlocking interest groups representing the interests of capital gain.

Diversity of viewpoints is not guaranteed by numerical diversity.

We need assurance that diverse political and cultural points of view may be heard or democracy will calcify, and a bent, decrepit, stiff society is not one in which the truth can burst forth and circulate among the populace. Broadcasting is a medium of property and money in which technology most often furthers the presentation of tired and obvious views, thereby insulating us from contact with really potent ideas. It seems reasonable that society ought to make some provision for their inclusion. Rhetorical appeals are essentially appeals to the kind of society we will inhabit. Appeals to the marketplace of communication technology will configure our culture in a more constricted, less diverse, and intellectually poorer fashion than appeals to access to the marketplace of ideas. The rhetorical appeal to the fairness doctrine advances the interests of expanding the open and antagonistic exchange of ideas, while the rhetoric of the contras appeals to the discretion of the visible hand of the broadcaster, trusting him or her to choose which views serve the public interest.

NOTES TO CHAPTER 8

1. H. Kelsen, *Pure Theory of Law*, trans. M. Knight (Berkeley: University of California Press, 1970), pp. 173-74.

2. Ibid., p. 62.

3. Ibid., p. 193.

4. Ibid., p. 199.

5. Ibid., p. 46.

6. Ibid., p. 84.

7. Ibid., p. 103.

8. Ibid., p. 202.

9. Ibid., p. 218.

10. William J. Brennan Jr., "Reason, Passion, and 'the Progress of the Law,'" *Cardozo L. Rev.*, 10:3, 1988, p. 16.

11. See J. Derrida, *"Devant La Loi,* in A. Udoff (ed.), *Kafka and the Contemporary Critical Performance* (Bloomington: Indiana University Press, 1987), pp. 128-149.

12. J. Derrida, "The Principle of Reason: The University in the Eyes of its Pupils," *Diacritics* 19:3, 1983, p. 9.

13. Ibid., p. 8.

14. J. Derrida, *Limited Inc*, trans. S. Weber and J. Mehlman (Evanston, IL: Northwestern University Press, 1988), p. 92.

15. J. Derrida, *"Declarations of Independence,"* trans. T. Keenan and T. Pepper, in *New Political Science*, 7, p. 10.

16. See P. Gabel, "The Phenomenology of Rights-Consciousness and the Pact of Withdrawn Selves," *Texas L. Rev.*, 62, 1984, pp. 1563-1599.

17. Brennan, "Reason, Passion, and 'the Progress of Law,'" pp. 3-23.

18. Ibid., p. 22 (emphasis added).

19. Ibid., p. 7.

20. Ibid., p. 7.

21. Ibid., p. 17.

22. B.C. Schmidt, Jr., *Freedom of the Press vs. Public Access* (New York: Praeger, 1976), p. 27.

23. *Red Lion Broadcasting Co. v. FCC*, 395 U.S. 367, 89 S. Ct. 1974 (1969).

24. *Miami Herald Publishing Co. v. Tornillo*, 418 U.S. 241, 94 S. Ct. 2831 (1974).

25. 395 U.S. 367, 89 S. Ct. 1974, 1806 (1969).

26. 418 U.S. 241, 94 S. Ct. 2831, 2838 (1974).

27. *CBS v. DNC*, 412 U.S. 94, 148 (1973), cited in Schmidt, *Freedom of the Press*, p. 243.

28. 395 U.S. 367, 89 S. Ct. 1974, 1798 (1969).

29. The FCC revoked the doctrine in 1987.

30. 395 U.S. 367, 89 S. Ct. 1794, 1799 (1969).

31. Ibid., p. 1806.

32. Ibid., p. 1807.

33. *Associated Press v. U.S.*, 326 U.S. 1 (1945).

34. 395 U.S. 367, 89 S. Ct. 1794, 1808 (1969).

35. B. Woodward and S. Armstrong, *The Brethren, Inside the Supreme Court* (New York: Avon Books, 1979), p. 71.

36. Ibid., pp. 227, 305, 318, 320, 373, and 481.

37. 418 U.S. 241, 94 S. Ct. 2831, 2835 (1974).

38. *Tornillo v. Miami Herald Publishing Co.*, 287 So. 2nd 78 (1973).

39. 412 U.S. 94, cited in 418 U.S. 241, 94 S. Ct. 2831, 2838 (1974).

40. Schmidt, *Freedom of the Press*, p. 13.

41. Ibid., p. 57.

42. K. Burke, *A Rhetoric of Motives*, (Berkeley: University of California Press, 1969), p. 23.

43. *Syracuse Peace Council v. Television Station WTVH*, 99 F.C.C. 2d 1389 (1984), recon. denied, F.C.C. 85-571, remanded sub nom. *Meredith Corporation v. Federal Communications Commission*, 809 F. 2d 863, 13 *Media L. Rep.* 1993 (1987). *Syracuse Peace Council v. Television Station WTVH*, 2 F.C.C. Rcd 5043 (1987).

44. *Meredith Corporation v. Federal Communications Commission*, 13 *Media L. Rep.*, 1993, 1995 (quoting Meredith).

45. *Syracuse Peace Council v. Television Station WTVH*, 2 F.C.C. Rcd. 5043 (1987).

46. Meredith provided response time to the SPC while the complaint was pending. *Meredith Corporation v. Federal Communications Commission*, 13, *Media L. Rep.* 1995.

47. See, for example, D. Kennedy, "Form and Substance in Private Law Adjudication," *89 Harvard L. Rev.* 1685 (1976); D. Kennedy, "The Structure of Blackstone's Commentaries,' *28 Buffalo L. Rev.* 205 (1978); R. Unger, *The Critical Legal Studies Movement* (1986); Unger, *Knowledge and Politics* (1975); D. Kairys (ed.) *The Politics of Law* (1982). "Critical Legal Studies Symposium," *36 Stanford L. Rev.* 1 (1984).

48. Derrida attempts to deconstruct the writings of authority to see better upon what grounds they claim to justify the classical liberal tradition. His analyses result in interpretations, seeking out conflicts not recognized by the authors themselves, whether they be novelists, philosophers, painters, linguists, lawyers, or framers of constitutions. The grammar of any system of discourse allows for dissemination of conflicting values and ideas.

49. Derrida, *Limited Inc.*, p. 148.

50. *In re* the Handling of Public Issues Under the Fairness Doctrine and the Public Interest Standards of the Communications Act, 48 F.C.C 2d 1 (1974) (hereinafter cited, 1974 Fairness Report).

51. Report Concerning General Fairness Doctrine Obligations of Broadcast Licensees, 102 F.C.C.. 2d 143 (1985) (hereinafter cited, 1985 Fairness Report).

52. *Brandywine-Main Line Radio, Inc. v. Federal Communications Commission*, 473 F. 2d, 46 (1972).

53. *Telecommunications Research Center v. Federal Communications Commission*, 13 *Media L. Rep.* 1881, 1894 (1986).

54. I am indebted to J. Frug's analysis in "Argument as Character," 140 *Stanford L. Rev.* 181 (1987).

55. Federal Communications Act of 1934, 48 Stat. 1082, 307 (a) (1934).

56. Great Lakes Broadcasting Co., 3 F.R.C. Ann. Rep. 32, 33 (1929).

57. B. Ramberg, "The Supreme Court and Public Interest in Broadcasting," 8 *Communications and the Law* 11, 13 (1986).

58. Report on Editorializing, 13 F.C.C. 1246, 1256 (1949).

59. 1974 Fairness Report, 48 F.C.C. 2d 1, 11.

60. Ibid., 10 (quoting Committee for the Fair Broadcasting of Controversial Issues, 25 F.C.C.. 2d 283, 292 (1970).

61. 376 U.S. 254, 270 (1964).

62. Policy Statement on Comparative Broadcast Hearings: Comparative Factors Discussed and Clarified, 1 F.C.C. 2d 393, 394 (1965).

63. *Federal Communications Commission v. Pottsville Broadcasting Co.,* 309 U.S. 134, 137 (1940).

64. *Red Lion Broadcasting Co. v. Federal Communications Commission,* 395 U.S. 367, 390.

65. *Associated Press v. United States*, 326 U.S. 1, 20 (1945).

66. *Red Lion Broadcasting Co. v. Federal Communications Commission,*

395 U.S. 367, 389.

67. Ibid., p. 394.

68. 1974 Fairness Report, 48 F.C.C. 2d 1.

69. Ibid., p. 8.

70. Ibid., p. 17.

71. The Cullman rule refers to a situation in which a broadcaster airs one side of a controversial issue and no sponsor for an opposing view can be found. The broadcaster must provide free airtime for the opposing point of view if opposing party cannot pay.

72. 412 U.S. 94 (1973).

73. Ibid., 182 n. 12 (Brennan, J., dissenting) (quoting *Abrams v. United States*, 250 U.S. 616, 630 (1919), (Holmes, J., dissenting).

74. Ibid., p. 187.

75. Ibid., p. 154 (Douglas, J., concurring).

76. 1985 Fairness Report, 102 F.C.C. 2d, 153 n. 36.

77. *Red Lion Broadcasting Co. v. Federal Communications Commission*, 395 U.S. 367, 393.

78. 102 F.C.C. 2d, p. 202.

79. Ibid., p. 204.

80. Ibid., p. 204.

81. Ibid., p. 214.

82. Ibid., p. 169.

83. Ibid., p. 193.

84. *Meredith Corporation v. Federal Communications Commission*, 13 *Media L. Rep.*, 169 (1987) (quoting *Federal Communications Commission v. League of Women Voters of California*, 468 U.S. 364, 376-77 n. 11) (1984).

85. Ibid., p. 2002.

86. *Syracuse Peace Council v. Television Station WTVH*, 2 F.C.C. Rcd 5043 (1987).

87. Ibid., p. 5053.

88. *Red Lion Broadcasting Co. v. Federal Communications Commission*, 395. U.S. 367, 390.

89. See L. Powe, *American Broadcasting and the First Amendment* (Berkeley: University of California Press, 1982), p. 199. Powe argues that public ownership of the airwaves does not secure the right of government to regulate, that is, censor, the airwaves. Citing *Hague v. Committee for Industrial Organization*, 307 U.S. 406 (1939), Powe points out that regulations will be tested on the same grounds as regulation of private enterprise. His point seems to be that there should be no First Amendment difference between regulation of government (airwaves) and privately owned (printing presses) resources. However, the fairness doctrine is not censorship, and government regulations of broadcasters are subject to reasonable limitations in relation to the rights of others as speakers, *Public Utilities*

Commission of the District of Columbia v. Democratic National Committee, 343 U.S. 451, 462, 464 (1952). Additionally, the government has put itself in a position with broadcasting "of participating in the challenged policy as to make the Government itself responsible for its effects," *Columbia Broadcasting System v. Democratic National Committee,* 412 U.S. 94, 181 n. 12 (Brennan, J., dissenting).

90. *Brandywine-Main Line Radio, Inc. v. Federal Communications Commission,* 473 F. 2d 16, 45 (1972).

91. Kennedy, "The Structure of Blackstone's Commentaries," p. 359.

92. Kennedy, "Form and Substance in Private Law Adjudication," p. 1773.

93. *Associated Press v. United States,* 326 U.S. 1, 20.

94. 1985 Fairness Report, 102 F.C.C. 2d, 143, 200-21.

95. Ibid., p. 172.

96. In August 1988, CBS' New York station shifted the time slot for the *Evening News.* The 6:30 p.m. time slot is less coveted as it attracts fewer viewers than 7 p.m. The head of CBS-owned stations said it made sense as a programming move because the game show replacing it, *Win, Lose or Draw,* is more compatible with the show that follows, *The Wheel of Fortune.* General Electric hardly inspires more confidence. This is a corporation that in 1986 paid $2 million in civil penalties for defrauding the government over defense contracts. G.E. has been convicted of price-fixing and rigging bids on government contracts in violation of antitrust law.

Author Index

Subject Index